"LOEX" of the West: Teaching and Learning in a Climate of Constant Change

FOUNDATIONS IN LIBRARY AND INFORMATION SCIENCE, Volume 34

Editors: Thomas W. Leonhardt, *Director of Library Technical Services, Bizzell Memorial Library, University of Oklahoma*

Murray S. Martin, *University Librarian and Professor of Library Science Emeritus, Tufts University*

Foundations in Library and Information Science

Edited by **Thomas W. Leonhardt**, *Director of Library Technical Services, Bizzell Memorial Library, University of Oklahoma* and **Murray S. Martin,** *University Librarian and Professor of Library Science Emeritus, Tufts University*

Volume 1.
The Mexican American: A Critical Guide to Research Aids
Barbara J. Robinson, *University of California Library, Riverside* and
J. Cordell Robinson, *California State College, San Bernardino*

Volume 2.
A Practical Approach to Serials Cataloging
Lynn S. Smith, *University of California Library, Riverside*

Volume 3.
The Microform Revolution in Libraries
Michael R. Gabriel, *Mankato State University* and **Dorothy P. Ladd**, *Boston University Library*

Volume 4.
China in Books: A Basic Bibliography in Western Language
Norman E. Tanis, David L. Perkins and **Justine Pinto**, *California State University Library, Northridge*

Volume 5.
Budgetary Control in Academic Libraries
Murray S. Martin, *Pennsylvania State University Libraries*

Volume 6.
Cost Analysis of Library Functions: A Total Systems Approach
Betty Jo Mitchell, Norman E. Tanis and **Jack Jaffe,** *California State University Library, Northridge*

Volume 7.
(Omitted From Numbering)

Volume 8.
Management of a Public Library
Harold R. Jenkins, *Kansas City Public Library*

Volume 9.
(Omitted from Numbering)

Volume 10.
Collection Development in Libraries: A Treatise
Edited by **Robert D. Stueart,** *Dean, Graduate School of Library and Information Science, Simmons College-Boston* and **George B. Miller, Jr.,** *Assistant Director for Collection Development, University of New Mexico Libraries*

Volume 11.

Introduction to Serial Management

Marcia Tuttle, *University of North Carolina, Chapel Hill*

Volume 12.

Developing Collections of U.S. Government Publications

Peter Hernon, *Graduate School of Library and Information Science, Simmons College, Boston* and **Gary R. Purcell**, *Graduate School of Library and Information Science, University of Tennessee, Knoxville*

Volume 13.

Library Management Without Bias

Ching-Chih Chen, *Graduate School of Library and Information Science, Simmons College, Boston*

Volume 14.

Issues in Personnel Management

Murray S. Martin, *Pennsylvania State University Libraries*

Volume 15.

Information Needs of the 80s.
Libraries and Information Services Role in Bringing Information to People Based on the Deliberations of the White House Conference on Library and Information Services

Edited by **Robert D. Stueart**, *Graduate School of Library and Information Science, Simmons College, Boston*

Volume 16.

ALMS: A Budget Based Library Management System

Betty Jo Mitchell, *California State University Library, Northridge*

Volume 17.

Options for the 80s
Proceedings of the Second National Conference of the Association of College and Research Libraries,
October 1-4, 1981, Minneapolis, Minnesota

Edited by **Michael D. Kathman**, *College of St. Benedict and St. John's University* and **Virgil F. Massman**, *James J. Hill Reference Library*

Volume 18.

The Library Services and Construction Act:
An Historical Overview from the Viewpoint of Major Participants

Edward G. Holley and **Robert F. Schremser**, *School of Library Science, The University of North Carolina at Chapel Hill*

Volume 19.

Fundraising for Nonprofit Institutions

Edited by **Sandy Dolnick**, *Executive Director, Friends of Libraries, U.S.A.*

Volume 20.

Changing Technology and Education for Librarianship and Information Science

Edited by **Basil Stuart-Stubbs,** *School of Librarianship, University of British Columbia*

Volume 21.

Videotex and Teletext: New Online Resources for Libraries

Michael B. Binder, *Director of Libraries, Fairleigh Dickinson Library*

Volume 22.

Research Libraries and Their Implementation of AACR2

Edited by **Judith Hopkins,** *Technical Services Research and Analysis Officer, Central Technical Services, University Libraries, State University of New York at Buffalo* and **John A. Edens,** *Director, Central Technical Services, University Libraries, State University of New York at Buffalo*

Volume 23.

An Encyclopedia of Film Festivals

Robert A. Nowlan and **Gwendolyn Wright Nowlan,** *Southern Connecticut State University*

Volume 24.

A Guide to the Literature of Electronic Publishing: CD-ROM, DESKTOP Publishing, and Electronic Mail, Books, & Journals

Edited by **Michael R. Gabriel,** *Mankato State University Library*

Volume 25.

Technical Services in Libraries: Systems and Applications

Edited by **Thomas W. Leonhardt,** *Holt Library, University of the Pacific*

Volume 26.

Collection Management: A New Treatise

Edited by **Charles B. Osburn,** *Ameila Gayle Gorgas Library, University of Alabama* and **Ross W. Atkinson,** *Cornell University Library*

Volume 27.

The Role of the American Academic Library in International Programs

Edited by **Bruce D. Bonta,** *The University Libraries, Pennsylvania State University* and **James G. Neal,** *University Libraries, Indiana University*

Volume 28.

Academic Library Budgets

Edited by **Murray S. Martin,** *University Librarian and Professor of Library Science Emeritus, Tufts University*

Volume 29.

Academic Libraries and Training

Edited by **Maryruth Phelps Glogowski,** *Associate Director, E.H. Butler Library, State University College at Buffalo*

Volume 30.

A Guide to Library Service in Mathematics: The Non-Trivial Mathematics Librarian

Edited by **Nancy D. Anderson,** *Mathematics Librarian, University of Illinois at Urbana-Champaign* and **Lois M. Pausch,** *Geology Librarian, University of Illinois at Urbana-Champaign*

Volume 31.

Issues in Collection Management: Librarians, Booksellers, Publishers

Edited by **Murray S. Martin,** *University Librarian and Professor of Library Science Emeritus, Tufts University*

Volume 32.

Diversity and Multiculturalism in Libraries

Edited by **Katherine Hoover Hill,** *Dry Memorial Library, Erie Community College*

Volume 33.

For the Good of the Order: Essays in Honor of Edward G. Holley

Edited by **Delmus Williams,** *University of Akron,* **John Budd,** *University of Missouri, Columbia,* **Robert E. Martin,** *Louisiana State University,* **Barbara Moran,** *University of North Carolina, Chapel Hill,* and **Fred Roper,** *University of South Carolina, Columbia*

"LOEX" of the West: Teaching and Learning in a Climate of Constant Change

Edited by: THOMAS W. LEONHARDT
Director of Library Technical Services
Bizzell Memorial Library
University of Oklahoma

Emerald

United Kingdom – North America – Japan
India – Malaysia – China

Emerald Group Publishing Limited
Howard House, Wagon Lane, Bingley BD16 1WA, UK

British Library Cataloguing in Publication Data
A catalogue record for this book is available from the British Library

ISBN: 978-0-7623-0099-0
ISSN: 1876-0562 (Series)

CONTENTS

FOREWORD xiii

INTRODUCTION
Loretta Rielly xv

WELCOMING ADDRESS TO "LOEX" OF THE WEST: CULTIVATING THE ELECTRONIC LANDSCAPE—FIVE CHALLENGES FOR LEADERSHIP
Todd S. Hutton xix

GLACIER OR AVALANCHE? SHIFTS IN THE ELECTRONIC, EDUCATIONAL, AND LIBRARY LANDSCAPE
Lizabeth A. Wilson 1

DESIGNING INSTRUCTION ON THE ELECTRONIC FRONTIER: LEARNING STYLES, INSTRUCTIONAL DESIGN, AND ELECTRONIC INFORMATION ACCESS SYSTEMS
Randall Hensley and Mary Ellen Litzinger 19

GODZILLA VS. KING KONG: A TEAM APPROACH TO TRAINING ON INTERNET RESOURCES
Vicky Pengelly 35

INTERNET INSTRUCTION AT THE UNIVERSITY OF MONTANA
Barry Brown 59

WITHOUT A NET: SUPPORTING OURSELVES IN A TREMULOUS ATMOSPHERE
Jeris Cassel and BethAnn Zambella 75

LIBRARY INSTRUCTION FOR FACULTY: TRAINING IN THE USE OF ELECTRONIC RESOURCES
Gale Burrow and Cynthia Snyder 93

INCORPORATING INFORMATION TECHNOLOGIES INSTRUCTION IN AN EXTENDED EDUCATION PROGRAM FOR WORKING ADULTS
Hélène Lafrance and Bonnie Gratch 105

THE LITERATE LIBRARIAN AND INFORMATION TECHNOLOGY: OVERSELLING THE INTERNET
Thomas W. Leonhardt 125

INTERNET RESOURCE DISCOVERY: THE ROLE OF CRITICAL THINKING
Craig Gibson and John Meade 137

INTERNET: THE GOOD, THE BAD, AND THE UGLY
Billie Joy Reinhart and Gary B. Thompson 147

REMOTE ACCESS AND ACTIVE LEARNING IN CONTEXT: TEACHING AT TIME AND PLACE OF NEED
Lori Arp, John Culshaw, and Keith Gresham 153

TEACHING THE LIBRARY AND ELECTRONIC RESOURCES ON TELEVISION
Naomi Lederer 171

THE GATEWAY TO INFORMATION: MEETING THE BI NEEDS OF 54,000 STUDENTS (NOT TO MENTION FACULTY, STAFF, AND COMMUNITY USERS) WITHOUT WORKSHOPS, FLYERS, OR STAFF ASSISTANCE
Fred Roecker 197

USE OF MACROMEDIA DIRECTOR™ AND QUICKTIME™ FOR MULTIMEDIA CLASSROOM PRESENTATIONS
Paul T. Adalian, Jr. 207

GRACE UNDER PRESSURE: COPING WITH MULTIPLE DATABASE PERSONALITIES
Linda Friend and Bonnie Osif 217

ABOUT THE AUTHORS 231

INDEX 237

FOREWORD

The publication of the first official "LOEX" of the West conference proceedings expands the regional audience of the conference to a national audience and beyond. This volume is the result of serendipity resulting from participation in a conference on library instruction, something I am only peripherally informed about. I was interested in the call for papers because of the emphasis on the electronic landscape and change, two areas that seem intertwined and almost synonymous in libraries of the late twentieth century. I was surprised and gratified to see just how much thought and energy is being put into library instruction in an electronic environment. The organizers of this conference are to be congratulated for the array of speakers they were able to assemble, and the speakers are to be thanked for turning their oral presentations into written documents for publication after the conference had ended.

When I approached the organizers of the conference about the possibility of publishing the proceedings, they agreed that the quality of the papers had been high, and that it was worth pursuing. Loretta Rielly was especially helpful to me in putting out reminders about deadlines and kindly supplied an introduction.

Practitioners in library instruction will find this a helpful, encouraging collection of papers. Students and librarians unfamiliar with library instruction would do well to read these papers carefully, too, and perhaps join in with their colleagues in further adapting technology to the betterment of all library services.

Thomas W. Leonhardt
University of Oklahoma
1995

INTRODUCTION

Loretta Rielly

The first official "LOEX" of the West, "Cultivating the Electronic Landscape: Teaching and Learning in a Climate of Constant Change," was held at Willamette University in Salem, Oregon, June 9-10, 1994. Its roots, however, lie in an Evan Farber workshop, "Faculty and Librarians: Colleagues in Education," held at Willamette two years earlier and attended by librarians, teaching faculty, and academic administrators from Idaho, Washington and Oregon. The positive response to that workshop prompted the sponsoring institutions (Linfield College, Oregon State University, and Willamette University) and the Oregon chapter of the Association of College and Research Libraries to recommend that the profits be used for a second regional library instruction conference.

When we began planning "Cultivating the Electronic Landscape," we knew that wanted to create opportunities for participants to meet in informal settings to share experiences, ideas, and concerns.[1] Each of us had attended a national LOEX conference and felt its format of nationally-recognized speakers and small group sessions with plenty of time to meet (especially over meals) was one to emulate. When we approached Linda Shirato about using the LOEX name, she agreed and subsequently supported us by publishing both the call for contributors and the conference information; she also referred potential participants and contributors to us. Although there was and is no formal connection between the national LOEX and "LOEX" of the West, this support and the use of a well-known, well-respected name helped contribute to its success.

We also agreed that we wanted to emphasize issues related to instruction in an electronic environment. The amount of computer-accessible information is multiplying at an astronomical rate, and librarians are devoting increasing amounts of time to teaching students to use electronic information resources effectively. The explosion of information resources coupled with rapid technological growth presents new challenges *and* new opportunities. We wanted to acknowledge the challenges and showcase the ways libraries and librarians are making the most of the opportunities.[2]

In her keynote address, "Glacier or Avalanche? Shifts in the Electronic, Educational, and Library Landscape," Lizabeth Wilson likens librarians to adventurers who can survive in a shifting landscape. She highlights the "options, opportunities, and strategies that will reshape libraries. . . user-centeredness, the use of technology to transform learning, new alliances and partnerships, experimentation as an organizational model, the library as collaboratory, user self-sufficiency, inclusiveness in library staff and programs, and the emergence of the value-added librarian."

Randall Hensley and Mary Ellen Litzinger turn our attention to the learner in "Designing Instruction on the Electronic Frontier: Learning Styles, Instructional Design, and Electronic Information Access Systems." They suggest that the searching of electronic databases encourages users to develop individual mental models of system structure, to become "subject catalogers," in effect. The models developed represent the application of individual (or group) learning preferences to information seeking, a sophisticated cognitive process, the successful practice of which depends more than ever on effective instruction.

In "Godzilla vs. King Kong: A Team Approach to Training on Internet Resources," and "Internet Instruction at the University of Montana," Vicki Pengelly and Barry Brown present a successful collaboration between the library and the computing center to provide hands-on internet instruction for students, faculty, and staff at the University of Montana. Begun in 1990, their courses have evolved from one class on electronic mail to a series of 17 classes offered each semester, course-integrated instruction, department workshops and seminars, and credit courses.

Eleven contributed papers address the components of instruction: the content, the methodology, the learner, and the instructor. Jeris Cassell and BethAnn Zambella share the experiences of an ad hoc group of librarians at Rutgers University who came together to develop workshops on electronic resources and have subsequently become a peer support group for training and sharing of tips and techniques. Non-traditional groups of learners are addressed in two papers: Gale Burrow and Cynthia Snyder present Claremont Colleges' program for training academic faculty in the use of electronic resources, while Bonnie Gratch and Helene LaFrance describe an extended education program for adults at St. Mary's College.

Several papers tackle the Internet. Thomas Leonhardt cautions us against imbuing technology with powers it may not have now or in the future; we need to teach the Internet—and information technology—as the tool it is, not as an end in itself. Craig Gibson and John Meade advocate a critical thinking approach that emphasizes decision-making frameworks, "cognitive maps," problem-solving methods, and critical evaluation of sources. Billie Reinhart and Gary Thompson discuss ways to teach critical thinking skills in evaluating Internet information and provide a set of criteria to be used in the evaluative process.

Electronic technology has increased our repertoire of teaching methods and changed the way we teach. Lori Arp, John Culshaw, and Keith Gresham examine electronic classroom facilities and recommend practical, technological, and pedagogical considerations for determining the appropriate setting to meet an instructional need. Naomi Lederer relates the challenges of teaching a televised course at Arizona State University and offers practical solutions to problems she has encountered. Fred Roecker shares information about the development and objectives of Ohio State University's Gateway to Information, an electronic gateway to resources and a self-instructional tool. Paul Adalian describes a multimedia program he has created using MacroMedia Director™ and QuickTime™ movies that enhances learning in one-shot and credit classes. And the students get to wear 3-D glasses! And, finally, Linda Friend and Bonnie Osif offer suggestions on how to accommodate the many interfaces that instructors and students alike must learn to deal with while tracking down needed information.

Looking back at the initial planning for "Cultivating the Electronic Landscape," it sometimes seems like a scene from a Judy Garland and Mickey Rooney movie—"Let's put on a show!" When the registration reached 125 and we were still getting calls, we began to realize we had a hit! In response to requests to "do it again," "LOEX" of the West will be a biennial conference held at different locations throughout the west, with the University of Washington sponsoring and hosting the 1996 meeting in Seattle. In a profession that values both, we are very pleased to have shared instructional innovations and begun a regional tradition.

NOTES

1. The conference planning committee consisted of Loretta Rielly, Oregon State University; Jan Davis Tudor, Willamette University; and Susan Barnes Whyte, Linfield College.
2. All the papers presented at the conference are reproduced here with the exception of "Library Instruction and the Internet: Why Us?" The presenters—Sarah Beasley, Oregon State University; Roy Bennett, Western Oregon State College; Isabel Stirling, University of Oregon—did not feel they could adequately replicate in print a lively, participative discussion among panelists and audience.

WELCOMING ADDRESS TO "LOEX" OF THE WEST:
CULTIVATING THE ELECTRONIC LANDSCAPE—FIVE CHALLENGES FOR LEADERSHIP[1]

Todd S. Hutton

After looking over the conference program and noticing the imaginative titles of the sessions, I could not help wondering if my brief remarks should have been titled "King Kong, Godzilla, Glaciers, Avalanches, and the Good, the Bad, and the Ugly—A Library Instruction Conference or a Science Fiction Writers Gathering After Two Delirious Days on Mt. Hood?" The images that the session titles evoke, while fanciful and fun, should also remind us that the new Information Age—and I am one who is convinced that humankind has just entered a new age that will span the next couple of centuries—will present imposing challenges for society in general and the information professions in particular. Many of these challenges will likely come at us like monsters and avalanches. Others will approach with the relentlessness of a glacier.

My immediate challenge in preparing for this address was deciding what to say to a group of professionals who are (or should be) society's vanguard for taming the monsters and turning the potentially destructive power of the avalanches and glaciers into a positive force. In keeping with the theme of challenges, I offer one: I ask you to take aggressive leadership and decisive action on five issues.

1. Equal and affordable access: With the coming privatization of the national information infrastructure and the entry of such players as TCI and Bell Atlantic on the Internet scene, equal access to information will become an even greater concern than it is today. We are already seeing, in this nascent Information Age, a further drawing of the line between the "haves" and "have nots," be they individuals, colleges, or public schools. Each of you as an individual, your respective libraries, and the American Library Association must demand of policy makers—at the local, state, and national levels—equal and affordable access to electronic information. You must work for it politically and fight for it in your own budget processes. We know that access to information can empower people. Without equal and affordable access, this country is ensured of perpetuating an information-economic underclass.
2. Library instruction as critical thinking instruction: As emerging information technologies make the concept of the virtual library more of a reality, the role of the librarian must become even more the role of a teacher. Equal and affordable access to electronic information will mean little if people are not taught how to evaluate information sources and how to apply critical thinking and inquiry skills to their searches for information. I have already seen students inundated with more information than they can handle. Many also are unable to distinguish reliable sources of information from those of a more spurious nature. And these students may be considered among the information elite today! A new version of the old adage about leading a horse to water seems to apply well to many students today. The problem with information access is no longer a matter of getting the horse to drink. It might best be expressed now as "How ya gonna keep 'em from trying to sip from Old Faithful?" Librarians must educate young people and adults alike about how to

choose the sources from which they will sip, how to do a taste test of the water they have sampled, and how to dive in when the water is really good.

3. Critical thinking about critical thinking instruction: If librarians are to become master teachers of critical thinking in the evaluation of information, they must also be engaged in self-directed improvement of practice. I like to think of this in terms of what Lawrence Stenhouse referred to as "critical action research," that is, the application of social science research methods for self-assessment and self-improvement of teaching.[2] This will require becoming more learner-centered than we tend to be in higher education. The focus of such critical assessment should be on how people learn (learning modalities/styles) and how well they learn, rather than on processes and resources. The latter can, of course, be one element in the assessment of how, and how well, patrons apply critical thinking to the task of gaining access to information. The aim of self-assessment should be to answer the questions, "How do you know what you are doing is effective?" and "How are you using the information to inform and improve your practice?"
4. Pro-active outreach and flexible service delivery: As the "virtual library" becomes both a depository for and a window onto the world of information and as the Internet becomes a commercial marketplace, librarians must find ways to go to their patrons, rather than waiting for their patrons to come to them for instruction in gaining access to electronic information. For public librarians, this might mean, for example, expanding the function of the bookmobile to become an "Internetmobile." Imagine bookmobiles of the future offering instruction in Internet navigation strategies, using on-board computers connected to the Internet via cellular or infrared transmissions or bookmobiles providing electronic document delivery from sources such as CARL, via similar technology. The diversity of patrons will increasingly demand a diversity of outreach activities by academic librarians. For academic programs, utilizing distance education methods, "distance library services," and "distance instruction in information access techniques" should become the norm. On campuses with

residential and commuter populations, pro-active service delivery should become standard practice.

5. Continuity of library instruction: Critical thinking for information access should become a lifelong learning skill requiring reinforcement and renewal. Greater continuity of instruction among kindergarten through 12th grade, public libraries, and academic libraries will promote more effective teaching and learning of information retrieval and evaluation skills. Library alliances and professional meetings can become venues for coordinating instructional methods and library instruction services and for sharing instructional techniques found to be effective with different populations. By introducing greater continuity into library instruction at different stages of learning, librarians of the future can avoid one of the plights of American education today—"trickle-down" blame for the poor basic skills of many of our citizens. Since the ability to get access to and critically evaluate information will be seen increasingly as a basic skill, the library profession has an opportunity to take a leading role in shaping how this basic lifelong skill will be taught throughout a person's lifetime.

Taking aggressive leadership in relation to these five issues will mean assuming a more prominent role as teachers and a more aggressive role as influencers of public policy. I believe that your expanding roles as teachers and trainers in critical thinking and problem solving for effective, lifelong use of information resources will help define the library profession in the Information Age and ensure its place among educational and information professions. I wish you the best for a successful conference.

NOTES AND REFERENCES

1. The text was expanded and adapted from welcoming remarks at the "LOEX" of the West Conference in June 1994.
2. Lawrence Stenhouse, *An Introduction to Curriculum Research and Development* (London: Heinemann Educational Books, 1975); Jean Rudduck and David Hopkins, *Research as a Basis for Teaching: Readings From the Work of Lawrence Stenhouse* (London: Heinemann Educational Books, 1985).

GLACIER OR AVALANCHE?

SHIFTS IN THE ELECTRONIC, EDUCATIONAL, AND LIBRARY LANDSCAPE

Lizabeth A. Wilson

I was born and raised a flatlander. I am comfortable with the landscape of the flatlands. I know the moods and nuances of each season. In the flatlands, you can always see where you are going. It is hard to get lost in a land where vistas are broad and wide. You can even tell in advance when it is going to rain by watching the rhythmic rustling of the corn fields as the winds begin to kick up.

The beauty that surrounds you in the flatlands is so subtle that it can go unnoticed unless you stop long enough to look around and take it all in. There are no grand gestures, just little things that, combined, create a certain splendor. The changes, focused along the horizon, are constant; they are governed by the seasons, the weather, or the cyclical nature of farming, or by all three at once. There is a sense of stability in the flatlands and the assurance that life and its routines will endure the storms that pass through. A quick look will not reveal everything; just as a quick look out your car window while traveling down Interstate 57 will not allow you to see the landscape that surrounds you. It is the second glance that will help you to appreciate this flatland.[1] I lived for many years in a landscape that required a second glance.

Two years ago, I moved to Seattle, to the Pacific Northwest, to a landscape that requires only a first glance to take your breath away. The first time I drove to work at the University of Washington, I came to the top of a hill on 45th Street and was stunned by an unobstructed view of the Olympic Mountains richly bathed in the morning light. I slammed on the brakes, shrieking to a stop, and gasped. I have since wondered how many other flatlanders have nearly caused an accident as I did that day.

Looming above all who live in Seattle is Tahoma, the majestic Mt. Rainier. The mountain is so splendid that an entire university is planned around the view. As an early Rainier climber Philemon Beecher Van Trump wrote:

> I obtained my first grand view of the mountain in August 1867, from one of the prairies southeast of Olympia. That first true vision of the mountain, revealing so much of its glorious beauty and grandeur, its mighty and sublime form filling up nearly all of the field of direct vision, swelling up from the plain and out of the green forest till its lofty triple summit towered immeasurably above the picturesque foothills, the westerly sun flooding with golden light and softening tints its lofty summit, rugged sides and far-sweeping flanks—all this impressed me so indescribably, enthused me so thoroughly, that I then and there vowed, almost with fervency, that I would some day stand upon its glorious summit, if that feat were possible to human effort and endurance.[2]

Van Trump fulfilled his vow three years later in 1870 when he climbed to the top of the mountain with Hazard Stevens guided by the Yakima tribesman Sluiskin. I, too, was filled with the fervent desire to climb Mt. Rainier after my first visit to the mountain, only to have that desire tempered when I read that people actually die during the climb.

My move from the landscape of the second glance to the landscape of first gasp has made me more and more aware of the nuances of each landscape, of the cues, the special forces, and the differences. Before my move, I didn't think much about the landscape. Now I find myself continually comparing and thinking and looking and wondering what other landscapes I might be missing. It is only when you step out of one landscape and move into another that you fully appreciate the forces that defined and shaped your environment before.

I'd like to step out of the immediate landscape of our individual libraries and take a look at the larger environment in which we teach, work, and learn—the electronic, library, and educational landscape. I hope to provide a view that maybe won't take your breath away, or cause you to slam on the brakes, but hopefully to take a second glance and look closer at the shifting landscape complete with both slow moving glaciers and unpredictable avalanches.

FORCES OF CHANGE

What is shaping our landscape? We are bombarded by major forces that are altering the landscape in which academic libraries exist including: changing users, information technology, social frameworks, educational forces, and economic realities.

Changing Users

Of all the transitions taking place, none is more important than the dramatic shifts in our population. These shifts are reflected in the decline of the traditional college-age population; an increase in older, part-time, and returning students; an increasing ethnic mix; and the influx of international students. We are drawing students from a changing immigrant population. Prior to 1970, immigrants came predominately from Western and Eastern Europe. Today most travel from Latin America and Asia. These demographic shifts have regional variations. Some states, such as Washington, are experiencing unprecedented population growth due to the baby boom echo and westward and northerly migration. With this growth comes increased pressure on some universities and colleges to expand the number of students they admit. Students from this increasingly pluralistic pool come to our campuses with diverse experiences, motivations, learning styles, educational demands, personal obligations, and financial situations.

In addition, our users are becoming invisible. With the availability of networks and more and more information available remotely, the numbers of individuals who never come through our doors to use the library will increase. But at the same time, our turnstile counts continue to increase, evidence of the growing importance of the library as a people place. This seemingly contradictory phenomenon is not unlike electronic shopping. While the QVC network expands, people continue to crowd into Nordstroms or meander through Seattle's Pike Place Market. The thousand year old tradition of going to the market (the social need filled by shopping) is not readily replaced by interactive television, just as remote access to information does not replace the library as a gathering place for people and ideas.

Information Technology

Increasing numbers of us are living in Toffler's electronic cottage with its microcomputers, VCRs, car phones, modems, fax machines, and CD-ROM players. Ninety-five percent of American homes have a VCR. This pervasive use and availability of technology has increased the public's expectations of libraries and the people who work in them. Media and information technologies have converged in multimedia—a fusion of technologies and solutions for combining text, illustrations, photographs, sound, voice, animation, and video in a new dynamic form.

There are many stories of how technology has transformed how we work. I used to say that Federal Express changed my life, then it was the fax machine, and now it is the Internet, a technology that is time and place independent. With the equalizing power of the Internet, it no longer matters about the size of your institution, where you are, or who you are. It only matters that you have access. No one is geographically disadvantaged on the Internet. With the help of navigational tools such as Gopher, Archie, Veronica, Jughead, Mosaic, WAIS, and the World-Wide Web, you are limited only by your imagination and stamina. But with these ever evolving tools, by the time we approach competency, changes are made, and we are back to being novices. The constant state of being a rookie is something that's hard to swallow for us the information experts.

Information technology has exacerbated the problem of information overload. Access is no longer the issue—excess is. In a technology forum held at the University of Washington, an education professor pleaded with the librarians in attendance to save him from drowning in information. He said the solution to this whole information saturation mess was to quadruple the number of librarians. He stressed that librarians are the ones who know how to handle information and to make it valuable. Futurist Paul Saffo agrees in a 1994 article in *Wired:*

> The future belongs to neither the conduit or content players, but those who control filtering, searching, and sense-making tools we will rely on to navigate through the expanses of cyberspace.
> In the world of hyperabundant content, point of view will become the scarcest of resources.[3]

(If you haven't discovered the magazine *Wired* yet, do take a look. I've heard it said that if you only read two journals make them *Wired* and the *Chronicle of Higher Education.*)

Information technology has brought profound changes in publishing and scholarly communication. Books on demand, custom publishing, and textbooks (or, as some have called them, pedagogical polyester) will be extinct by the year 2000 when such texts will be modified, customized daily, and zapped across the network or produced using multimedia.[4] In libraries, we have moved from automation to innovation to transformation.

Social Frameworks

The students entering our libraries have spent their formative years in a world that has undergone profound social change. These changes are most visible in the increasingly information-based society, global interdependence, and the accelerated pace of change. Today we live in an information-based society in which information increases geometrically, and no one person can keep pace with it. As Paul Saffo suggests:

> Think of information as a wave about to engulf us and about the need to learn to surf for information. Information surfers, who can develop knowledge and understanding out of large information flows, will be the pathfinders, applying new intellectual skills and working with more powerful information tools.[5]

The world is shrinking. Communication technology and microelectronics have moved the peoples of the world metaphorically, although not necessarily physically or intellectually, closer together. We live in a globally interconnected world in which geographical, psychological, social, and environmental phenomena are all interdependent. Few of us will forget watching television as the Berlin Wall was toppled or as Chinese students at American universities faxed information to protesters in Tiananmen Square to avoid the official news blackout and not marvel at how technology has made the world an electronic village. In addition to working with individuals in our own institutions, we are increasingly collaborating with others across the country and around the world as if they were in the next room. Instructional, research, and geographical barriers are now easily overcome. There are fewer disadvantages caused by lack of physical proximity.

Change has always been inevitable, but never has the world operated at the accelerated pace it does today. As historian Arthur Schlesinger said:

> This cumulative increase in the rate of change has been *the* decisive factor in the making of the modern world.[6]

John Secor, Chief Executive Officer of Yankee Book Peddler, a supplier of scholarly materials and collection management services to libraries, reminds us that:

> Change is not a 1990s phenomenon. Change is ageless. Organizations fail in periods of great change because leaders let obsolescence set in. Leaders and managers stop thinking and focusing people on opportunities.[7]

People have to learn to go with the flow and realize that there are no answers that will last for eternity.[8]

Educational Mandates

Educational mandates emanating from a seemingly infinite number of commissions have called for broad reform. Central to these reports is the concern that we are neither educating students in the basics or how to function in the modern world. Skills and information become dated quickly, making it difficult to know what should be taught. Educators are in agreement that students should no longer be expected to master a finite set of skills, but rather learn how to learn so that learning becomes a lifelong process.

One of the increased demands on students is the ability to sort through and evaluate millions of bits of information. To be successful, they must be able to make good decisions about the consumption of information. Critical thinking—deciding what to believe or how to act—has become a survival skill. To be personally empowered, individuals need sophisticated information management skills.

Changes in the curriculum are reshaping our campuses. We are witnessing a move away from textbooks and reserved readings toward resource-based teaching. We are beginning to see these changes reflected in accreditation processes. Accrediting agencies are no longer fixating on volume count but on outcome-based evidence that the library is contributing to the information literacy of students. It remains to be seen, however, what long-term impact these shifts in accreditation will have on how we do business.

There is a wide-spread perception that the quality of undergraduate education has deteriorated. Whether or not this is true doesn't matter. The view is strongly held by legislators, parents, students, and funding agencies. The fallout is seen in legislative mandates for faculty workload studies, distrust of higher education, and the public's call for accountability.

We have also experienced a major paradigm shift in the thinking and research on how people learn. As Lori Arp has synthesized,[9] the old traditions tell us:

> [T]he learner is an empty vessel, a blank slate; that learning is an additive process; that learning is measured by changes in behavior alone; and that the teacher is the expert authority (the sage on the stage).

The new traditions tell us:

> [T]hat the learner comes to learning with his/her own schemata; that the learner constructs and transforms knowledge; that learning is not additive, that learners move back and forth between parts and wholes and wholes and parts; and that the teacher is a coach, modeler, facilitator (the guide on the side).

Not unlike how the logger's world in the Pacific Northwest has changed, this new tradition throws our first-learned teaching and learning behaviors into disarray. The paradigm is toppled as we are challenged to reform, rethink, and restructure how we teach and work.

Economic Realities

Can America afford its colleges, universities, and libraries? And if it can, will it chose to? From all the budget cutting going on across the country, the answer seems to be no. We are cutting costs, eliminating programs, restructuring, facing deficits, and getting very lean. I suggest to you that this is not just one of those cyclical funding blips.

We can't afford to do business as usual. Bigger is no longer better. Bigger may make us less viable. Funding for research is changing. The major change is an incipient trend toward the federal agencies setting the topics to be studied. This increased emphasis on targeted research is driven by the desire of elected officials to have relatively rapid and accountable social value for dollars spent. In libraries, we talk about access or ownership, but we don't fully understand the economic, research, or social implications.

We're challenged to find less expensive ways to deliver instruction through distance education, sharing academic departments among universities, and off-loading information once delivered by a professor in the classroom to educational technology. Will we have an excess of professors? Will there be an excess of librarians?

We have shared cataloging on a national basis through bibliographic utilities. What happens now that we can share reference and instructional expertise and services over the Net? The new *kanbrain* systems have the potential to make classrooms and training and teaching departments obsolete.[10] At the heart of kanbrain development is the rapid spread of performance support systems. A shift to kanbrain systems may replace the warehousing of knowledge in classrooms and libraries and degreed experts with just-in-time intelligence and on-demand hyperlearning.

OPPORTUNITIES

What do all these changes mean for us as we try to navigate our way up the mountains or across the crevasses in our environment?

These changes and shifts mean that opportunities are everywhere. In a landscape of little change, the opportunities are proportionally small. In a landscape of dynamic shifts, myriad opportunities surround us, if only we can keep our footing long enough to see them.

A leading business school did a study that showed that its graduates did well at first, but in 10 years, they were overtaken by a more street-wise, pragmatic group. The professor who ran the study gave this reason: "We taught them how to solve problems, not recognize opportunities."[11]

Peter Drucker underscores the pivotal importance of listening for the knock of opportunity when he writes about the "Five Deadly Business Sins":

> The last of the deadly sins is feeding problems and starving opportunities. For many years, I have been asking new clients to tell me who their best performing people are. And then I ask, "What are they assigned to?" Almost without exception, the performers are assigned to problems—to the old business that is sinking faster than had been forecast. Then I ask, "And who takes care of opportunities?" Almost invariably, the opportunities are left to fend for themselves. All one gets by problem-solving is damage containment. Only opportunities produce results and growth.[12]

What are our opportunities in this shifting landscape full of avalanches, crevasses, and glaciers? They are many and varied: user-centeredness, using technology to transform, alliances and partnerships, experimentation, collaboratory, self-sufficiency, inclusiveness, and value-added librarians.

User-Centeredness

Most libraries say they serve users. In reality, most of them serve themselves.[13] We need to understand that simply making our libraries more manageable is not the answer. In doing so, we may end up serving ourselves better but at the expense of the user. First we need to acknowledge that taking care of the user is a priority. Second, we have to turn that acknowledgment into action. We have to not only talk the talk but walk the talk.[14]

In the user-connected library, quality services and user satisfaction are goals shared by *all* staff, not just the director or the head of public services. Focus is explicitly on the information and communication needs of users. Services are emphasized through ongoing assessment, user feedback, empowerment of staff to solve problems, a high level of staff interaction with users, differentiated service which responds to diverse needs, and library functions and operations organized to facilitate, *not hinder*, the attainment of the user self-sufficiency. All staff have the constancy of purpose to strive to understand user needs and expectations and develop responsive programs. Our success hinges on becoming user-connected.

Community Analysis

How do we walk the talk? Community analysis and needs assessment is the key.

To be user-centered, we need to review who our users are, define our services, measure user satisfaction, assess user needs, and position our libraries to make wise use of resources, to select the best from a growing array of options, to reach out and get feedback from our invisible users, to develop a customer orientation, to set in place mechanisms for continuous improvement, and to market services realistically. Most importantly, we need to engage our staff and our users in a decision-making dialog on what new services and programs will be introduced, and what we will no longer do.

Community analysis must be sustained on an ongoing and operational basis. We need to develop in-house measurement and evaluation expertise through staff development initiatives, purchase expertise where appropriate, and commit funds to support this expertise. We must make assessment an administrative and operational priority by tying it to funding and goal setting. We must demonstrate to users the direct benefit of listening to them. And we must dispel the myth, change the attitude, that assessment is an add-on, something extra, something that is not part of our jobs.

One of my favorite Gary Larson cartoons depicts Satan and his cohorts laughing as they read submissions to hell's suggestion box as the damned toil in the flames. When we work to connect with users and tell them we care about their input, we are obliged to do something with what they tell us, unlike the suggestion box in hell.

For the first time in nearly a century when reference services were first introduced in academic libraries, we have the chance to redesign our libraries and, consequently, the whole campus information landscape in fundamental ways. We must include users in the process. User involvement is crucial because in the shifting information landscape, we have, perhaps for the first time, serious competitors. We are no longer the only game in town. We no longer have a captive audience.

Technology to Transform

Technology has revolutionized the look and feel of our libraries. How technology is introduced and used are defining opportunities. We have the opportunity to showcase, integrate, and innovate with technology. We need to share technology in a non-prescriptive manner where experimentation is the norm. Technology as a transforming opportunity does not mean presenting technology for technology's sake but for its potential to transform access, learning, and research.

The virtual library is no longer the futurist's dream. Educational technology is allowing us to distribute instruction and training anytime, anywhere. Z39.50 is becoming a functioning reality. Full-text is no longer a theoretical issue; it is an operational challenge. Internet has become integrated into our workblood. Adaptive technology is breaking down barriers. The digital revolution is over. We are living it.

Alliances and Partnerships

Just as we have learned that no one library can operate in a collection vacuum, so we have realized that we cannot provide effective programs without collaboration with others on and off campus. But collaboration can create confusion. We must know what business we are in, otherwise, we will go down many a blind alley for the sake of cooperation.

What business are we in?[15] Ten years ago, we might have said to collect and organize knowledge and to teach users how to use library resources effectively. Today we might say to provide access to information wherever it resides worldwide, to package this information with value added, and to teach and guide users how to access, interpret, and use it.

During a period of rapid change, the rules are changing just as quickly. The greater the number of players who come to the table who might know some of the rules, the higher the probability that we will solve problems and identify new opportunities. Cooperation and shared visions are fundamental to successful partnerships among computing centers, academic departments, support services, development offices, vendors and suppliers, university administration, libraries, and users.

We have the opportunity to add value to more endeavors than ever before within our own institutions and beyond. By building alliances and partnerships within the university, between universities, with schools, with public libraries, and with our suppliers and users, we can avoid a destructive academic slugfest.

Experimentation

We must embrace the opportunity to create environments where new approaches and structures are encouraged, and innovation and risk-taking are rewarded. It is not just the responsibility of the library director to create this environment; it is a responsibility we all share.

In the business world, it is said that it takes 60 product ideas to come up with one successful one. Are we allowing ourselves 59 failures for each success? Are we creating environments that allow us to take these risks?

In environments that foster risk taking, fluid organizational structures are paramount. Traditional structures defined by function or departmental affiliation no longer work. We must get out of what Michael Hammer and James Champy, authors of *Reengineering the Corporation,* call *functional silos*—work boundaries that compartmentalize and segment our organizations.[16] The hierarchy has lost much of its usefulness. The impacted wisdom group is no longer wise.

The best environment for creative work is on scale with the extended family where people can find autonomy within a larger whole. Groups need to be brought together based on a common goal. The structure must allow for project development, foster collaboration, and create a safe haven for ideas and experimentation. We need to publicly applaud individuals who take risks and encourage people to fall in love with change. We need to applaud ourselves. We need to practice pro-active innovation and listen to those on the fringe. As Larry Wilson of Pecos River Learning Center says:

> You'll always do what you've always done if you always think the way you've always thought.[17]

Collaboratory

At a National Science Foundation workshop in 1989, Joshua Lederberg proposed an alternative structure for teaching and research called the collaboratory.[18] The collaboratory is envisioned as an advanced, distributed infrastructure which uses technology to relax the constraints of distance, time, and even reality. It supports and enhances intellectual teamwork in both research and teaching. There is growing consensus that the next major paradigm shift in computing is in the direction of the collaboratory. Perhaps the collaboratory provides us with an infrastructure, the "tooling," for learning organizations and libraries.

The library as collaboratory is a teaching facility, not a book warehouse. All services, programs, and resource decisions are evaluated in terms of how they support the learning organization. As Joan Bechtel suggests, the most appropriate metaphor for the emerging paradigm of libraries is a conversation.[19] She suggests that both views of the library as a warehouse and as the heart of the university are equally archaic. Storing books is *one* of many services libraries provide. The heart of the intellectual life is more likely to be in a group of friends or among colleagues. Libraries do collect people and ideas and facilitate conversation among them. The preservation of crucial conversations serves not only to preserve the record but more importantly to ensure the continuation of significant conversations already in progress. We can make a persuasive case for institutionalizing collaborative learning with bricks and mortar by designing spaces that facilitate conversation among people and ideas.

In order to cope with the overwhelming information choices, users of all levels and backgrounds need quality filtering mechanisms—critical thinking skills. We need to use methods that are effective in addressing these higher level cognitive demands.

The shortcomings of the "I-lecture-you-listen" approach, the most prevalent teaching method in higher education, is becoming increasingly problematic because of the information explosion, curricular reform, and increasing diversity of learners and workers. Many educators have successfully used collaborative learning approaches to address these new learning demands. Collaborative learning is an umbrella term for a broad array of teaching and training methods that are learner-centered rather than teacher-, librarian-, or lecture-centered. Collaborative learning is based on several assumptions: that learning is an active, constructive process; that learning depends on rich contexts—schemata; that learners are diverse; and that learning is inherently social.

There are several approaches of particular interest to librarians:[20] cooperative learning, problem-centered techniques, peer teaching, discussion groups, and learning communities.

At the University of Washington, we are involved in an exciting collaborative endeavor to build electronic learning communities. The initiative is called UWired and it seeks to integrate electronic communication and information navigation skills into instruction and learning. Targeting a pilot group of freshmen and faculty for intensive technology instruction and use, UWired will serve as a prototype for integrating technology into teaching and learning. Bringing together librarians, computing experts, faculty, and students, its purpose is to create an electronic community in which communication, collaboration, and information technology become an ongoing, integral part of teaching and learning.

Self-Sufficiency

Libraries say they support user self-sufficiency. I challenge you to go into any of our libraries and see if you don't experience anxiety and heart palpitations when you have to use the library as a user. We have new opportunities to promote user self-sufficiency if we only take a second glance. We need to take signage seriously and use it wisely. We need to look at space through the user's eyes. We need to provide opportunities for self-orientation through audio, interactive video, and even virtual reality methods. We need to design our systems and interfaces with a goal of user self-sufficiency. We need to break down the barriers we continue to build. We need to build what Michael Gorman calls the "BI-less" library so we can get on with the business of education.[21] We have the tools to allow our users to be self-sufficient. Are we using them?

Inclusiveness

We not only have the opportunity but the obligation to create places in which all of our users, regardless of background or experience, are comfortable. We need to embrace and reflect diversity through our staff, programs, and priorities.

The library must address the different learning styles of its users and employees as our classrooms and workplaces become increasingly multicultural. Our classrooms and workplaces have always been diverse as there is diversity even in seeming homogeneity, but only recently has this been acknowledged. We must do what Ellen Broidy has asked—teach as if people really mattered.[22]

We need to create environments in which individual contributions and visions are highly valued. The quality of programs is a direct outgrowth of our staff. As the late library visionary Hugh Atkinson was fond of saying—success is not a zero sum game. There is room for everyone to succeed. An environment which allows each to contribute her or his best, which welcomes diversity and values individual integrity and input, is required if any of us are to succeed. We have the opportunity to enrich our landscape through a global orientation with respect to curricula, collections, services, users, and our colleagues.

Value-Added Librarian

How valuable are librarians? What is it that librarians offer that no one else can bring to the table of opportunity?

Librarians know how to organize information and know how to create the interface between the information that they have organized and the user. That interface may take the form of the reference interview, system design and embedded filters, or instruction and education.

Anne Lipow offers a job description for the twenty-first century that describes this value-added librarian.[23] She calls for:

> [A]n advanced degree in librarianship, with a specialization in user-agent systems; depth of knowledge about resources and research issues; energy and enthusiasm for solving client's informational problems; ability to thrive in conditions of ambiguity and rapid change; skilled in question handling and instructional techniques; demonstrated knowledge of applications of current and emerging technology as it contributes to meeting the needs of researchers; ability to plan, design, and evaluate systems; ability to communicate clearly, knowledgeably and personably, orally, and in writing with a variety of client constituencies and colleagues; demonstrated ability to work both independently and as part of a team. Salary: Comparable to compensation in other value-added professions such as medicine and law.

Value-added librarians are advocates, consultants, designers, and educators. As advocates, they represent the user in the creation of information systems and policies and safeguard equal access to information and intellectual freedom. As consultants, they advise and guide users in problem solving and provide an informed context for decision making. As designers, they create actual and virtual collections and construct information systems that require little or no learning time. As educators, they teach and empower individuals to manage the information process.

CONCLUSION

We teach and learn in the environment of higher education. At times, we may perceive this landscape to change at glacial speeds, especially when responding to outside forces. Some elements of our environment do move as slowly as the ancient Nisqually Glacier on Mt. Rainier, but others shift as quickly as the unexpected avalanche. Avalanches and glaciers exist simultaneously on Mt. Rainier. Like hundreds of adventurers who have traversed crevasses on the Nisqually Glacier, we can survive and flourish in our shifting landscape.

The key is to keep in touch with our environment. Some forces and elements will be obvious, like the landscape of the first gasp that forces us to slam on the brakes. Others require a second glance, like the view you see from your window as you drive down the interstate in the flatlands. Whether you must take a second look or a first gasp, look for the opportunities that abound in the shifting landscape. When you feel you are walking into a blizzard of information overload and unknowns, unable to see what is before you, try turning around. You will find that new opportunities are right behind you, in unexpected places, in the shifting electronic, library, and educational landscape.

NOTES AND REFERENCES

1. The concept for the second glance and this paraphrased passage are from the "Preface," Larry Kanfer, *On Second Glance: Midwest Photographs* (Urbana and Chicago, IL: University of Illinois Press, 1992).
2. As cited in Dee Molenaar, *The Challenge of Rainier: A Record of the Explorations and Ascents, Triumphs and Tragedies on the Northwest's Greatest Mountain* (Seattle, WA: Mountaineers, 1971), p. 34.
3. Paul Saffo, "It's the Context, Stupid," *Wired* (March 1994).
4. David L. Wilson, "Textbook Publishers Struggle to Embrace New Technologies," *Chronicle of Higher Education* (May 18, 1994): A21.
5. Paul Saffo, "Surfing for Information," *Personal Computing* (July 1989): 213-224.
6. Arthur M. Schlesinger, Jr., "The Challenge of Change," *New York Times Magazine* (July 27, 1986): 20.
7. John R. Secor, "Precarious Crossroads: Time to Take the Road Less Traveled," manuscript of paper delivered at the Oklahoma Conference (March 4, 1994): 4.
8. Tom Peters as quoted in Thomas Kiely, "Unconventional Wisdom," *CIO* (December 15, 1993-January 1, 1994): 26-27.
9. Lori Arp, "An Introduction to Learning Theory," in *Sourcebook for Bibliographic Instruction*, edited by Katherine Branch (Chicago: Association of College and Research Libraries, 1993), pp. 5-15.
10. Lewis J. Perelman, "Kanban to Kanbrain," *Forbes ASAP* (June 6, 1994): 85-95.
11. Roger von Oech, *Roger von Oech's Creative Whack Pack: 64 Creative Thinking Strategies* (Stamford, CT: U.S. Games Systems, Inc., 1989).
12. Peter F. Drucker, "The Five Business Sins," *Wall Street Journal* (October 21, 1993): A16.
13. This statement was paraphased to fit libraries from Rosabeth Moss Kanter, "Think Like the Customer: The Global Business Logic," *Harvard Business Review* (July-August 1992): 9.
14. Secor, "Precarious Crossroads," p. 8.
15. John Secor calls this question in "Precarious Crossroads," p. 9.
16. Michael Hammer and James Champy, *Reengineering the Corporation: A Manifesto for Business Revolution* (New York: HarperCollins, 1993), p. 28.
17. Larry Wilson as quoted in Daniel Coleman, *The Creative Spirit* (New York and London: Dutton, 1992), p. 134.

18. Joshua Lederberg as cited in James J. Duderstadt, "Redrawing the Boundaries," *The University Record* (University of Michigan) (December 7, 1992), 5.

19. "Mime and Supermine: Collaborative Learning and Instructional Technology," *EDUCOM Review* (March/April 1994): 63.

20. Lori Arp, Sharon Mader, Mary Jane Petrowski, and Lizabeth Wilson, "Cooperative Learning: A Guided Discovery Workshop," in *The Impact of Technology on Library Instruction,* edited by Linda Shirato (Ann Arbor, MI: Pierian Press, 1995), pp. 21-75.

21. Michael Gorman, "Send for a Child of Four! or Creating the BI-Less Library," *Library Trends* (Winter 1991): 354-362.

22. Ellen Broidy, "Celebrating Diversity: Teaching Library Skills as if People Mattered," in *Reaching and Teaching Diverse Library User Groups,* edited by Linda Shirato (Ann Arbor, MI: Pierian Press, 1989).

23. Anne Grodzins Lipow, editor, *Rethinking Reference in Academic Libraries* (Berkeley, CA: Library Solutions Press, 1993), pp. 201-205.

DESIGNING INSTRUCTION ON THE ELECTRONIC FRONTIER:

LEARNING STYLES, INSTRUCTIONAL DESIGN, AND ELECTRONIC INFORMATION ACCESS SYSTEMS

Randall Hensley and Mary Ellen Litzinger

It has occurred to us that the theme of this conference—"teaching and learning in a climate of constant change"—describes not only the technology we work with but also the people who use our resources. As librarians and teachers we are being constantly challenged to provide instruction that is timely, relevant, and appropriate for groups of users who appear to be constantly changing. These groups are different from each other, and we know that they are certainly different from the users we encountered when we joined the profession 22 years ago.

We have also realized with disheartening frequency that the teaching techniques that served us well in the past are no longer quite as effective. Like many of you, we have modeled our teaching techniques after the strategies that work well for us as learners. For example, Mary Ellen has a strong preference for visual learning, and she has been conditioned to learn from lectures. Consequently, her classes and workshops are interlaced with slides and overheads and feature her doing most of the talking. We have never stopped to consider whether the way we teach is appropriate for all the groups with whom we work. We assumed that because we were teaching reasonably well, the people in our classes were also learning reasonably well. It was only when we realized that several of the people who attended our classes subsequently appeared confused and bewildered at the reference desk that we began to question this assumption. We found ourselves asking this question, which succinctly explains the nexus of our problem: "Isn't it time to stop confusing teaching with learning?"

Put another way, what this question suggests is that proficient teaching by itself does not ensure effective learning. What is needed is a consideration of how individual students prefer to learn and a commitment to using this information to inform our classroom teaching. What we would like to do is share with you some of the research that's been done in the area of learning style preference and suggest some ways you can incorporate this information into the instructional design of your classroom activities. We will not be able to exhaustively cover each style in such a short time, but hopefully we will be able to raise your awareness of the different learning styles that may lurk about in your classrooms and stimulate you to discover new and innovative ways to design learning activities that support your instruction.

We would like to focus our consideration of learning style preferences on three questions:

Question 1: "What is a learning style?" The phrase "learning style" appears with such amazing frequency in the literature of instructional design that it's in danger of losing its meaning. We will try to provide a basic definition for you.

Question 2: "What learning styles do individuals prefer?" There is an extensive body of research that supports the idea that individuals develop unique learning preferences. We would like to describe three of these preferences and suggest teaching strategies that will allow you to accommodate these preferences into your classroom.

Question 3: "What learning styles do groups prefer?" A body of research has emerged in the last 15 years which identifies the learning preferences of various societal groups. While there is by no means universal agreement on the outcomes of this research, we would like to share some of the data with you and suggest ways you can use this information in designing your classroom activities.

WHAT IS A LEARNING STYLE?

The term "learning style" describes the different ways in which children and adults prefer to think and learn. Each person develops a unique set of pervasive, consistent behaviors or approaches to learning. These approaches are based on the way a learner thinks about and reacts to a situation and together these preferences influence the development of a learning style. In general, a learning style is composed of three processes: (1) cognition, the process of acquiring knowledge; (2) conceptualization, the act of processing information; and (3) affective behavior patterns, the combination of motives, judgments, values, and emotions that help one decide to perform a specific action. Let us examine each of these processes in more detail

Cognition is the process of answering the question, "How do I know?" It involves the interaction of two activities: perceiving and acquiring knowledge. Perception is the initial stage of cognition and involves using our senses to receive and discern information. Complementing perception is the process of acquiring, or gaining, knowledge. Some people prefer to use abstract sources such as research data to discover information. Others prefer to read or listen to someone else's description. And some learners are sensory specialists who prefer to receive information using their hearing, sight, or touch.

People also differ in how they think about or conceptualize the information they acquire. Some people are convergers, always looking for connections among seemingly unrelated events. Others are divergers, for whom one idea triggers a multitude of new ideas which seem to occur simultaneously. Some people order their thoughts in a linear sequence while others structure thoughts in randomly patterned clusters. "Thinking speed" also influences learning style: some people think quickly and verbalize their thoughts spontaneously. Others are slower and more reflective, pausing between thoughts and speaking in elliptical drawn out sentences.

Differences in affective behavior patterns such as motivation, decision-making style, values, and emotional preferences also define a learning style. Some people are motivated by an internalized value system of their own design, while others are driven by external motivation, such as the opinions of neighbors or friends. Some learners strive to please others, while others ignore or rebel against external demands. Some learners make decisions logically and rationally, while others make decisions focused on their perceptions and emotions. Individuals have varying emotional investments in education as well. Some learners are emotionally involved in everything they do and prefer an emotionally charged classroom where the teacher is a high-energy, dynamic presenter. Others students are more "emotionally neutral," and they work best in a low key environment.

The important thing to remember about learning styles is that all styles are valid because they are the result of legitimately developed behavior patterns. To deny learners access to environments which support their preferences is to deny learners part of their identity.

Learning styles can be grouped into three general areas: (1) cognitive, those styles that focus on how we perceive and process information from our environment; (2) affective, those styles that focus on emotional motivation and values; and (3) kinetic, those styles that deal with physical motion. Because of the importance of cognitive processes to successful electronic information access, we will confine the remainder of our discussion to the styles in this area.

WHAT LEARNING STYLES DO INDIVIDUALS PREFER?

First, we would like to discuss a group of learning styles that identify individual learning preferences without regard to gender, age, or multicultural group. While several styles have been identified in the literature, three preferences have been well researched and documented: (1) field sensitivity/independence; (2) sensory preference; and (3) experiential learning preference. The following is a brief discussion of each preference group.

The term "field sensitivity/independence" (often referred to as "field dependence/independence") describes the degree to which people can differentiate an object from its background. If you can identify a single object embedded in a complex of other figures, you have a tendency toward field independence. If you need someone to point the figure out to you, you're more likely field sensitive. The concept of field sensitivity/independence was first recognized by Herman Witkin during World War II.[1] Witkin was asked to determine why certain pilots became physically disoriented and crashed their planes when they lost contact with the ground. Witkin theorized that a pilot's ability to distinguish an objective from its surrounding environment could predict his ability to maintain correct physical orientation while flying. After the war, Witkin expanded his study to include the effect of field dependence/independence on different aspects of personality. He discovered that a tendency for field sensitivity/independence develops separately from intelligence, while still influencing the development of one's social behavior. Specifically, Witkin's research uncovered these correlations.

Field independent learners tend to develop sequential and structural thinking patterns, can easily learn material that is inanimate and impersonal, are not easily affected by others opinions, and tend to persist in completing unstimulating tasks. Field sensitive learners often exhibit improvisational and intuitive thinking, can easily learn material that has a predominantly human, and social content, have a good memory for verbally presented ideas and information, are influenced by an authority figure's self-confidence or self-doubt in performance, and tend to withdraw from unexciting tasks.

What strategies can you incorporate in your teaching to accommodate field sensitive/field independence preferences? When working with field-sensitive learners, it is helpful to focus on student needs rather than an instructor-generated agenda, acting as a consultant/coach in the classroom rather than authority figure and approaching each class as an informal opportunity to encourage discussion. In contrast, field independent learners prefer their instructors to use a formal, lecture-oriented approach in the classroom and respond well to impersonal rewards like grades. When working with independent learners, instructors should encourage individual achievement, emphasize facts and principles, and try to remain as emotionally detached as possible in the classroom. These strategies are summarized in Figure 1.

Another way to think about individually-based learning styles is to consider which sensory channel—auditory, visual, or kinetic—a learner prefers to use sending and receiving messages.[2] Auditory learners use their voices and ears as primary modes for

Preference	Attributes	Instructional Strategies
Field Independence	• Able to distinguish specific information from total picture • Exhibits sequential, structural thinking patterns • More easily learns materials that are inanimate and personal • Not easily affected by others' opinions • Persists with unstimulating tasks	• Focus on task at hand • Foster modeling behaviors in the classroom • Use formal, lecture oriented teaching approach • Use impersonal rewards • Encourage individual achievement • Emphasize facts and principles • Remain emotionally detached in the classroom
Field Sensitivity	• Perceives information as part of a whole • Exhibits improvisational and intuitive thinking • More easily learns materials that have human, social content • Good memory for verbally presented ideas and information • Influenced by authority figure's confidence/doubt re: performance • Withdraws from unstimulating tasks	• Focus on student needs • Act as consultant in the classroom • Use an informal approach, elicit discussion • Use personal rewards, especially praise • Encourage group achievement • Identify with the class and its tasks • Narrate and humanize concepts

Figure 1. Preferential Learning Styles: Field Independence/Sensitivity

learning. They remember what they hear, and they want to verbalize confusion and enthusiasm and attend to all the noises around them. Although they are easily distracted by any kind of noise, they are also uncomfortable with silence and will often talk to fill the "silence gap." Visual learners want to see things written down. They prefer a pleasant and orderly physical environment—these are the people who have orderly desks and decorate their workspaces. They review and study material by reading over notes, recopying and reorganizing them in outline form. If you are the sort of person who has to "neaten up" your work area before you tackle a major writing project, then you are probably a visual learner. Kinesthetic learners tend to act out a situation. They handle materials constantly, tend to jump up and down in a classroom (if they are a younger learner), and fidget when asked to sit for a period of time. As these learners get older, they tend to take notes to keep their hands busy, but they never re-read them.

There are several instructional design strategies you can use to accommodate each sensory learning preference. When working with an auditory learner, encourage discussion to channel all that verbal enthusiasm into productive learning situations. It's also important to control classroom sound level as much as possible for the auditory learner. When working with a visual learner, build on the affinity for visualization by using charts and diagrams to express concepts. Use overhead transparencies and handouts—it is not a redundancy to handout printed versions of your overheads to the visual learner. Another strategy is to provide a copy of your lecture notes to students after your class is finished. When working with the kinesthetic learner, provide lots of experimentation and "hands-on" practice. These students are the ones who will be touching the keyboard before you have finished introducing yourself. Spend a minimal time on lecture, trying instead to accomplish your teaching through the use of "guided design" exercises structured so that key concepts and principles will become obvious as the students progress through each example. These strategies are summarized in Figure 2.

Preference	Attributes	Instructional Strategies
Auditory	• Remembers what he/she hears • Verbalizes confusion & enthusiasm • Attends to all noises and distractions	• Encourage class discussion • Control sound level as much as possible
Visual	• Comfortable with orderly physical environment • Organizes materials and workspaces • Seeks out diagrams and pictures to increase understanding	• Use diagrams and charts to express concepts • Liberally use overhead transparencies and handouts • Provide lecture notes after class
Kinetic	• Constantly handling materials • Jumps up and down in class • "Fidgets" when forced to sit down • Makes lots of notes but rarely uses them	• Include experimentation and "hands on" practice • Minimal use of lecture • Provide "guided design" exercises

Figure 2. Preferential Learning Styles: Sensory Preferences

Finally, it is important to consider how each learner processes the learning experience that you offer in the classroom. This way of looking at learning styles, called "experiential learning," was popularized by David Kolb, a faculty member at Case Western Reserve University, who identified a cycle of four different experiential learning style preferences.[3] In this model he identified two major dimensions of learning—perception and processing—and said that learning results from the interaction between the way people perceive and then process what they perceive. He described a continuum of experience for both processes. At one end of the perception continuum are people who perceive through concrete experience and at the other extreme are people who perceive through abstract conceptualization. As he continued his research, he discovered that people process information on a continuum as well. Some learners process information through active experimentation while others process through reflective experimentation.

The juxtaposition of the two continuums led Kolb to describe a four-cycle model of learning styles: (1) divergers who prefer to perceive information through concrete experience and process information using reflective observation; (2) assimilators who prefer to perceive information through abstract conceptualization and process information using reflective observation; (3) convergers who prefer to perceive information through abstract conceptualization and process information using active experimentation; and (4) accommodators who prefer to perceive information through concrete experience and process information using active experimentation.

Each phase of the Kolb's experiential cycle has discreet attributes that are supported by specific instructional strategies. (Note: These strategies are summarized in Figure 3.) Divergers understand an experience by analyzing it and frequently ask "Why?" rather than "How?" or "What?" The divergent learner must understand how a specific learning experience will affect him/her and is particularly sensitive to his/her own feelings about the learning experience as well as those of fellow classmates. These learners profit from peer feedback and discussion situations and perceive an instructor as a potential coach/helper who will provide personalized counseling. Assimilators are driven to integrate new experiences with what they already know and carefully observe a

Preference	Attributes and learning strength	Preferred learning situations
Diverger (Concrete/Reflective)	• Searches for personal meaning through experience and intuition • Understands an experience by analyzing it • Frequently asks "Why?" • Must understand how learning will affect him/her • Sensitive to feelings and people	• Learning from new experiences, games, role plays • Peer feedback and discussion • Personalized counseling • Teacher as coach/helper
Assimilator (Abstract/Reflective)	• Driven to integrate new experiences with what he/she already knows • Carefully observes before making judgments • Frequently asks "What?" • Wants accurate information and immediately organizes that information into concepts and theories • Views things from different perspectives	• Lectures • Opportunities to take an observer role • Objective tests that measure one's knowledge of an issue • Teacher as guide/master
Converger (Abstract/Active)	• Seeks applications for what he/she learns • Learns by thinking • Prefers logical analysis of ideas • Asks "how does it work?" • Systematic planning • Deductive thinking - acting on the basis of one's understanding of a situation	• Theory readings • Study time alone • Clear, well-structured presentation of ideas • Teacher as a communicator of information • Allow time for experimentation and practice
Accommodator (Concrete/Active)	• Analyzes current learning for relevance and significance • Learns by doing • Asks "What if?" • Actively seeks relationships and connections between concepts • Synthesizes relationships into knowledge • Comfortable with unresolved complexities • Likes being the "devil's advocate"	• Provide opportunities to practice and receive feedback • Small group discussions • Provide projects and individualized, self-paced learning activities • Act as a performance role model

Figure 3. Preferential Learning Styles: Experiential Learning Cycle

situation before making judgments. They want accurate information that they can immediately organize into concepts and theories. Lectures are an effective teaching strategy for these learners, and they tend to view teachers as guides and masters who can supply an endless store of information. Convergers seek applications for what they learn and are constantly asking the question, "How does this work?" They analyze new experiences deductively, acting on the basis of their understanding of a situation. These learners appreciate a clear, well-structured instructional presentation followed by plenty of time for experimentation and practice. Accommodators analyze each new learning situation for relevance and significance and actively seek relationships and connections between concepts, synthesizing these relationships into new knowledge. They are comfortable with unresolved complexities and have the ability to get things done, often taking risks in the process. These students enjoy playing "devil's advocate" and often preface their questions with the phrase "Why doesn't the system...?" These students thrive if given individual, self-paced learning activities with generous opportunities for practice and feedback.

WHAT LEARNING STYLES DO GROUPS PREFER?

A body of research has emerged in the last 15 years which identifies the learning preferences of various societal groups. While there is by no means universal agreement on the outcomes of this research, we would like to share some of the data with you and suggest ways you can use this information in designing your classroom activities. For clarity's sake, we have divided the research into three areas which represent what we traditionally think of as "diversity-based" groups: (1) gender; (2) age; and (3) multicultural/ethnic group. Let us quickly review some of the research findings.

Recent research about women and computers indicates that a gender gap exists in the way students use computers for information gathering.[4] A "we-can-I-can't" syndrome exists, suggesting that female students think that computer proficiency is possible for groups of women working together yet impossible for individual women to accomplish. This negative attitude persists despite conventional instructional intervention such as hands-on classes and lectures. To counteract this perception, instructors are encouraged to create a socially engaging physical environment (structure "learning in the round" discussion groups instead of lectures), design interactive discussion groups in which women are encouraged to participate, develop team-based exercises where women have the opportunity to work with other women, use female-based analogies and examples during lectures and demonstrations, and ensure that females have the same access to computers and CD-ROM equipment as males.

"Non-traditional" or "adult" students who don't fit the traditional 18-22 age profile are an increasingly visible presence on most campuses. These students have different life experiences than the traditional college student and have correspondingly different learning needs as well.[5] Adult students tend to be self-directed learners who bring a rich store of personal experiences to each learning situation. They are oriented to problem solving and specific task completion rather than focusing on a particular subject and tend to be motivated more by internal incentives such as curiosity than by external rewards such as grades. These learners appreciate a more collaborative and personalized teaching style where the instructor becomes the coach and facilitator rather than the expert who constantly lectures.

Recent research in multicultural learning differences suggests various correlations between cultural groups and learning preferences.[6] For example, Caucasian females, tend to display field-sensitive tendencies, while Euro-American and Asian-American males display field-independent tendencies. Certain groups, such as African-American students and Chicano students, have a strong orientation to learning through socialization and group interaction, while Native-American students display a preference for visual learning. The most effective solution for accommodating these differences is to create a continuum of instructional experiences that represent the breadth of experiential learning styles (see Figure 3). Indeed, to our way of thinking, this solution provides a guide for accommodating any difference in learning style, be it individually or group-based. In the typical library instructional situation, you do not have the luxury of residential instruction of three 50-minute periods for 15 weeks a year. You certainly don't have time to administer learning style inventories, and usually you have to guess what styles might be in your class. But if you become accustomed to mixing the instructional experiences you include in your classes, you will be farther along the path of providing "something for everyone."

Why should we think about learning styles when we teach electronic information access? We think its importance lies in the nature of electronic literature searching, which is a highly developed cognitive task. The card catalog, with its stationary drawers and controlled subject headings, took much of the creativity out of literature searching. Patrons were dependent on the subject headings that librarians gave them to identify information on a topic. Unless the patron was extremely energetic, chances are that he or she would not go jumping from drawer to drawer trying to match lists of materials from a variety of subject headings to develop bibliographies.

Electronic information access changes all of that. With the advent of keyword and Boolean searching, each patron can become, in effect, his own subject cataloger, no longer dependent on the Library of Congress to guide him through a morass of literature. The degree to which patrons can successfully fulfill that function for themselves depends on how well they can perform three tasks: (1) perceive and define the information they need; (2) analyze the diverse bits of information they find and synthesize that analysis into a coherent "information solution" to a problem; and (3) develop an effective "mental model" of each electronic system they use and identify which system will most effectively and efficiently provide the information they need. These activities are "cognitive-intensive" and their successful practice depends more than ever on effective instruction. And as we have demonstrated, there are several learning styles that exist for processing cognitive information. By offering only one style of instruction to our patrons, we risk disenfranchising a significant number of our users. As we dramatically change how we present information to our users, so must we also change how we present our instruction.

APPENDIX

Active Learning Experience

This presentation includes an extended workshop period that allowed workshop participants to apply their understanding of learning styles to a series of scenarios. The scenarios were instructional design dilemmas that offered opportunities to apply expertise while demonstrating an appreciation of the learning styles presentation.

Groups of participants were created in order to work on the scenarios. More than one group worked on each scenarios so that participants could observe alternative approaches to similar instructional situations. A presentation of each group's design, a facilitated discussion with the audience, and a summary of key aspects of effective design concluded the workshop.

This active learning approach was designed to provide an experience in applying learning style theory to actual instructional design and to demonstrate the variety of design approaches inherent in the application of learning style theory.

The scenario format was as follows:

Goal:
Audience
  Size
  Experience
  Attributes
Time Allotted for Instruction
Skills to be Developed
Practice Activities/Feedback Opportunities
Facilities and Materials (include environmental concerns such as room configuration, light, sound)
How Do Your Activities/Opportunities and Facilities/Materials Accommodate the Attributes of Your Group?

The goals, audience, and time allotted portions of the scenarios were provided by the presenters. Participants completed the subsequent sections of the scenarios.

The scenarios provided were:

Goal: Be able to access various gophers on the Internet.
Audience
  Size: 10 international studies graduate students
  Experience: print information resources
  Attributes: primarily female, primarily divergers, primarily auditory learners, primarily field dependent
Time Allotted for Instruction: 3 hours

Goal: Be able to begin literature search for doctoral dissertation.
Audience
  Size: 15 first-year graduate engineering students
  Experience: heavily computer-oriented with little familiarity with American libraries

Attributes: international students, primarily Asian and 75% of group is male, divergers, visual and kinetic learners, and field independent

Time Allotted for instruction: 3 hours

Goal: Be able to find magazine articles about a current topic.

Audience

Size: 30 lower division undergraduate students

Experience: familiar with print version of Reader's Guide and online catalog

Attributes: primarily Asian, Hispanic, and black students, primarily divergers with preference for kinetic learning, primarily field independent

Time Allotted for Instruction: 90 minutes

Goal: Be able to locate research articles from psychology journals.

Audience

Size: 220 undergraduate students

Experience: can locate books in online catalog

Attributes: traditional, full time students, 18-22 years old, even distribution of male and female, mix of Kolb learning styles, mix of learning modalities, mix of field independence and field dependent learners

Time Allotted for Instruction: 50 minutes

Goal: Be able to evaluate the value of a research article in anthropology in terms of author expertise, discipline discourse, and quality of argument.

Audience

Size: 20 upper division undergraduates, returning adult students

Experience: world processing skills

Attributes: mixture of male and female, primarily convergers, mixture of auditory and kinetic learners, primarily field independent

Time allotted for Instruction: 90 minutes

Goal: Be able to locate statistical and other current supportive information for persuasive speeches.

Audience
Size: 25 upper division undergraduates
Experience: can use online catalog and CD-ROM periodical indexes
Attributes: traditional full time students, 18-22 years old, mix of male and female, primarily accomodators with preference for auditory learning, primarily field independent learners
Time Allotted for Instruction: 50 minutes

Goal: Be able to research background of Christian symbolism in medieval art.
Audience
Size: 40 lower division undergraduates, mixture of traditional age and older than average students
Experience: online catalog familiar
Attributes: primarily female, ethnically mixed, mix of convergers and accomodators, primarily visual learners, mix of field independent and field dependent learners
Time Allotted for Instruction: 50 minutes

Goal: Be able to begin work on senior thesis about a Japanese cultural topic.
Audience
Size: 5 senior undergraduate students
Experience: extensive print source experience, minimal online experience
Attributes: all white males, older than average, primarily assimilators, preference for visual learning, field dependent learners
Time Allotted for Instruction: 2 hours

NOTES AND REFERENCES

1. H. Witkin and C.A. Moore, *Field-Dependent and Field-Independent Cognitive Styles and Their Educational Implications* (Princeton, NJ: Educational Testing Services, 1975).

2. W.B. Barbe and R.H. Swassing, *Teaching Through Modality Strengths: Concepts and Practices* (Columbus, OH: Zaner-Bloser, 1979), p. 20.

3. D.A. Kolb, *Experiential Learning* (Englewood Cliffs, NJ: Prentice-Hall, 1984), p. 25.

4. F. Jacobson, "Gender Differences in Attitudes Toward Using Computers in Libraries: An Exploratory Study," *Library and Information Science Research* 13 (1991): 277.

5. S.M. Merriam, "Adult Learning: Where Have We Come From? Where Are We Headed?" in *An Update on Learning Theory*, edited by S.M. Merriam (San Francisco: Jossey-Bass, 1993), p. 5.

6. J.A. Anderson and M. Adams, "Acknowledging the Learning Styles of Diverse Student Populations: Implications for Instructional Design," in *Teaching for Diversity*, edited by L.L.B. Border and N.V. Chism (San Francisco: Jossey-Bass, 1992), p. 5.

GODZILLA VS. KING KONG:

A TEAM APPROACH TO TRAINING ON INTERNET RESOURCES

Vicki Pengelly

Am I Godzilla or King Kong? I'm not certain, but in reality the team approach to teaching Internet resources that I will describe here has gone quite smoothly, not at all like the movie whose title I used for this paper. You may not get the entire picture in living color, but I hope you'll get a vivid image of our approach.

Here at the University of Montana our curriculum on wide-area network resources comprises seven courses, briefly listed below (and described in more detail in the appendixes). Our team approach to presenting this material has proved valuable on our campus:

1. Introduction to Wide Area Networks,
2a. Unix Mail for WANderers,
2b. VMS Mail for WANDerers (participants generally take just one or the other, depending on which computer system their account is on),
3. Computer Conferences and Electronic Journals,
4. Library Catalogs and Databases,

5. Publicly Accessible Files and Electronic Books,
6. Gopher, WAIS, and World-Wide Web, and
7. WANderings (wrap-up session).

RAISING MONTANA: THE SETTING

The University of Montana is Located in Missoula, a community of about 50,000 people in the western part of the state. Despite the forbidding names of some local points of interest, like Hellgate Canyon and Rattlesnake Wilderness, students are flocking to UM like never before. Last year's record high enrollment of 10,800 will easily be eclipsed by this year's predicted count of 11,700.

When they aren't sending e-mail or "telnetting" to library catalogs, our faculty, staff, and students may be kayaking, mountain climbing, skiing—well, you get the idea. Oh, and watching movies, too. Of course, they also teach, study, do research, and keep the university going.

THE BAUDFATHER: A BRIEF HISTORY OF OUR NETWORK ACCESS

About four years ago, the staff of Computing and Information Services (CIS) arranged for uucp access on our campus. Access was available only through our Unix machine (at the time a VAX 11/785), and we exchanged e-mail by making a phone call in the middle of the night to transmit messages (first to the University of California—Davis and later to Apple.com). We didn't teach any classes on wide-area network resources then but helped people get started through one-on-one consultation. Sometimes, we got the feeling that the faculty wanted to send their Mafia friends to visit us because it was so frustrating for them to have to wait (at least overnight or sometimes a few days) for a response to their e-mail.

Then, almost three years ago, we got full Internet access through a research grant obtained by a professor in the School of Forestry, and we have also joined NorthWestNet. At present, anyone with an account on our central computers has access to most of the Internet resources (the exceptions are explained later). The general-purpose central systems are a DECsystem 5500 running Ultrix and a VAXcluster running VMS. The clustered machines are VAX

6000, model 510s. Numerous other machines, such as VAX 3400s, provide specialized service (e.g., to the residence halls' staff).

For the past few years the university president has allocated funds to provide every faculty member with a microcomputer. During the past year, we have witnessed the installation of a fiber-optic backbone on campus and now are striving to hook up all the offices during the next couple years. Our library has been hooked up to the backbone to expedite the automation of their holdings and the delivery of catalog information to the rest of campus. A couple of other crucial buildings have also been wired in the last few months.

In the meantime, people dial in via phone lines, use the computer labs on campus, or obtain access to the central computers (and thus to Internet resources) through existing hard-wired lines.

A CLASS IS BORN: HOW WE DECIDED TO COLLABORATE

When we first obtained full Internet access, we taught one class, which focused mainly on exchanging electronic mail. It also briefly mentioned such resources as FTP and Telnet, but we weren't really sure how many people on campus would have a need for those tools. Certain faculty members seemed very interested in the resources (in fact, they had been begging for network access for years), but it seemed hard to convince other people that these tools might prove useful to them.

One of the people who attended an early class on network mail was Barry Brown, our science librarian. After taking that class, Barry approached me about a cooperative effort between the library and CIS. He proposed that he and I offer a series of classes on Internet resources. I liked his idea for several reasons:

1. Traditionally there had been little interaction between the staff in CIS and the library. Without knowing anything about the history of relations between our two departments, I knew I wanted to contribute toward increased cooperation.
2. I anticipated that people would be asking about bibliographic information, such as library catalogs and databases,

that I wasn't very familiar with, but Barry and other librarians would be well acquainted with.

3. I had limited experience teaching with another instructor and thought it would be beneficial to improve my teaching methods by observing someone else's style and by being part of a team.

Beginning in the spring of 1991, Barry and I offered a series of three classes, and later expanded it to the series of seven classes listed previously. Additional changes are planned for fall semester 1994 (see Appendix B). We haven't made it big in the entertainment industry yet, but we are enjoying the classes.

A ROOM WITH NO VIEW: THE LAB AND EQUIPMENT

In a given semester we offer all our classes in the same computer lab (one of six labs maintained by Computing and Information Services). The specific lab may vary from one semester to the next. We usually have an overhead projector and screen so that we can display instructions. Participants are expected to do hands-on exercises, trying out the instructions we give.

When we first started giving these classes, the lab had 16 Zenith Z-29 terminals, which sometimes worked. The room was not configured well for instruction (with some terminals facing the outside walls and others facing each other in the center of the room). The lab we have used most recently has 20 DECstation 212P 286 PCs, each with a VGA monochrome monitor, a hard drive, and a 3.5" floppy drive (this lab was updated to 486s right after the "LOEX" conference). The machines are networked with Pathworks.

AROUND THE WORLD IN 80 DAZES: OUR APPROACH

Our approach is briefly outlined here. More detailed class outlines and sample handouts are provided in the appendixes. Currently we divide the material into seven separate classes. Participants are not required to take all the classes or to take them in any particular order. However, we strongly recommend that they take the whole series, and we find that many people do so.

We teach people how to log in, how to connect to a database or how to subscribe to a LISTSERVer, for example. But, beyond the mechanics, we stress the use of directories and "finding aids," the way catalogs and databases are organized, bibliographic searching techniques. We stress the functions of the Internet, not just the procedures of getting to a particular bit of information. We try to show people how they can begin to teach themselves about the resources.

Again, the detailed outlines are provided in the appendixes.

PLAIN STRAINS AND AUDIBLE SQUEALS: GOING OUT OF OUR WAY TO GIVE EXTRA HELP

In addition to our regularly scheduled short courses, we also provide follow-up individualized consulting for people who want more details than we can provide in class. Our front-line help desk in CIS has seen a tremendous increase in the number of questions related to Internet resources. By implication our consultants at the help desk are assiduously learning as much as they can about these resources, and they have been some of our most active users of the Internet.

Another service we offer, whenever we have time, is to provide special presentations for individual departments. For example, Barry and I gave a class for the faculty in foreign languages and literatures. Other departments receiving special presentations include the School of Business and the division of biological sciences. Some of these presentations are intended to pique the interest of the faculty; we want them to consider these resources as a way to enhance their tools for research (e.g., using library catalogs and databases via Telnet) or as a way to collaborate with colleagues (via e-mail) without the expense of a phone bill or a plane ticket. Other presentations focus on helping students in academic classes use Internet resources for their major or for a particular course.

These specialized presentations also allow us to focus on tools of interest specifically to a particular group. For example, the faculty who teach German and are training K-12 teachers might be interested in the Usenet news group k12.lang.deutsch-eng. One technique we use is to subscribe to a relevant LISTSERV ahead of time and then display some of the more interesting messages and responses. In preparing for these presentations, we boost our knowledge of the Internet, and we provide a service to the faculty by filtering some of the information they might otherwise have to wade through themselves.

THE WIZARD OF AWES: HOW HAVE WE BENEFITTED FROM THIS JOURNEY?

Our approach has proved beneficial in a number of ways. Like Dorothy on her way to Oz, I have been very thankful to have a friend to travel with on the yellow brick road of Internet resources. Barry is an energetic colleague with a good sense of humor and good organizational skills. I have learned a lot from his teaching style and his knowledge of the Internet. I am thankful that he took the initiative to get our cooperative effort going.

I like to think our efforts have contributed toward greater cooperation between the library staff and CIS. For example, staff members from our two departments collaborated in planning and designing the campus Gopher (and continue to collaborate with regard to its maintenance). The staff in both departments are interested in managing, transmitting, cataloguing, and otherwise processing information; it makes sense that some cooperative efforts could benefit us all and the rest of our campus.

During class I am Barry's built-in teaching assistant. I can go around the room and see whether people are following his instructions. If someone gets stuck, I can try to help out while he continues with the instructions for the other members of the class. Similarly, he plays the TA's role when I'm giving my spiel.

You might say we have each received a heart, a brain, and some courage along the way. Now, if I could just get some sparkly red shoes!

THE SEVEN YEAR GLITCH: WHAT CAN GO WRONG?

So far the whole experience has sounded pretty rosy. However, we do run into a few glitches now and then. At the end of some of our classes, we have occasionally found ourselves quoting Marilyn Monroe: "Golly!"

We have reorganized the courses several times and have reshuffled the topics covered in each class. The main problems we've encountered include the following:

1. Mixed audience: We don't have enough staff or time to offer more than one series of classes. Thus, in one group we might have some individuals with Unix accounts and some with VMS accounts. The operating system commands are different and the way people address their network mail is different (for example, on our VMS system we run MX for sending network mail). The mail features and file features differ a great deal on the two systems. Furthermore, up to this point, some resources have been restricted to one system or the other. We have had Usenet news groups only on our Unix machine and the VAX Notes conferencing program only on the VMS system. This intermingling invariably causes some confusion. We have tried various ways of dealing with this issue (such as having the VMS people simply tune out while the Unix people try a few commands or having each group sit on a different side of the room). Our solutions have been less than satisfactory, and we are in the midst of deciding whether we should offer completely separate classes to the two groups.
2. Equipment problems: The lab we use has equipment problems at times. The problems are intermittent and unpredictable (of course) but sometimes render the equipment totally useless. We are in the process of installing new connections and network software that we hope will alleviate these problems. In spite of the difficulties we have often used the same lab because it is best suited to our needs (because of the number of machines provided, the access to central computers, and the proximity to our offices).
3. Redundancy: So far we have not required that people take the "Introduction to Wide Area Networks" before coming to the classes on library catalogs and computer conferences. Thus, there is some unavoidable redundancy in the classes. For example, in the class on computer conferences we go over the procedures for electronic mail since people must

use mail to subscribe to LISTSERVs. We don't give as much detail on mail in that class as we do in the introductory session, but for someone who attends both classes, there is redundancy. (Of course, I like to think of it as helpful review.)

4, Lack of time: One comment we consistently receive on our class evaluations is that people would like the classes to be longer so that they can spend more time going over the resources. We would like to offer longer classes or perhaps more sections, but we simply do not have the staff to do so right now. As it is, Barry and I are stretched so thin that we find it difficult to meet often enough to discuss revising our course outlines or to do needed research into new resources. At the present time, we are just striving to give the best, albeit brief, introduction we can.

BACK TO THE FEW SURE: OUR GOALS FOR IMPROVEMENT

We're always learning, always revising our courses, always striving to improve. Some ideas we're currently considering are:

1. Next fall semester we plan a major rearrangement of the classes. See Appendix B for details.
2. We are considering whether to hold completely separate classes for people on the Unix system vs. those on the VMS system.
3. We may want to make the introductory class a requirement for attending the later classes. Or we might have one eight-hour class that people could sign up for if they have no experience with the resources. And then we would also keep offering the current series of classes for those who need to pick and choose (perhaps someone already knows mail and just needs to learn about library catalogs). In fact, it would be easy to envision a semester-long course for academic credit.
4. We sincerely hope the equipment problems are behind us because they have been a major source of frustration.
5. We are looking for ways of improving service on campus, which will have implications for our classes. For example,

we are considering "gatewaying" LISTSERV conferences to e-mail.

THE PRINCESS FRIED: COURSE EVALUATIONS AND MISCELLANEOUS COMMENTS

At the end of every class we hand out evaluation forms and ask the participants to return them to us. A sample evaluation form will be provided with the course handouts.

Generally our evaluations have been quite positive. People often comment that they would like to spend more time learning about the Internet resources. In a separate paper, Barry Brown discusses the results of a follow-up survey we did recently.

We usually have a pretty good mixture of faculty, staff, and students in our classes. So far, we have seen more graduate students than undergraduates. This trend is partly a result of the undergraduates having limited access to the central computers in the past (they had to be enrolled in a class that required getting an account, or they had to request an account through their major department). Undergraduates now have the ability to build their own accounts (once they officially register) and, as a result, we are seeing increased interest in the Internet resources among undergraduates.

If or when instructors start using the Internet as a teaching tool, we may get a demand for instruction that far exceeds our capability to provide it.

IT'S A MAD, MAD, MAD, MAD WHIRL: CONCLUSION

What have we learned from all this? In today's environment of networked information, libraries and computer centers are natural allies, and their staff have complementary talents and expertise. Our goal has been to pro-actively provide enough instruction to enable individuals to begin exploring the Internet and continue independent learning.

With my harried schedule (which is just like yours, I'm sure) and with the overwhelming and ever-increasing amount of information on the Internet, I feel as frantic as some of the characters in the movie whose title I have alluded to in this section.

But, it has been edifying and fun to be involved in teaching these classes. And I definitely believe there are treasures to be found on the Internet. I will continue to search them out, not just for me, but for our clients on campus, whom Barry and I want to serve by inviting them along on the treasure hunt.

I look forward to hearing what people at other schools are planning for their Internet training in the next few months or years (who can plan that far ahead in this field?!?).

Appendix A gives details of the course descriptions and outlines we were using at the time of the "LOEX" meeting in June of 1994. We have since altered our courses quite drastically; the current course descriptions are shown in Appendix B. Course outlines, handouts, and other materials are provided on the University of Montana's Gopher and on our FTP host. Use the following URLs to obtain those materials. The specific file names that correspond to each course are given below in the detailed course outlines.

APPENDIX A

Course Descriptions and Outlines Used Spring Semester 1994

gopher://wilcox.umt.edu/University of Montana information/Computing & Information Services/Training Materials/Internet/*

ftp://ftphost.umt.edu/internet/training/*

Brief Course Descriptions

- Offered weekly, each semester, in chronological order.
- Participants encouraged to take all of them.
- Joint instruction by librarian and computing services instructor.
- "Hands-on" emphasis; classes held in computer labs.
- Equipment: overhead projector and screen.
- Maximum number of participants: 20; minimum number: 5.
- Prerequisites:
    a. a central computer account, and
    b. familiarity with login procedures and some fundamentals

1. Introduction to Wide Area Networks (50 minutes)
   Learn about the information services and resources available on MUSEnet, Usenet, BITNET, and the Internet. An overview of each network will be presented, and some hands-on examples will be explored.

2a. Unix Mail for "WANderers" (80 minutes)
   Become familiar with basic commands and procedures for sending, receiving, and manipulating e-mail and files (focus is on pine mailer). An understanding of mail commands and procedures is essential for efficiently accessing WAN information resources. Note: if you sign up for this class, then you don't need to sign up for VAX Mail for "WANderers."

2b. VMS Mail for WANderers (80 minutes)
   Become familiar with basic commands and procedures for sending, receiving, and manipulating e-mail and files. An understanding of these commands and procedures is essential for efficiently accessing WAN information resources. Note: if you sign up for this class, then you don't need to sign up for Unix Mail for "WANderers."

3. Computer Conferences and Electronic Journals (80 minutes, which has proven to be too short!)
   From the scholarly to the personal, whether you're interested in the evolution of bonehooks in Indonesia or the Grateful Dead, there is very likely an electronic journal or computer conference on the topic. Find out how to overcome geographic isolation and communicate with colleagues around the world and how to use these new computer-mediated communication tools as information resources.

4. Library Catalogs and Databases (80 minutes)
   There are over 500 library catalogs and databases online in a wide variety of countries available free of charge over the Internet. Learn how to find directories, use the "telnet" command to interactively access these databases, and strategies for conducting bibliographic searches.

5. Publicly Accessible Files and Electronic Books (80 minutes)
   There are thousands of files (full text, numeric, image, sound, software) online, in a wide variety of countries,

available free of charge over the Internet. Learn how to locate files and use the "ftp" command to retrieve them.

6. Gopher, WAIS, and World-Wide Web (80 minutes)
   Learn about the latest tools to evolve on the Internet. These information servers provide access to a wide variety of Internet resources using a common interface and commands.
7. WANderings (50 minutes)
   The final class of this series offers the chance to tie up any loose ends that were left floating in cyberspace during the first six classes and the chance to explore in greater depth some of the topics that were briefly introduced in the other classes. Bring your questions and ideas for exploration.

Instructional Outlines

1. Introduction to Wide Area Networks (50 minutes)

Librarian:

I. Welcome, introduction, our series of courses
II. Internet, MUSEnet (the Montana University System Education network), Usenet, and BITNET
   - overview and explanation
III. Information resources available on the Internet
   - list and explanation of resources
   - examples of how individuals use the Internet
IV. Sources for help
   - print guides
   - online sources
   - people to call

Computing Services Instructor:

V. Local situation
   - history of access to various networks
   - current campus network
   - set up of machines, hardware, and different operating systems
   - greater pathway (UM-NWnet-NSFnet-etc.)
   - caution: networks are dynamic!!
VI. Options for connecting to the network

- campus network: different labs and wired buildings
- dial-up from campus
- dial-up from home

VII. Network etiquette

VIII. Two ways of looking at the network
- tools (commands and procedures)
- tasks (what you can accomplish)

IX. Directed search (hands-on exercise)
- Freenet
- other quick examples, such as earthquake activity

Handouts:

- information sources on the Internet, general sources for help, and network etiquette
  file: intro-help-etc.txt
- two ways of looking at WAN resources: tools vs. tasks
  file: intro-tools.txt
- glossary of terms for Wide Area Networking
  file: intro-glossary.txt
- login instructions specific to lab where class is held in
  No files (instructions specific to University of Montana)
- script for logging on to Freenets or for other hands-on exercises
  file: intro-exercises.txt
- evaluation form
  file: eval-old.txt

2a. Unix Mail for "WANderers" (80 minutes)

Computing Services Instructor:

I. Welcome, introduction, our series of courses

II. Unix operating system and mail commands

III. Directed search (hands-on exercise)
- sending mail
- reading mail
- replying
- editing, cutting, pasting, forwarding, deleting

IV. Customizing your mail environment
- how to create signature files
- how to turn off announcements of incoming mail

- the "talk" command and how to turn it off
- creating "aliases"

V. Internet, MUSEnet, BITNET, and UUCP
- mail addresses (sending and receiving)
- procedures for sending mail messages

VI. Directed search (hands-on exercise)
- send mail over the Internet, if participants have addresses

VII. Advanced mail programs for Unix (if time and interest)
- Elm

Librarian:

VIII. White pages resources
- explanation and description
- various services

IX. Directed search (hands-on)
- search a white pages service

X. Privacy issues and "Alias Servers"

Handouts:

- Unix operating system and mail commands
  file: mail-unix.txt
- brief description of additional mail programs (Elm)
  No handout, no files
- accessing WAN from UM (how to address messages, etc.)
  No file (instructions specific to University of Montana)
- evaluation form
  No additional files (see above under Intro)

2b. VMS Mail for WANderers (80 minutes)

Computing Services Instructor:

I. Welcome, introduction, our series of courses

II. VMS operating system and mail commands

III. Directed search (hands-on exercise)
- sending mail
- reading mail
- replying, forwarding
- editing, cutting, pasting, forwarding, deleting

IV. Customizing your mail environment

- how to create signature files
- the "talk" command and how to turn it off
- creating "aliases"
- using the SET command to set personal name and other features

V. Internet, MUSEnet, BITNET, and UUCP
- mail addresses (sending and receiving)
- procedures for sending mail messages

VI. Directed search (hands-on exercise)
- send network mail if participants brought addresses to try

Librarian:

VI. White pages resources
- explanation and description
- various services

VII. Directed search (hands-on)
- search a white pages service

VIII. Privacy issues and "Alias Servers"

Handouts:

- VMS operating system and mail commands
  File: mail-vms.txt
- accessing WAN from UM (how to address messages, etc.)
  No files (instructions specific to University of Montana)
- Evaluation Form
  No new files (see above under Intro)

3. Computer Conferences and Electronic Journals (80 minutes)

Computing Services Instructor:

I. Welcome, introduction, our series of courses

II. Brief review of mail commands and network addresses

Librarian:

III). Computer conferences and electronic journals (Internet and BITNET)
- types of conferences and e-journals
- directories (scholarly and list of lists)
- moderated vs. unmoderated conferences

- computer-mediated communication (flaming, emoticons, etc.)
- conference etiquette
- LISTSERV vs. other types
- commands and procedures for subscribing to them
- searching archived conferences

IV. Directed search (hands-on)
- subscribe to a conference and to a journal
- check acknowledgments
- unsubscribe

Computing Services Instructor and Librarian:

V. VaxNotes conferences (local) and Usenet news groups
- overview
- commands

VI. Directed search (hands-on)
- split class by operating system
- computing services instructor leads those on VMS machine through VaxNotes example and librarian leads those on Unix machine through Usenet example

Handouts:

- Unix Mail brief review
  File: compconf-unixmail.txt
- VMS mail brief review
  File: compconf-vmsmail.txt
- Usenet news groups
  File: compconf-usenet.txt
- introduction to VaxNotes
  File: compconf-vaxnotes.txt
- script for subscribing to an Internet conference and an e-journal
  File: to be provided by librarian
- how to access directories for computer conferences and e-journals
  File: to be provided by librarian
- computer conference (LISTSERV) commands and searching archives
  File: to be provided by librarian
- evaluation form
  No new files (see above under Intro)

4. Library Catalogs and Databases (80 minutes)

Librarian:

I. Welcome, introduction, our series of courses

II. Overview of library catalogs, databases, CWISes
- description, type, features, abundance and location
- what you can do
- what you can't do
- why search them
- how to determine which one to use (e.g., subject collection guides)

III. Guides to library catalogs, databases, CWISes
- Art St. George Guide
- Billy Barron Guide
- Hytelnet (online and local)

IV. Searching library catalogs, databases, CWISes
- kinds of interfaces and how to get help
- search strategies, Boolean searching, proximity operators, etc.
- problems encountered
- advanced features

Computing Services Instructor:

V. Role of library vs. computing center
- technical vs. bibliographic assistance

VI. Terminal specific commands
- PC and telecommunications software differences
- keyboard features
- functions: printing, downloading, uploading

VII. Telnet and tn3270
- commands and examples

Librarian:

VIII. Directed search (hands-on)
- Hytelnet
- library catalog
- CWIS

Handouts:
- brief listing of Unix commands
  File: libcat-unix.txt

- brief listing of VMS commands
  File: libcat-vms.txt
- Telnet commands
  File: libcat-telnet.txt
- script for search of Hytelnet, library catalog, CWIS
  File: to be provided by librarian
- evaluation
  No new files (see above under Intro)

5. Publicly Accessible Files and Electronic Books (80 minutes)

Librarian:

I. Welcome, introduction, our series of courses

II. Overview of publicly accessible files and electronic books
- types of files and e-books and producers of them
- what you can do with them
- directories (Hytelnet, Archie, etc.)
- archive sites

Computing Services Instructor:

III. FTP commands and procedures
- commands for transferring files
- file structure of FTP hosts

IV. General file operating commands for local VMS, Unix machines
- using directories
- using a "temp" directory
- reading a file
- compressing and uncompressing a file
- printing a file
- deleting a file
- downloading a file (e.g., software)

V. Virus protection and safeguards

VI. Archie commands

VII. Directed search (hands-on)
- searching Archie
- using FTP to retrieve the file identified by Archie
- using FTP to peruse an archive site and retrieve a file

Handouts:

- Arrangement of files on FTP hosts
  No file (special diagram on an overhead transparency; produced in PageMaker)
- FTP commands and procedures
  File: pubfiles-ftp.txt
- Archie commands and procedures
  File: pubfiles-archie.txt
- script for searching Archie and using FTP to get a file and then reading it, plus overview of the procedures for FTP and Archie
  File: pubfiles-exer-etc.txt
- Evaluation
  No new files (see Intro above)

6. Gopher, WAIS, and World-Wide Web (80 minutes)

Librarian:

I. Welcome, introduction, our series of courses

II. Explanation of Gopher, WAIS, and WWW
- description and history
- what they do
- nformation resources available through them
- directories (e.g., Veronica, directory of servers)
- sources of information (e.g., Ed Krol's The Whole Internet, online)
- example of WWW

Computing Services Instructor:

III. Overview of Gopher, WAIS, WWW
- conceptual overview
- commands (e.g., bookmarks, saving information, interrupting searches)
- options of how to access (e.g., local Gopher, local Hytelnet, other Gophers)

IV. Directed search (hands-on)
- various Gopher resources
- a WAIS file
- World-Wide Web

Handouts:

- Gopher description and commands
  File: infoservers-gopher.txt
- WAIS description and commands
  File: infoservers-wais.txt
- WWW description and commands
  File: infoservers-www.txt
- evaluation
  No new files (see Intro above)

7. WANderings (50 minutes)

Computing Services Instructor:

I. Welcome, introduction
II. Questions or problems encountered

Librarian:
III. Review some of the "Internet Hunts"

Handouts:

- final evaluation for the whole series of courses
  No new files (see Intro above)

APPENDIX B

Course Descriptions for Fall Semester 1994

Internet Classes - University of Montana - Spring 1995

Dates and times listed below. All classes held in Liberal Arts 206, unless otherwise noted.

Instructors: Barry Brown, Mansfield Library (barry@selway.umt.edu); and Vicki Pengelly, Computing and Information Services (pengelly@selway.umt.edu)

Prerequisites: (1) a central computer account, (2) familiarity with login procedures and the fundamentals of using a central computer, (3) Pre-registration (x5455).

Suggestion: These classes are most beneficial when you take the entire series.

Introduction to Wide Area Networks, Tuesday, Feb.7, 3:10-4:00 p.m. Learn about the information services and resources available on the Internet, linking together millions of people from over a hundred countries. An overview will be presented and some hands-on examples will be explored. Find out what's out there, how to find it, and how to use it.

Unix Mail for "WANderers": beginning, Tuesday, Feb.14, 3:10-4:00 p.m.
Unix Mail for "WANderers": advanced, Tuesday, Feb.14, 4:10-5:00 p.m.
Those with accounts on Selway can become familiar with basic commands and procedures of the Pine program for sending, receiving, and manipulating e-mail and files. An understanding of e-mail is essential for using certain Internet resources. Note: If you sign up for this class, then you probably don't need "VMS Mail for WANderers."

VMS Mail for "WANderers": beginning, Thursday, Feb.16, 3:10-4:00 p.m.
VMS Mail for "WANderers": advanced, Thursday, Feb.16, 4:10-5:00 p.m.
Those with accounts on Lewis can become familiar with basic commands and procedures of the VMS mail program for sending, receiving, and manipulating e-mail and files. An understanding of e-mail is essential for using certain Internet resources. Note: If you sign up for this class, then you probably don't need "Unix Mail for WANderers."

Gopher and WAIS, Tuesday, Feb. 21, 3:10-4:00 p.m.
World-Wide Web, Tuesday, Feb. 21, 4:10-5:00 p.m.
These network tools provide organization and allow easy navigation of Internet information resources and often alleviate the need for knowing computer addresses or using protocols such as Telnet and FTP. Learn what each tool does and how best to use them. Special "client software" (e.g., Turbogopher, Mosaic, Cello, etc.) for each will be discussed.

Windows Applications: Winsock and Netscape, Thursday, Feb. 23, 3:10-4:00 p.m.
Note: This lecture/demonstration will be held in Mansfield Library 285.

The tools described are not available in the labs on campus, but this session is offered for those who may have their own access to these tools. Access the Internet via TCP/IP and Netscape, and learn about the Windows graphics interface to the Internet. Netscape is among the first and best of the Mosaic-type Internet applications. This session will show you how to set up TCP/IP access and how to configure and run Netscape. This graphics interface allows you to view pictures, hear audio files, and view video clips from locations all over the world.

Computer Conferences: BITNET and Internet, Tuesday, Feb. 28, 3:10-4:00 p.m.
Computer Conferences: Usenet Newsgroups, Tuesday, Feb. 28, 4:10-5:00 p.m.
From the scholarly to the personal, whether you're interested in the evolution of bonehooks in Indonesia or the Grateful Dead, there is very likely an electronic journal or computer conference on the topic (and if there isn't, maybe you should start one). Find out how to overcome geographic isolation by participating in online discussions and communicating with colleagues around the world.

Windows Applications: WS_FTP and QVTNET, Thursday, March 2, 3:10-4:00 p.m.
Use Winsock to open several excellent Windows Internet applications QVTNET is one of the best Telnet programs. It will allow you to open a stable connection with the Mainsfield Library LaserNet or other libraries throughout the world. WS_FTP will let you download binary and ASCII files from some of the best sites worldwide.

Library Catalogs and Databases, Tuesday, March 7, 3:10-4:00 p.m.
Online Bookstores, Electronic Books, Journals, and Newspapers, Tuesday, March 7, 4:10-5:00 p.m.
There are over 1,000 library catalogs and databases from over 70 countries, many online bookstores and hundreds of e-books, e-journals, and e-newspapers available free of charge over the Internet. Learn how to find directories, use the "telnet" command and Gopher to interactively access these resources and strategies for conducting bibliographic searches.

Publicly Accessible Files: beginning, Tuesday, March 21, 3:10-4:00 p.m.
Publicly Accessible Files: advanced, Tuesday, March 21, 4:10-5:00 p.m.
There are thousands of files (full text, image, numeric, sound, software) from a wide variety of countries, available free of charge over the Internet. Learn how to locate them (with "archie"), retrieve them (with "ftp"), uncompress them, and use them.

Interactive Communication (IRC, MUDs, etc.), Tuesday, March 28, 3:10-4:00
(Additional prerequisite: an account on Gibson)
WANderings, Tuesday, March 28, 4:10-5:00 p.m.
Learn about interactive communication tools and role playing simulation environments - Talk, IRC, MUDs, MOOs, etc. will be explained and used. The final class in this series, WANderings offers the chance to review questions from previous classes and tie up any loose ends left floating in cyberspace and the chance to explore in greater depth some of the topics that were briefly introduced. Electronic style guides for network information, general information search strategies, and how to "keep up with it all" will be discussed.

INTERNET INSTRUCTION AT THE UNIVERSITY OF MONTANA

Barry Brown

I have been engaged in collaborative Internet instruction for over three years at the University of Montana. My initial motivation for collaborating with Vicki Pengelly and her unit, Computing and Information Services (CIS), was prompted largely by a fear of librarians being preempted or marginalized after hearing that the assistant head of CIS was going around campus providing demonstrations and talks about searching library catalogs on the Internet. No one else in the library at that time was using BITNET or the Internet. And CIS was very restrictive in allowing access to the networks. There was a form that had to be filled out and a "legitimate need to use" justification had to be provided before an account was issued. The magic phrase was "instructional need" (e.g., "I have an instructional need to participate in scholarly computer conferences and to search databases," etc.). Being a new librarian fresh out of library school I had experience with using computer networks, wanted to continue to learn about them and was anxious to expose the campus community (and my fellow librarians) to the value of networked information. I also suspected that, as more people became aware of networked information resources, they would demand network accounts, and widespread access would have to occur. Realizing that if the library did not react quickly that there was a good chance of CIS moving ahead on its own with Internet instruction. Believing that librarians were the natural instructors of how to use library catalogs and networked information resources, I approached CIS about a collaborative instructional effort. Immediately after beginning to work together, it became apparent that there were a number of very positive benefits from our alliance.

After discussions with CIS and wanting to proceed with Internet instruction under the umbrella of the existing CIS instructional program (free "short courses" offered each semester), I informed my administrators and asked for their support. It was decided that I could proceed with Internet instruction since I was not asking to be relieved of any other existing duties. This has continued to be the case up to the present. Currently, I would like to institutionalize the program and decide, as a library, whose responsibility it should most logically be.

The evolution of our instructional network classes series is shown in Appendix A. The order of their listing is the specific series order in which they are covered. Changes in their order (e.g., Gopher and WWW moved from the end to the beginning) reflect new ideas of how best to introduce Internet information resources. The trend has been to offer more and more different classes over the years. Current discussions are continuing about adding a "create your own WWW Homepage" class and ar "html editing" class. Two new classes, taught by another librarian, have recently been offered on Windows applications. We hope to involve additional instructors as new classes are offered. Classes have been offered every quarter/semester (including summers) for the last three years. Early classes tended to be two hours long. Current classes are 50 minutes each with two different consecutive classes typically offered each week during the course series (see Appendix B for full descriptions, times, and listings of current classes). Summer classes are fewer and longer (i.e., typically three classes, each two hours long). Participants are encouraged to take the entire series but are not required to. Classes are offered only once each semester but given enough staffing it would be desirable to repeat them at different times throughout each semester.

All classes are team taught by a librarian and a computing and information services instructor. The classes have always incorporated lecture (with an overhead projector) and hands-on instruction (with every student at a computer station). Ideally each class has an equal amount of lecture, directed hands-on experience, and undirected individual hands-on exploration. Early classes incorporated live demonstrations projected overhead with an LCD panel, but this was discontinued and said to be an ineffective use of class time. Each new class offered was typically taught to librarians first. This served both to troubleshoot a class and to make librarians aware of what new information resources would be covered. We have always emphasized the information resources available on the network (i.e., tasks instead of tools). We have tried to provide a context for the network as well as the how-to skills for searching network information. We hope to instill a sense of adventure and confidence in using the network and impart specific search strategies for using network information resources.

Specific challenges for network instruction at the University of Montana include two different network operating systems (Unix and VMS), widely varying computer/network skill levels of class participants (usually our only prerequisite for registering for a class is to have an account), and widely varying computer lab equipment and network setups.

One measure of our success might be the number of people coming to the classes (the number has increased each year). But other factors are undoubtedly influencing attendance. Attendance was sparse during the initial years despite a considerable advertising. There was a distinct jump in class attendance after the publication of a series of student newspaper articles discussing pornography on the Internet. Additionally, 1993 was described as the year of the Internet in the media, and this widespread coverage has continued. In the last year, class attendance has remained high (e.g., last semester we had almost 50 people attempt to register for almost every class). Use of the campus computer network has grown tremendously in the last two years as measured by a variety of statistics. The number of accounts has gone from 500 to 2,000, the average number of concurrent users has grown from 25 to 75, and the average daily connect time in hours has gone from 180 to 560. Classes are limited to 20-26 participants depending on the number of computers in the lab where the classes are being held; all others are registered for the "wait list" and allowed to participate as space permits. This is because each class has a hands-on emphasis and the goal is to have each participant actively using a computer.

Evaluation forms are distributed during each class. One of the benefits of collaborative instruction is the chance to debrief after each class and get some idea of how it went. Class structure and content are constantly being revised every time it is taught. Before each semester there is a discussion of whether to add any new classes or rearrange any existing classes. While considering whether to make classes longer or shorter and how to accommodate those individuals who want a series of classes vs. just a single refresher class, we decided to give a comprehensive survey to individuals who participated in three or more classes during fall semester 1993 and spring semester 1994.

The survey results are listed in Appendix C. Response to the survey was low. The lowest response rate was from students probably because it was given at the end of the semester. The majority did not choose to be anonymous. University staff members are the largest audience for the course and contributed the most to the survey. One of the challenges of offering Internet courses at the University of Montana has been accommodating the two different network operating systems—Unix and VMS. The survey indicates that most participants are either on the Unix system or have accounts on both systems, therefore we could probably deemphasize VMS. Most survey respondents attended four or more classes with attendance fairly consistent up until the last class. The network resources that are used the most are gopher and e-mail followed by library catalogs. The survey was given before campus computers loaded WWW client program such as Lynx. There was no clear pattern of which resources they wanted more instruction with—except for ftp. Participants felt that the classes had helped improve their expertise with network resources (the average self-rated level almost tripled after the classes), but most ranked themselves quite low overall. There were a few comments about slowing down the pace of the classes. Majority preferred short, single topic courses. The survey results helped shape our current course offerings and content.

The types of collaborative network instruction offered at the University of Montana include:

- short courses,
- course integrated instruction,
- department workshops and seminars,
- conference workshops,
- credit course—"Cyberspace Information Research Methods," HC295, 3 credits,
- continuing education credit course (proposed).

The short courses are offered each semester (see Appendix B). The course integrated instruction is subject specific and done at the request of the instructor. We are limited more by time and staffing than by opportunity. With a little more advertising of our services, we could easily generate more teaching opportunities. With a campus population of almost 12,000 students, we obviously can't train all the students. We need to train the trainers, and have started with other librarians and faculty members who have taken our classes and are now training on their own. The diverse departments represented by these faculty, who are actively incorporating Internet instruction and information resources into their classes, include biology, economics, environmental studies, foreign languages and linguistics, health and human performance, journalism, and political science. Those are just the ones that I know about; there may well be others. As with traditional library assignments some of the Internet assignments that I see students struggling with that are from these faculty members are well thought out and others are exercises in frustration.

The benefits of collaborative or team teaching are numerous. Vicki Pengelly and I try to formally engage in peer coaching by critiquing each other's style and the content of our presentations. This was originally done by meeting each week to discuss how the previous week went, but it is now usually done through e-mail. Each of us tries to learn from the other and improve our teaching abilities. Having someone to walk around the lab and troubleshoot problems or give individual attention while the other instructor leads participants through a directed, hands-on example has proven invaluable. After continuous instruction for every academic session for over three years, having a partner can help enthusiasm as high as it should be and help stimulate each other to keep up with it all. The networks are very dynamic, so constant continuing education is required. Occasionally, the redundancy has helped when one person is sick or otherwise committed. Having a librarian and a computing services instructor involved in team teaching brought together very complementary, different skills. Originally, we capitalized on those skills by having Pengelly (CIS) concentrate on technical issues, while I covered information resources and search strategies. However, the longer we teach together the less we differentiate between who does what.

In our introductory class we have always explained positively the different services provided by the library vs. the computing center. Last fall at the annual NorthWestNet meeting (a regional Internet provider), there was a special series on libraries and computing groups. There were many interesting and provocative discussions over the three days of sessions. I heard a computing center director say, "The library is just another customer like the physics department," and I heard a library director state, "The computer center is just another campus agency service provider like the business office." I think that both of those statements are seriously misguided. With the advent of networked information resources there is an increasing overlap in the role of libraries and computing centers and both can benefit from an alliance.

Before beginning our Internet classes there was little interaction at the University of Montana between the library and Computing and Information Services. The interaction that did occurr was often negative or competitive. Since our classes began interaction and cooperation have been mostly positive and have included: developing a campus information technology plan, organizing information technology conferences, sponsoring Internet teleconferences, developing a campus gopher, providing dial-in access support for the library catalog and CD-ROM network, exchanges between the library reference desk and computing help desk for observation, and providing a public Internet station. The real measure of success for our collaborative Internet instruction will be perhaps if it becomes institutionalized and when both organizations continue formal collaboration after one, or both of us, stops being involved.

APPENDIX A

Evolution of Network Classes at the University of Montana

Winter Quarter 1991

- Wide Area Network Access

Spring Quarter 1991

- Introduction to VMS
- Information Resources on the Internet: Library Catalogs and Databases

Fall Quarter 1991

- Introduction to Unix
- Introduction to VMS
- Wide Area Networks
- Searching Library Catalogs and Databases Via Internet
- Computer Conferences, E-Journals, and Publicly Accessible Files

Fall Semester 1992

- Introduction to Unix
- Introduction to VMS
- Wide Area Networks
- Computer Conferences and E-Journals
- Searching Library Catalogs and Databases Via Internet
- Publicly Accessible Files
- Information Servers: Gopher, WAIS, World-Wide Web

Spring Semester 1993

- Introduction to Wide Area Networks (WAN)
- Unix Mail for WANderers
- VMS Mail for WANderers
- Computer Conferences and E-Journals
- Library Catalogs and Databases
- Publicly Accessible Files and E-Books
- Gopher, WAIS, World-Wide Web
- WANderings

Spring Semester 1995

- Introduction to WAN
- Unix Mail for WANderers
- VMS Mail for WANderers
- Gopher and WAIS
- World-Wide Web
- Windows Applications: Winsock and Netscape
- Computer Conferences: LISTSERVs
- Computer Conferences: Usenet
- Windows Applications: WS_FTP and QVTNET
- Library Catalogs and Databases
- Online Bookstores, Electronic Books, Journals, and Newspapers
- Publicly Accessible Files: Beginning
- Publicly Accessible Files: Advanced
- Interactive Communication: IRC, MUDs, etc.
- WANderings

APPENDIX B

Internet Classes, University of Montana, Spring 1995[1]

Dates and times listed below.
Instructors: Barry Brown, Mansfield Library (barry@selway.umt.edu); and Vicki Pengelly, Computing and Information Services (pengelly@selway.umt.edu)
Prerequisites: (1) a central computer account, (2) familiarity with login procedures and the fundamentals of using a central computer, (3) pre-registration (x5455).
Suggestion: These classes are most beneficial when you take the entire series.

Introduction to Wide Area Networks, Tuesday, Feb.7, 3:10-4:00 p.m.
Learn about the information services and resources available on the Internet, linking together millions of people from over a hundred countries. An overview will be presented and some hands-on examples will be explored. Find out what's out there, how to find it, and how to use it.

Unix Mail for "WANderers": beginning, Tuesday, Feb.14, 3:10-4:00 p.m.
Unix Mail for "WANderers": advanced, Tuesday, Feb.14, 4:10-5:00 p.m.
Those with accounts on Selway can become familiar with basic commands and procedures of the Pine program for sending, receiving, and manipulating e-mail and files. An understanding of e-mail is essential for using certain Internet resources. Note: if you sign up for this class, then you probably don't need "VMS Mail for WANderers."

VMS Mail for "WANderers": beginning, Thursday, Feb.16, 3:10-4:00 p.m.
VMS Mail for "WANderers": advanced, Thursday, Feb.16, 4:10-5:00 p.m.
Those with accounts on Lewis can become familiar with basic commands and procedures of the VMS mail program for sending, receiving, and manipulating e-mail and files. An understanding of e-mail is essential for using certain Internet resources. Note: if you sign up for this class, then you probably don't need "Unix Mail for WANderers."

Gopher and WAIS, Tuesday, Feb. 21, 3:10-4:00 p.m.
World-Wide Web, Tuesday, Feb. 21, 4:10-5:00 p.m.
These network tools provide organization and allow easy navigation of Internet information resources and often alleviate the need for knowing computer addresses or using protocols such as telnet and ftp. Learn what each tool does and how best to use them. Special "client software" (e.g., Turbogopher, Mosaic, Cello, etc.) for each will be discussed.

Windows Applications: Winsock and Netscape—Thursday, Feb. 23, 3:10-4:00 p.m.
NOTE: Instructor: Bill Elison, Mansfield Library. This lecture/demonstration will be held in Mansfield Library 285.
The tools described are not available yet in the labs on campus, but this session is offered for those who may have their own access to these tools. Access the Internet via TCP/IP and Netscape, and learn about the Windows graphics interface to the Internet. Netscape is among the first and best of the Mosaic-type Internet

applications. This session will show you how to set up TCP/IP access and how to configure and run Netscape. This graphics interface allows you to view pictures, hear audio files, and view video clips from locations all over the world.

Computer Conferences: BITNET and Internet, Tuesday, Feb. 28, 3:10-4:00 p.m.
Computer Conferences: Usenet Newsgroups, Tuesday, Feb. 28, 4:10-5:00 p.m.
From the scholarly to the personal, whether you're interested in the evolution of bonehooks in Indonesia or the Grateful Dead, there is very likely an electronic journal or computer conference on the topic (and if there isn't, maybe you should start one). Find out how to overcome geographic isolation by participating in online discussions and communicating with colleagues around the world.

Windows Applications: WS_FTP and QVTNET, Thursday, March 2, 3:10-4:00 p.m.
NOTE: Instructor: Bill Elison, Mansfield Library. This lecture/demonstration will be held in Mansfield Library 285.

Use Winsock to open several excellent Windows Internet applications. QVTNET is one of the best telnet programs. It will allow you to open a stable connection with the Mansfield Library LaserNet (CD-ROM network) or other libraries throughout the world. WS_FTP will let you download binary and ASCII files from some of the best sites worldwide.

Library Catalogs and Databases, Tuesday, March 7, 3:10-4:00 p.m.
Online Bookstores, Electronic Books, Journals, and Newspapers, Tuesday, March 7, 4:10-5:00 p.m.
There are over 1,000 library catalogs and databases from over 70 countries, many online bookstores, and hundreds of e-books, e-journals, and e-newspapers available free of charge over the Internet. Learn how to find directories, use the "telnet" command and Gopher to interactively access these resources and strategies for conducting bibliographic searches.

Publicly Accessible Files: beginning, Tuesday, March 21, 3:10-4:00 p.m.

Publicly Accessible Files: advanced, Tuesday, March 21, 4:10-5:00 p.m.
There are thousands of files (full text, image, numeric, sound, software) from a wide variety of countries available free of charge over the Internet. Learn how to locate them (with "archie"), retrieve them (with "ftp"), uncompress them, and use them.

Interactive Communication (IRC, MUDs, etc.), Tuesday, March 28, 3:10-4:00 p.m.
WANderings, Tuesday, March 28, 4:10-5:00 p.m.
Learn about interactive communication tools and role playing simulation environments—Talk, IRC, MUDs, MOOs, etc. will be explained and used (Prerequisite: account on Gibson). MUDs are not just dungeons and dragons. There are many educational and research MUDs, MOOs, etc. Some people think that they are the future interface for the Internet.
The final class in this series, WANderings offers the chance to review questions from previous classes and tie up any loose ends left floating in cyberspace and the chance to explore in greater depth some of the topics that were briefly introduced. Electronic style guides for network information, general information search strategies and how to "keep up with it all" will be discussed.

APPENDIX C

Internet Short Courses: Follow-Up Evaluation

# of respondents from fall semester 1993 =	4 out of 20 = 20%
# of respondents from spring semester 1994 =	13 out of 33 = 39%
	total = 17 out of 53 = 32%

1. % that signed name =
   14 out of 17 = 82%
2. Survey Respondents — Registered For Course

Survey Respondents	Registered For Course
Staff = 9	22
Staff Faculty = 6	12 Faculty
UG = 1	10 UG

Grad = 0	8 Grad
Other = 1 (Special Librarian)	1 Other
3. Accounts on:	
Unix system only: 5	
VMS system only: 2	
Both systems: 9	
Other: 1	
4. Classes attended:	
Intro	I I I I I I I I I I
Unix Mail	I I I I I I I I I
VMS Mail	I I I I I
Conferences/LISTSERV/ Usenet	I I I I I I I
Lib. Catalogs/Telnet	I I I I I I I I I I
Files/FTP	I I I I I
Gopher/WAIS/WWW	I I I I I I I I I I
Wrap-up	I I I I
Can't remember which ones	I

\# of respondents who attended 4 or more classes = 9
(more than half)

5. Resources they are using:	
Freenets	
e-mail	I I I I I I I I I I I I I I
LISTSERVs	I I I I I I I I
Usenet	I I I I I
Telnet	I I I I I I I I I
Library catalogs, databases, CWISes	I I I I I I I I I I
FTP	I I I I
Archie	
Gopher	I I I I I I I I II I I I I
WAIS	I
WWW	I I
Other (state BBS, METnet)	I
6. Would like more instruction with:	
Freenets	I

e-mail	
LISTSERVs	I
Usenet	
Telnet	I
Library catalogs, databases, CWISes	I
FTP	I I I I I
Archie	I I
Gopher	
WAIS	I
WWW	I
ALL	I I I I I
Mosaic	I
More Practice	I I

7. Rate your level of expertise with Internet resources:

		1	2	3	4	5	6	7	8	9	10	
Before the classes:	novice	12	2	2								expert

average = 1.4

		1	2	3	4	5	6	7	8	9	10	
After the classes:	novice		3	7	1		1	4				expert

average = 4.1

8. What would have made this course series more profitable for you? How can it be improved (e.g., balance of lecture vs. hands-on, pace of courses, examples used, etc.)? Address your reply to the entire series or to specific classes. If you are referring to particular class(es), please note which ones:

Comments:

- Every little bit helps in the process, whether it is hands-on or lecture.
- When I started the series, I had just learned how to get into Selway (Unix system), so everything that was taught was brand new. The courses seemed to move very quickly, but then again it was totally new material. I think the classes benefitted me most by giving me confidence to go into the Internet and try things for myself. Now, after feeling much

more comfortable with the Internet, I would like to go back and retake the same courses. The only suggestion I can make is possibly more time for hands-on experience.

- Courses need to be longer and in "off-hours" when class commitments don't conflict.
- I liked the classes. My biggest problem was the difficulty in accessing Internet via modem. It takes a long time to get in and discourages practicing much less regular use. I am currently trying to get online—I've been at it 25 minutes and have not been successful. Once I got in on the first try, the longest I've taken is 75 minutes—average is about 30-45 minutes.
- Would have liked more hands-on experience, but with so much info to cover, it would be difficult.
- Class was pretty fast paced, could be slowed down.
- Great class!
- Perhaps a follow-up series to get into a deeper exploration of the Net.
- There is so much available that the mass amount of information you must cover can be baffling. If we could cover just a few resources each semester, but more intensely and thoroughly, I think it would be much more useful. Of course, for a "free course," this was wonderful.
- Slower pace would be helpful. Also, if we could have had concrete projects of our own to work on to make it more meaningful. Although I didn't know enough to ever come up with any ideas of what to do with the network.
- For WAIS, etc., I needed the whole series and not just one class. For Library Catalogs, etc., more time for supervised searching and possibly handout for F keys (e.g., F2, F10, etc.) to move within the catalog.
- I only attended one lecture, it was helpful. The handouts on the various subjects have allowed me to get started. I would like to see some kind of course designed for those with some hands-on experience where questions could be answered but not take as much time as the regular courses.

9. It is common for the enrollment to decrease as the semester drags on. However, perhaps scheduling or some other factors also affected the enrollment. Do you prefer short, single-topic courses

(like we offered this semester) or would you rather have long, comprehensive courses (e.g., three 3-hour courses) each semester? Please comment on the scheduling or any factors affecting enrollment.

Comments:

- I think its easier to take an odd hour to sit in a class, three hours is almost a half av day of work!
- I liked the schedule; unfortunately towards the end of the series, I was in the process of hiring, filling in, and training a new staff member.
- Short, single-topic courses. After an hour, you don't remember much. And we need more practice just using what we learned.
- Single-topic courses.
- This format was fine!
- Prefer short, single-topic courses.
- I liked the ongoing series of classes.
- I would prefer the shorter one-hour courses.
- Short, single-topic.
- Prefer short, single-topic. Still need to be productive at my office.
- Long, but nights on Saturday.
- three 3-hour long courses.
- I prefer long, comprehensive courses. It is difficult to predict when a meeting or other commitment will come up, causing me to miss a class.
- I was luckily able to attend throughout the semester, so obviously this format worked for me. However, if the three-hour sessions would allow us to more thoroughly explore each topic, rather than skimming, I would be all for it.
- Either way.

NOTE

1. Current course listings and instructional outlines available via ftp at: ftphost.umt.edu /pub/papers/internet/training.

WITHOUT A NET:

SUPPORTING OURSELVES IN A TREMULOUS ATMOSPHERE

Jeris Cassel and BethAnn Zambella

THE MUDDLED STATE OF CONSTANT CHANGE

In a preface to his novel *What Maisie Knew*, Henry James wrote the following passage which seems apropos to the technological age:

> The effort really to see and really to represent is no idle business in face of the *constant* force that makes for muddlement. The great thing is indeed that the muddled state too is one of the very sharpest of the realities, that it also has color and form and character, has often in fact a broad and rich comicality.[1]

"The great thing is indeed that the muddled state too is one of the very sharpest of the realities..." The realization of the muddled state of technology, the Internet, and the national information infrastructure seems to be the essence of this conference. That this muddled state "has color and form and character" is the essence of what we are trying to grasp within the state of constant change that all of us are experiencing in our valiant efforts to learn and to teach. It is within our valiant efforts that we must see, in fact, "broad and rich comicality" as we prepare ourselves to teach others and discover that, upon the *very* day for which we have been preparing and awaiting to share our vast storehouse of knowledge, the *very* source upon which that knowledge is based has changed! Comical? Yes, if you have a good sense of humor and a true sense of flexibility! At these moments, which are increasing in frequency, we must remember Marshall McLuhan's wisdom and foresight in 1967 when he wrote, "Learning, the educational process, has long been associated only with the glum ... Our time presents a unique opportunity for learning by means of humor ..."[2] One of the questions frequently asked by the Rutgers University Libraries search committees to interviewees is: "Do you have a tolerance for ambiguity?" It is a question that has provoked knowing smiles, nervous laughs, and serious questions. This question is not rooted in the poignancy of constant change we have been experiencing within a technological environment and teaching and learning within that environment, but it is rooted in a system that is in constant change and within which individuals remain at various levels of change. Perhaps we should revise the question to "Do you have a tolerance for constant change?" Or better yet, "Do you have a tolerance for muddlement?"

The muddled state of constant change in and proliferation of tools, sources, and access and the ambiguities in the meanings of these for the role of certain library positions gave impetus to the formation of the Electronic Resources Committee at the Rutgers University Libraries. The purposes of this paper are to share with you the evolution and role of this committee in a tremulous atmosphere and practical and theoretical perspectives on the group process. It is our hope that you can learn from our experience, and we can learn from you as you respond to this presentation of that experience.

GEOGRAPHY AND STRESS

In a geographically dispersed university campus with 18 libraries, three university computing services, one library systems department, and approximately 50,000 students, the advantages and disadvantages of electronic information sources are profound.

With a large number of undergraduate students, an increasing number of so-called "non-traditional" students, varying levels of graduate students, and a large mix of residential and commuting students in a world in which good, fast information determines success (and therefore becomes power), the pressure on academic librarians to get up to and keep up to speed on the wide world of electronic sources increases.

With the decrease in mediated online searching and with the increase in end-user electronic resources, the coordinators of online services were seeing the need for a shift in their responsibilities and the coordinators of bibliographic instruction were seeing the need to address the instructional aspects of the rapidly expanding resources. There was a definite need for security, support, and sharing of information evidenced by questions and concerns raised by a few librarians. The online services coordinators (the title varies within the Rutgers libraries) were asking, "Why aren't we ever involved in discussions and decisions related to end-user searching services?" Indeed, there was a fear of extinction—the same fear that must have been pivotal in the planning for the 1993 American Library Association Midwinter Machine Assisted Reference Section (MARS) Hot Topics Discussion Group forum on whether or not online searchers were dead. It appeared that we were no longer considered essential or important at a time when there was a great potential for the use of our knowledge, experience, and skills. At the same time, bibliographic instruction coordinators were increasingly feeling pressure of the responsibility of learning all of the new electronic resources rapidly appearing within our libraries in order to incorporate them into instructional sessions. Both groups felt left out of the decision-making process regarding electronic resources in the libraries. After raising a few questions among ourselves and administrators, these two groups were joined together to pool their skills, talents, and resourcefulness.

EVOLUTION OF A COLLEGIAL PEER SUPPORT GROUP

In fall 1992, the associate university librarian for graduate and undergraduate services asked the bibliographic instruction coordinators and the online services coordinators from the six major libraries of the university, representing the three dispersed geographical locations of the university, to work together as an ad hoc committee of the library faculty Standing Advisory Committee on Public Services (SACOPS). These two groups formed what eventually become known as the Electronic Resources Committee. The official charge to the committee was to develop system-wide electronic workshops to be presented in the spring of 1993 with, ideally, pilot workshops for December 1992. What this meant was that we were to plan and prepare a program of workshops that would be offered on all of our campuses—Camden, Newark, and New Brunswick (where there are four geographically dispersed campuses: the College Avenue Campus, Busch Campus, Douglass/Cook Campus, and Livingston Campus). A part of this charge included preparing one or two handouts to cover all electronic resources at the Rutgers University Libraries and to involve a number of librarians in teaching electronic resources by preparing teaching guides or scripts. The premises of the workshops were that: (1) everyone needed to know the basics regardless of level and discipline, and (2) the workshops needed to be held in convenient locations and at various times for a diversity of users.

Fall/Winter 1992—Spring 1993

This joint committee of bibliographic instruction coordinators and online services coordinators began meeting in October 1992. Attitudes that frequently prevail within groups given charges prevailed: (1) here is a chance to prove ourselves, (2) here's our chance to experiment, and (3) let us do the task we have been given and get it over with. After a couple of meetings of this highly energized group, it was clear that we would not have pilot workshops in December. Nevertheless, we decided relatively quickly upon the following guidelines for the workshops:

a. Workshops would begin the third week of the semester.
b. Each of the six libraries would present three workshops, providing a total of 18 workshops for the spring semester.
c. The workshops would be introductory workshops open to anyone affiliated with Rutgers University.

d. The workshops would focus on library databases, meaning those databases paid for by the libraries that were available through INFO, the Rutgers University campus-wide information system.
e. The workshops would be approximately one hour in length.
f. Projection equipment would be used for all workshops.
g. Individuals were to register for the session, but walk-ins would be welcomed.

In view of the desire to produce one or two handouts covering all of the electronic resources at the Rutgers University Libraries, the group gathered and reviewed handouts from across the libraries. The consensus was that handouts be designated, or new ones be prepared, for use with the workshops; preparing one or two handouts to cover all electronic resources at RUL seemed unworkable; materials related to the workshops should be the same color; and the online help features provided with the electronic sources should be emphasized in the class sessions. Generally, there should be less focus on the production of handouts and more on the development of and use of online features in electronic resources.

Over a couple of months, we planned and prepared a packet of information for presenting one-hour, system-wide workshops on electronic resources. We decided that we would offer two different workshops—one covering the RUL online catalog (IRIS), Innopac (used for acquisitions and serials control), and CARL (Colorado Alliance of Research Libraries) UnCover and another covering RLIN (Research Libraries Information Network) bibliographic and CitaDel files. The committee spent much effort and time in the planning and preparation of the sessions to reduce the burden of these processes on individuals and to establish some consistency in presentations. The committee prepared both summary and detailed outlines, sample exercises, and handouts for each workshop, as well as a calendar of sessions, a publicity flyer, an evaluation form, and an attendance sheet.

This planning and preparation process was invaluable for both instruction coordinators and online services coordinators in that much information and expertise was shared. The amount of learning that occurred through discovery and active participation in our large group and small group meetings is immeasurable. We divided into two teams, with each team focusing on teaching outlines and workshop handouts. When the teams presented their outlines to the group, it was obvious that we had two different ways and philosophies of approaching the teaching outlines. One team presented a summary outline that provided highlights of the most important things to relay in a workshop—feeling that librarians doing the instruction could fill in their own examples and instructional ideas—and the other team presented a detailed outline, with the idea of providing a logical sequence for instruction. Each team was looking at what different library instructors might prefer in terms of a teaching guide. The result was that the group decided that having both a summary and a detailed outline for each workshop would be useful, so each team developed both.

As the entire group reviewed the outlines, there were exclamations such as "I didn't know that feature was available! Are you sure you can search that way? There are limitations to searching that way; it is better to teach this other way of searching..." Suddenly, we were discovering things about systems we had been searching for years, as well as for fairly new systems! We were learning from each other!

We were all seeing the variations in knowledge about and experience with systems we worked with everyday. We began to recognize the learning and teaching resources we had among ourselves. As a result, our meetings evolved into working and sharing sessions in a classroom, rather than around a meeting table, in which we could demonstrate, test, and experiment with searching techniques for the teaching guides and, generally, for our own edification. We were learning collaboratively, cooperatively, and actively. We were thinking critically about the electronic resources and, generally, about what we were doing.

Within a matter of months, this group expanded from an ad hoc committee focused on a particular task to a community of learning and inquiry and a peer support group. Faculty collegiality was reigning! The group had gained a reputation within the library system as a "fun and productive committee." Workshop evaluations indicated high satisfaction with the organization of, handouts for, and demonstration-lectures in the system-wide electronic workshops. Workshop attendees indicated that the workshops were a great idea!

Although we are a group that enjoys praise, we knew we could learn as much, if not more, from criticism of our workshops. There were suggestions that we have more publicity, more suitable settings where everyone could see the screen, provide hands-on workshops, provide more information about accessing from home or office, and deal with discipline-specific questions offline so that others are not left out of the conversation. The committee not only analyzed the comments of workshop participants, but also the instructors' experiences in providing the workshops. We also examined our assumptions in planning the workshops, regarding instructional method, teaching materials, librarian participation, attendees, and publicity.

The involvement of librarians within each library varied, depending on attendance at the workshops, schedules, coverage, and willingness. With the exception of one of our libraries, each workshop was conducted by one person. Our sciences library used a team approach in which one librarian provided the instruction while the other provided technical assistance for the demonstration. This was a means of providing greater attentiveness to the attendees and of preparing others within the library to conduct one of the workshops in the future.

The workshops were publicized in the university faculty newsletter calendar and the computing services newsletter. The "Workshops" option was created within the library menus on the campus network, flyers were posted at various locations on all campuses (e.g., libraries, Learning Resource Centers, Teaching Excellence Centers, departments, and student centers), and were available at the reference desks in each of the major libraries.

After analyzing the feedback and experiences from the first round of system-wide workshops, we set new guidelines for the next round of workshops. Of course, we had to agree among ourselves that, indeed, there would be a next round of workshops! Since we did not get a huge number of attendees, there were mixed feelings about expending the time and effort. These mixed feelings were magnified by a newcomer to the committee. The advent of this newcomer made us realize the cohesiveness we had established as a group over a period of about nine months. This individual proposed a total restructuring of everything we had done. Even though there was a certain level of agreement with the new ideas, there was resistance among the group who had worked together and had formed a collegial bond. Nevertheless, we were able to establish some compromises, and this newcomer is now a valuable member of the community of inquiry and learning. Our equilibrium was restored, and we moved forward.

Fall 1993

For the fall 1993 semester, the Electronic Resources Committee decided to increase the number of workshops offered, offer sessions during the first three weeks and the last few weeks of the semester (thinking that these times would correspond to the time when individuals would feel a need to know and a need to use the resources), provide both hands-on and demonstration/lecture workshops, increase the length of the sessions (demonstration lecture workshops were planned for one and a half-hour slots, while hands-on workshops were planned for two-hour slots), expand departmental mailings of flyers, and publicize the workshops through student newspaper advertisements.

As we began preparing for the next semester of workshops, the committee was asked to take on a new charge of developing an information literacy program outline by the beginning of the following fall. We agreed to take on the charge, but as we considered this responsibility in conjunction with planning for the next workshops, we heard that there might be changes with the databases being offered on the network in the fall, there would be general changes in the overall campus network, and computer accounts would be widely available to students. The committee began wondering how we could possibly plan ahead without knowledge of possible decisions or participation in the decision-making process.

It was August, and we still did not know about forthcoming events. Having developed a cohesiveness, the committee was able to turn a gripe session into a pro-active stance in the form of a letter to library administrators regarding our concerns and recommendations. This letter included an expression of our concerns over how the forthcoming changes might effect the committee's planning for fall workshops and our place in the information loop. An outline of representative questions, concerns, issues, and recommendations was forwarded to the administration. We included such questions as:

Who has responsibility for decision making and information sharing on the current development of the library branch of the campus network?

Is network access provided at the expense of walk-in service?

What student awareness mechanisms need to be developed in terms of network education?

What is the appropriate role of the Electronic Resources Committee with regard to planning and implementation of electronic resources on the campus network?

The letter included a reminder that the committee, primarily charged with developing instructional programs, comprises RUL librarians who have considerable experience with electronic resources (electronic/online services coordinators); librarians who have the most significant contact in educating end-users (bibliographic instruction coordinators); and librarians who routinely work the front lines of library service at Rutgers (reference librarians) and a reminder that the members are uniquely positioned to assist in configuring the electronic information systems for RUL. (Many librarians at Rutgers have dual position titles, such as bibliographic instruction coordinator/ reference librarian.)

The committee recommended that the charge for the group be broadened to include liaison work with RUL Systems Department to design user-friendly interfaces, including recommendations for subject-specific Gopher pointers to selected Internet resources, and a strong advisory role in the RUL acquisition of subject-specific electronic resources.

As a result of our letter, a Libraries INFO Advisory Committee was formed to address some of these issues. Three members of the Electronic Resources Committee, plus collection development librarians, systems staff, technical services librarians, and university computing services staff are represented within this group.

More New Ventures

During fall 1993, the Electronic Resources Committee worked together learning a new search interface for the RLG (Research Libraries Group) CitaDel databases and learning about the new Gopher client that was installed on the campus network. The group developed a preliminary outline for an information literacy program which involved discussing the concept of information literacy, its relation to library instruction, an analysis of our instruction activities, and familiarizing ourselves with significant literature and documents on the subject of information literacy. We arrived at this document through a group process, using brainstorming techniques and the Socratic method.

The group coordinated a total of 24 system-wide electronic workshops, six more than in the previous spring semester. Fifteen of the workshops, publicized as "The Rutgers Connection," offered an introduction to the functions and searching basics of IRIS, Innopac, and UnCover. The remaining nine workshops offered an introduction to the content and searching basics of the RLIN bibliographic (BIB) file and CitaDel files (NPA, PRA, and ABI) using the Eureka interface. The committee survived the unknown and the sudden changes! Once again, it regained its equilibrium and continued debating, sharing, discovering, and collaborating.

Instructional Approaches

We began using two instructional methods, demonstration/ lecture and hands-on. The workshops were held in computer labs at the various campuses, with arrangements for lab space and equipment setup done by Computing Services personnel. Two extra hands-on "The Rutgers Connection" workshops were provided at the request of Computing Services to cover the demand for this workshop.

A team approach was used for all hands-on workshops and for demonstration/lecture workshops. Teams used varying methods in conducting the workshops. In some instances, each librarian took equal responsibility for the instruction and in monitoring attendees working on the computers. In other instances, one librarian would provide the instruction and the other would serve in a supporting role at the computer and in monitoring attendees at the computers. For the practical workshops, the teams followed the same outlines/scripts used for the lecture/demonstration workshops. Some teams provided very brief introductions and worked through the script examples with the attendees working on the computers. Other teams provided lengthier lecture/ demonstrations and then a practical work session with a set of prepared exercises provided in written or oral form, or alternated lecture/demonstration and practical work throughout the workshop.

Participation

For the first time, librarians from different library units began forming the instructional teams for hands-on workshops (Central Technical Services and the sciences research library, humanities/ social sciences research library and an undergraduate library, and the Camden library and a New Brunswick undergraduate library). These occasions proved to be positive learning experiences for the teams involved.

Evaluations

Again, the workshops were rated with high satisfaction. Attendees indicated that their preferred instruction was in a hands-on session in lab and a class with demonstration, ranking far above learning on their own through trial and error; self-instructional guide; and a combination of class with demonstration and guide in library. General comments indicated that the workshops were very helpful, that allowing individuals a chance to explore and use new skills at intervals during the session was critical to success and that having practice exercises was good.

Based on comments of workshop attendees and on experiences at the workshops and at the reference desk, the committee once again set about preparing another round of workshops. Again, the workshops were revised. This time we focused on databases with similar content and purpose and provided an introductory workshop on the Internet. We recommended that subject-focused workshops be offered by subject specialists since they are more likely to be aware of the specialized databases on the Internet; that appropriate electronic resources be incorporated into all bibliographic instruction sessions since, currently, this seems the better way of reaching undergraduates; and that step-by-step user guides be developed for IRIS, Innopac, UnCover, and CitaDel files. The outlines and scripts prepared by the committee could be used as guides for the preparation of subject-focused workshops and for bibliographic instruction sessions.

We offered a total of 22 workshops. We called this series of workshops "The Rutgers Connection" with the following three segments: "You Can Access Subject Databases," "You Can Access Books," and "INFO: Gateway to the Internet." All but three of these were hands-on workshops. Since there had been an increase of public access terminals, the hands-on workshops were held in the public areas of the libraries—with the exception of the ones held in Camden and Newark campuses where it was just as convenient, if not more so, to use the Computing Services labs and with the exception of our Library of Science and Medicine where an electronic classroom had just been established.

The workshops were increased to approximately two hours and were presented throughout the semester, focusing on the weeks near the beginning and end of the semester.

FUTURE OF THE COLLEGIAL PEER SUPPORT GROUP

During spring 1994, the Electronic Resources Committee had a session devoted to reflecting on where we have been and what we have done, as well as the future activities and direction of the group. We reviewed the information literacy outline, the detailed outlines of instructional activities at individual Rutgers libraries, statistical and evaluations summary reports from the three semesters of electronic workshops, and other pertinent materials. The committee decided that it would focus on encouraging further information literacy with the instruction program by developing a partnership service in which teaching faculty and library faculty will enter into a contract regarding library instruction. It will be understood that when faculty fill out a request for a library instruction session that library faculty will provide appropriate resources for students to proceed with library research-related assignments, teach concepts, and provide active learning experiences. Teaching faculty will be required to attend the library session, provide students with library research-related assignments, and provide appropriate assignment materials and information to the librarian for session preparation.

The committee also recommended that workshops be provided for librarians in order to encourage and assist them in providing active learning instruction sessions, developing and providing appropriate paper and online documentation for online resources, pursuing the possibility of internships for peer counselors at library network terminals, continuing with system-wide electronic workshops (but offer only one workshop repeatedly—INFO: Gateway to the Internet), and supporting the development of self-instructional modules on the campus-wide network. We will look at how these systems can best be developed, identify transferable skills for incorporating into the modules, and identify items/information repeatedly requested that might be incorporated into the modules.

This outline of projects or goals indicates that members of the Electronic Resources Committee continue to value the experience of learning and working together as sub-groups focusing on workshop preparations, as teams presenting workshops focusing on electronic resources, and as a large group sharing ideas and experiences related to instruction, information literacy, and technology. It also indicates a desire and willingness of this group to continue expanding this experience and support beyond the group.

A PROCESS PERSPECTIVE

Creating a Community of Inquiry

While carrying out its official charges, the Electronic Resources Committee has accomplished many measurable goals, such as the various workshops and the beginnings of an information literacy program, that are helping everyone at the libraries cope with change. But the Electronic Resource Committee has also fostered immeasurable growth for committee members, helping us form a community of inquiry—a community that offers support, helps demystify, reduces risk, and critically assesses technology.

Supporting Ourselves

The Electronic Resources Committee serves as a peer support group where librarians can teach each other and swap tips and techniques. This open exchange of ideas creates an environment for incidental learning, particularly through group discussion and group work on projects. Beyerman has observed a similar phenomenon among nurses who serve on professional committees.[3] We have discovered that we continue to learn, even about technology that we consider well-known and knowable, such as our online catalog. Realizing that even the most knowledgeable and curious among us still do not know *everything* helps us feel less alone in our muddlement and also sensitizes us to the bewilderment our patrons must feel as they confront electronic catalogs and databases.

Our group helps abate the sense of aloneness we all tend to feel about our constant state of flux. It hardly seems possible that educated individuals such as librarians should think, "I am the only one who feels this way," and yet we obviously do. We are relieved and overjoyed to learn that a colleague shares our despair or hope. We flock to conferences such as this one in large part seeking a shared sense of unity with other librarians. Tom Kirk, a recognized leader in academic librarianship, said in a recent opinion piece, "I am not alone. We as a society and as a profession are navigating in uncharted seas. Like generations before us we are making up the rules as we go along."[4] Kirk seems to be reassuring himself as much as he hopes to reassure others.

The Electronic Resources Committee offers support to its members in ways that the individual's department or unit often cannot or will not. Members with similar job functions find others who really share their interests and who do not discourage new ideas simply because they might alter daily workloads. For example, a member might suggest implementing or deleting a layer or paperwork. Back home at the member's unit, the idea might be immediately shot down because of political turf and power issues; in the committee, members are less threatened and bring a fresh, less parochial outlook to problems. Committee work helps us view the library system more broadly; it can help us understand other positions, so that we can offer support that may be lacking at their home units.

Reducing Risk and Ambiguity

The constantly changing technological landscape keeps us forever at the edge of our competence. Kirk says we must accept the "level of risk involved" and "move on."[5] This is, of course, more easily said than done. As Sheil so aptly observes, "our immediate environment will always loom so large in our perceptions that any change in it will appear to be revolutionary."[6] Just as students in the classroom prefer to avoid tasks that involve ambiguity and risk, so do practicing professionals. The Electronic Resources Committee helps reduce the risk and ambiguity inherent in learning new things by providing a supportive environment and by structuring the learning process for other librarians.

Quoting Schon, authors Baskett and Marsick explain that all professionals function in a world "characterized by uncertainty, disorder, and indeterminacy."[7] This seems poignantly so for librarians. The knowledge we have garnered from our formal education assumes predictability and control of our environment, while in our professional lives we confront the exact opposite. We must accept that we can no longer know the answer to every question, and new models of knowledge can help us do just that. Baskett and Marsick say that the idea of "knowledge," as an accumulation of facts, is giving way to a concept of "knowing," which is created as people interact with their environments and gain closer and closer approximations of a sense of certainty.

Demystifying and Modeling

Approximating certainty is as close to knowing as many of us feel we may ever come. As information sources multiply, it gets harder and harder to claim universal expertise, yet we all have pieces of knowledge to share with one another. The members of the Electronic Resources Committee emphasize that we are *not* experts but recognize that we all have contributions to make. We hope to demystify the workings and teaching of technology for others, not by claiming to know all, but by working *with* them to collaboratively explore it all. We offer ourselves as models who are willing to take risks—not as experts.

Our modeling is an unconscious form of cognitive apprenticeship, as defined by Farmer, Buckmaster, and LeGrand which bridges theory into practice. The model articulates his or her thinking and often describes "tricks of the trade" for the learner.[8] In the Electronic Resources Committee, members take turns demonstrating the shortcuts and detours we have discovered along the information highway and explain to each other how we planned or stumbled upon our routes. We have also learned to share our instructional strategies through reflection and example.

In addition to modeling, group members use stories and anecdotes to reveal their knowledge to others and to reveal others' knowledge to themselves. One of our student information assistants recently asked me if she had been using the Internet. The question came up when her aunt, also a librarian, had asked her what she was doing with the Internet, and the student did not know. In fact, the student had been "on the Net" through our campus-wide information system. When I retell this story to others, I accomplish several things. I let you know in a non-threatening way that you, too, may have been on the Internet without knowing it; I reassure you that others are equally flummoxed by technology and its attendant terminology; and I share a piece of my working day with you. As Clarissa Pinkola Estes (the author of *Women Who Run With the Wolves*) says, "Stories strengthen and help turn around situations."[9]

Critically Assessing

As we share stories and demystify the process of learning about technology, we minimize the risk involved in learning. As our group increases in confidence, our ability to critically assess the technologies we are working with also improves. We began by learning to work around the shortcomings of the hardware and software we were given, but we are steadily gaining more of a voice in the purchasing decisions and design of systems. One small triumph was the formation of an advisory committee to propose changes in the library menu of our campus-wide information system. We do not accept technology in general uncritically—we also discuss when technology is appropriate and when, perhaps, more fundamental sources might be efficacious.

CONCLUSION

Our critical assessment also extends to the group itself. We have painted a rather idealistic picture of the committee, but it is not without its own problems. The Electronic Resources Committee is dealing well with concrete issues, such as hands-on workshops, but poorly with the theoretical, such as our looming information literacy program. Perhaps because we are a youthful committee, the group often shows an adolescent nature—suspicious of authority, yet eager to please, moody and unruly at times, still trying to build confidence in our own powers of decision-making. And yet we are a dynamic, democratic, creative, hard-working community that is accustomed to getting things done. We have made tremendous strides in some of our charges, small steps forward in others. But through it all, the process has helped us grow in immeasurable ways.

Process has overtaken product for us. The value of peer support, risk reduction, demystification, modeling, and critical assessment surpasses the temporary triumphs and trials of committee work. If the Electronic Resources Committee can help us become comfortable with unpredictability and can keep us balanced on the tightrope of information technology, it will have more than met *our* goals for the group.

NOTES AND REFERENCES

1. Henry James, Preface to *What Maisie Knew, In the Cage,* and *The Pupil* (reprint of 1908 edition published by Scribner, New York, as *The Novels and Tales of Henry James,* Vol. 11; Fairfield, NJ: Augustus M. Kelley, 1979), p. xiii.

2. Marshall McLuhan and Quentin Fiore, *The Medium is the Massage* (New York: Bantam, 1967), p. 10.

3. Kathleen Beyerman, "Committee Work: Serendipitous Teaching and Learning," *Journal of Continuing Education in Nursing* 21(1990): 18-22.

4. Thomas G. Kirk, "The Way I See It: College Libraries and the New Technology," *College and Research Libraries News* 55(1994): 197.

5. Ibid.

6. B.A. Sheil, "Coping with Complexity," in *Information Technology and Psychology: Prospects for the Future,* edited by Richard A. Kasschau, Roy Lachman, and Kenneth R. Laughery (New York: Praeger, 1982), p. 79.

7. H.K. Morris Baskett and Victoria J. Marsick, "Confronting New Understandings About Professional Learning and Change," in *Professionals' Ways of Knowing: New Findings on How to Improve Professional Education,* edited by H.K. Morris Baskett and Victoria J. Marsick (San Francisco: Jossey-Bass, 1992), p. 10.

8. J.A. Farmer, Jr., A. Buckmaster, and B. LeGrand, "Cognitive Apprenticeship: Implications for Continuing Professional Education," in *Professionals' Ways of Knowing: New Findings on How to Improve Professional*

Education, edited by H.K. Morris Baskett and Victoria J. Marsick (San Francisco: Jossey-Bass, 1992), pp. 41-49.

9. Gene Stone, "Clarissa Explains It All," *Playboy* (July 1994): 72.

LIBRARY INSTRUCTION FOR FACULTY:

TRAINING IN THE USE OF ELECTRONIC RESOURCES

Gale Burrow and Cynthia Snyder

The Libraries of The Claremont Colleges began offering presentations to faculty on access to and use of electronic resources in the spring of 1991. These presentations, as well as many of the libraries' CD-ROM databases and the campus network connections that made these and a wide range of other databases available, were made possible by a Knight Foundation grant to Claremont McKenna College and Pomona College.[1]

The presentations were planned by a committee of librarians and campus computer center staff and were offered at least once on each of the six Claremont campuses within the following 18 months. Each presentation lasted approximately two hours and focused on the online catalog and CD-ROM databases subscribed to by the libraries as well as external databases accessed through the Internet such as FirstSearch and MELVYL. Participants received a notebook which included information on available databases and connections, where to get help, discussions of related services such as instruction, screens captured and reproduced from demonstrated searches, and helpsheets for several databases. Since each session had a broad subject focus (humanities, social sciences, business and economics, government and statistics, science and technology), two librarians with appropriate subject responsibilities planned and led each presentation, adapting the outline and the notebook to suit the interests of their audience. Although none were exactly the same, each presentation followed what one faculty member called the "research model": first searching citation databases for articles, then searching the online catalog for periodicals needed and books on the subject, then broadening the search to external connections and databases. The "Presentation Overview," which served as the table of contents for the notebook, outlines a session. The pages that follow are reprinted from the notebook.

Throughout the entire process we learned several lessons—some obvious, some not so obvious. For instance, we learned to give clear, focused presentations and cover less material, not more. Our goal was not to overwhelm the audience. We learned that people knew less than we thought, so we needed to begin with the basics. We tried very hard not to use jargon. Also, through trials by fire, we learned to always have searches captured onto floppy diskette or on overhead transparencies ready for times when connections were not available or when they failed.

In choosing the people to present the sessions, there were several issues to consider. Most important was the comfort level of the presenter: some people do not like to speak in front of crowds. Also important were the the presenter's enthusiasm and familiarity with the subject matter. Finally, we asked, "How well does this person function under stress? If everything fails, can he/she recover and carry on?"

In contacting faculty to attend the sessions, we found we had to be very diligent. The libraries did a lot of initial advertising; librarians made many phone calls to deans and faculty and followed up with reminders. Following the sessions, we promptly answered any questions or requests for materials. Maintaining contact in the weeks or months after the sessions was equally important. We needed to share new developments and changes in databases and software to keep faculty up to date.

Also we, as librarians, learned much about the databases and connections, about faculty interests and needs, about campus computer centers and electronic access from preparing and presenting the sessions; and we took what we learned back to our jobs, thereby making us better librarians for the experience.

Although the presentations have changed over time as new resources have become available, we continue to offer these sessions to faculty. In addition to specific databases and database systems, we now include Gopher resources and will soon add the World-Wide Web. We vary our focus from campus to campus, depending on requests from faculty and advice from each campus academic computing center: some sessions emphasize a particular database or group of databases, others focus on a range of resources within a subject area. As long as access to and availability of resources continues to grow and change, these faculty sessions will remain an important part of our instructional and outreach program.

NOTE

1. For a more detailed discussion of the libraries' network implementation and development of faculty presentations, see Burrow and Gunter, "The CD-ROM Network at The Claremont Colleges: Implementation, Instruction, and Remote Access," *RSR Reference Services Review* 22(Summer 1994): 7-14, 30.

PRESENTATION OVERVIEW

I. Introduction
Expanding access to information through electronic resources
Database structure: records, fields, and interface
Connections

II. Using CD-ROM Databases

III. Blais, the Libraries' Online Catalog

IV. Using Databases Through the Internet

V. Conclusion
Who to contact for help
Time for questions

Appendix: CD-ROM

Connecting to the CD-ROM Tower
Getting Started with SocioFile
Getting Started with Ethnic NewsWatch
Descriptions of CD-ROM Databases
Logging Off CD-ROM Databases

Appendix: Other

Using Blais
Using the University of California's MELVYL
Internet Accessible Library Catalogs

PREPARING YOUR SEARCH STRATEGY

1. State your topic in one or two sentences.
2. Write down the key words that express each main idea or concept.
3. Break down phrases into single terms whenever possible. Only keep phrases when the concept is consistently described in a particular way (e.g., artificial intelligence).
4. Write down some possible synonyms for each concept.
5. Consider truncation and wildcards. For example, **legal*** would find
   legal
   legality
   legalize
6. Combine terms using **and** and **or**.
   OR to link similar or synonomous concepts:
      law? or legal?
   AND to find items with both concepts:
      abortion and law?
   parentheses to control the grouping of concepts:
      (law? or legal?) and abortion
7. Determine which databases to search.
8. Think about how to limit or modify the search if you retrieve too many or too few items. (You may need to browse a few of the items retrieved to look for alternate terms.)

SELECTING DATABASES

There are a variety of options to consider in choosing the databases for your searches. First, you will need to select databases with the appropriate subject coverage and time span. Below are some other considerations.

Content Type

Full-text	Citation
Shakespeare on Disc	Humanities Index

Physical Format

CD-ROM	Online
America: History and Life	Blais online catalog
MathSci Disc	Lexis-Nexis

Cost

No cost to user	User pays fees
ERIC	Philosophers' Index in Knowledge Index

Access

Network	In library
INSPEC on FirstSearch	Ethnic NewsWatch

Once you have selected the databases you need, become familiar with the database and its search system:

Look at the database structure. What fields does it contain? Are fields indexed by phrase, by keyword, by code?

Translate your search topic into a statement the database will understand. Take advantage of special database features (thesaurus, field-specific searching, etc.) to make your searching more effective.

Find out how the database search software specifies basic functions:

logical operations	(AND, OR, NOT, ANDNOT, +)
truncation	(* ? # !, single or multiple character wildcard)
set recombination	(S1, #1, [1])
proximity operations	(w/5, with, near, adj)
search history	(review, display sets)
index lookup	(F5, expand)
display	(F4, citn, all, S3/9/1-4)
print or download	(P, Alt/F3, output, type)

Assistance

For Questions About:	Contact:
Searching CD-ROMs Blais Library Menu	Honnold/Mudd Reference ext. 3959 Government Publications ext. 8800 Denison Library ext. 3941 Seeley G. Mudd Science ext. 8924 Sprague Library ext. 8920
Technical problems with CD-ROMs Blais Library Menu	Systems Department, Honnold/Mudd ext. 8014
Connections to CD-ROMs Blais Library Menu	Systems Department, Honnold/Mudd ext. 8014 Your Campus Academic Computing Center
Library Instruction	Gale Burrow, Coordinator of Library Instruction ext. 3987

GETTING STARTED WITH ETHNIC NEWSWATCH

Ethnic NewsWatch is a full-text database of newspapers and magazines from the ethnic minority press in America. It presents the "other side of the stories" from African-American, Arab/Middle Eastern, Asian-American, European/Eastern European, Hispanic/Latino, Jewish, and Native American points of view. The entire database is searchable in either English or Spanish. The database is updated quarterly.

SELECT A DATABASE

At the opening screen, use the **UP/DOWN Arrow** keys to choose a database. Press **ENTER** to select.

SELECT A SEARCH LANGUAGE (ENGLISH OR SPANISH)

Press **F9** to change the search language that appears on the screen.

SEARCH THE FULL-TEXT DATABASE

The Ethnic NewsWatch full-text search screen provides 10 searchable fields. All fields can be searched by typing in search word(s) or using the Browse Key (**F2**). You may type in more than one term in each field, using the operators AND, OR, or NOT to expand or limit your search.

AND Retrieves records in which all of the search terms appear.
Africa and apartheid

OR Retrieves all records containing either search term
pound or dollar

NOT Retrieves only those records which include the first term, but do not include the second term.
sports not football

Truncation To replace any number of characters in a search term use * (asterisk).
wom*n econom*

You can enter information in several fields. The more terms and fields you select, the more narrow the search will be.

DISPLAYING

Press the **F3** key to display a list of the search results. Use the **UP/DOWN Arrow** keys to highlight article titles.

Press **F2** to see the short citation. Press the **SPACEBAR** once for the full citation. Press the **SPACEBAR** again for the complete full-text article.

The left arrow key will move to the previous index record. The right arrow key will move to the next index record.

Press **CTRL** and **SPACEBAR** to select articles to print.

Press **F2** to return to the main list.

Press **F3** to return to the search screen to modify your search.

PRINTING

Press **F5**: Print. Use the spacebar to choose between Easy (one article) and Advanced (multiple articles) Print. Press **ENTER** to select.

Easy Print allows you to print the document on the screen, either the citation only, article only, or both. Use the **UP/DOWN Arrow** keys to choose and the **SPACEBAR** to select.

Advanced Print allows you to print one or more articles that you previously selected (by pressing **CTRL** and **SPACEBAR**).

DOWNLOADING

Press **F4**: Actions. Use the **UP/DOWN Arrow** keys to move to Export.

1. Press the **SPACEBAR** for "Export" options. Use the **UP/DOWN Arrow** keys and spacebar to move and select within the window. Press the **SPACEBAR** to choose and **ENTER** to select.
2. At Export Type, select "Formatted Text" to export the articles as they appear. Key in a name for the search at "File Name."
3. "Document Format" lets you choose between citation, index record, article, or citation AND article.
4. If you have selected articles to print or export, the system will default to "selected documents" at Document Range and export the documents you have chosen.

QUITTING

Press **F10**: Quit to return to the main screen.
Press **ESC** to return to the Menu.

SEARCHABLE FIELDS

Article Key Word

Since every word in the full-text articles is searchable, "Article Key Word" is often the best way to find articles which contain the information you want. Using the **UP/DOWN Arrow** keys, move the cursor to the "Article Key Word" field and type in the term(s) you want to search. Press **ENTER** to perform the search.

Article Subject

Ethnic NewsWatch contains a "Controlled Subject Vocabulary" designed to make it easier to search a single subject across the entire database. To browse the subject index use the **UP/DOWN Arrow** keys to move to the "Article Subject" field. Press the **F2**: Browse key. Use the **UP/DOWN Arrow** keys or type the first letters of your subject. Move the cursor to your desired subject and press the **ENTER** key to select. You can return to the Browse window to select additional terms. When you have selected all of the subjects wanted, press **ENTER** again and the system will perform the search.

Article Title

Every word in each title is searchable (except for words such as "of," "for," "in," "a," "an," etc.) Using the **UP/DOWN Arrow** keys, move the cursor to the "Article Title" field. Type in the key or major words from the title you want to search. Press the **ENTER** key to perform the search.

Author/Byline

This field contains the names of all authors, writers, syndicated columnists and other contributers. Using the **UP/DOWN Arrow** keys move the cursor to the "Author/Byline" field. Type in the name. You can enter names either first name then last name, or last name then first name. Do not use commas or other punctuation between first and last names. Press the **ENTER** key to perform the search.

Article Type

Articles are designated by one of the following categories or types

Article	Editorial	Movie Review	Interview	Theater Review
Column	Obituary	Book Review	Record Review	

Publication Date

Dates are displayed as mm-dd-yy. Date range searching is also possible using the greater than ($gt) or less than ($lt) keys.

$lt0991 would retrieve all articles before September 1991

$gt040191 would retrieve all articles after April 1, 1991

People (Names)

People given significant coverage in articles are listed in the "People (Names)" field. Names are entered (spelled) exactly as they appear in the original text of the article. Since some names may have more than one accepted spelling, that name may appear under two or more spellings. More than one name may be entered in the field if you are looking for articles in which both people are discussed.

Jackson Jesse and Cuomo Mario

Qaddafi or Khaddafi or Khadafy

Geographic Location

This field lists cities, counties, states, countries, continents, and geographic regions mentioned in the articles. They are entered exactly as they appear in the articles, with the exception of states which are entered with the two letter abbreviation when they follow a city or town.

Chicago, IL (city and state abbreviation)	**Dublin** (city only)
California (state only)	**Saudi Arabia** (country)
Middle East (geographic location)	**West Bank** (geographic region/section)
Africa (continent)	

Ethnic Group

You may enter the following designations in this field

African American	**Jewish**	**Hispanic**
Asian/Pacific Islander	**Arab/Middle Eastern**	
European/Eastern European	**Native American/American Indian**	

Publication Name

This field lists the name of every publication in the database. You can type in the name of the publication or press **F2**: Browse to display a list of the publications.

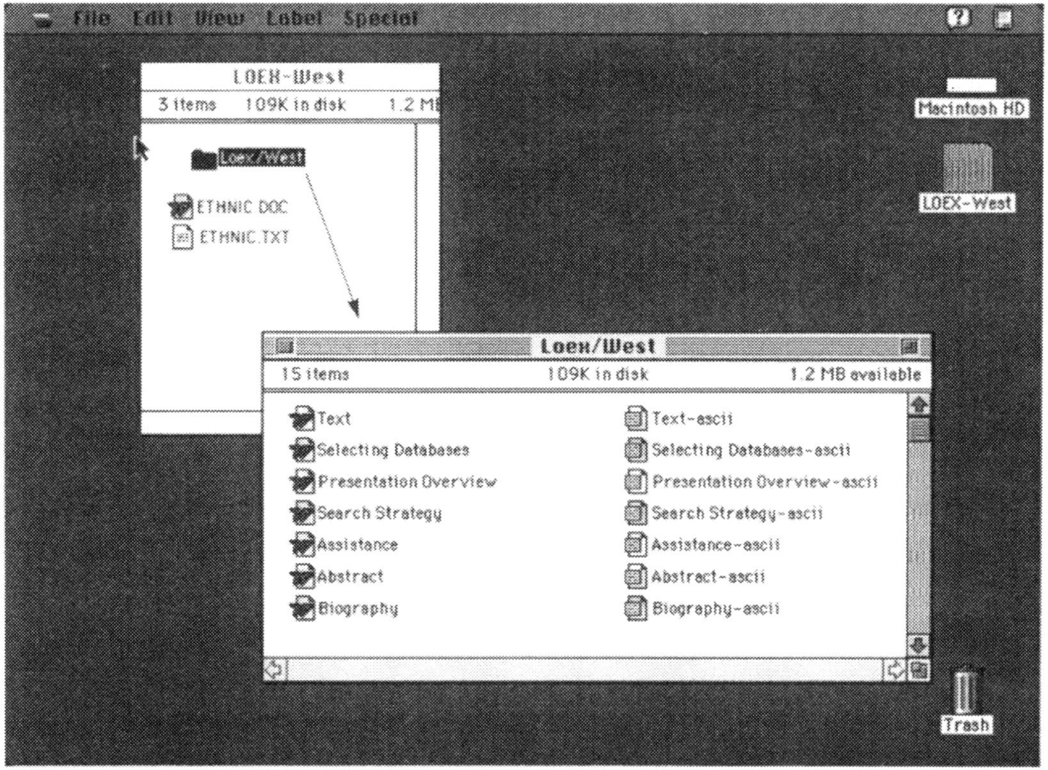

Computer Screen Art Work

INCORPORATING INFORMATION TECHNOLOGIES INSTRUCTION IN AN EXTENDED EDUCATION PROGRAM FOR WORKING ADULTS

Hélène Lafrance and Bonnie Gratch

BACKGROUND

Saint Mary's College is a private, Catholic, liberal arts college located in Moraga, California. It is operated by the Christian Brothers, a lay religious teaching order, and the current enrollment is approximately 4,200 students including 1,000 off-campus extended education students. The School of Extended Education, in existence since 1979, offers three major programs: bachelor of arts in management and in health services administration and masters of science in health services administration. The mission of the School of Extended Education is to provide educational programs to mature individuals whose needs are not met by the traditional, on-campus programs.

The goals of the extended education programs are both learner-centered (meaning to be aware of and responsive to the characteristics and needs of adult students) and outcome oriented. When we developed our library instruction component for these programs, we had to make sure that its goals matched and reinforced the goals of the overall program such as:

1. to recognize the unique learning situation of the experienced adult,
2. to ensure that the programs match with the external contexts within which the students are functioning,
3. to provide the competence and knowledge adults need in the world of work,
4. to enhance students' critical thinking skills.

One of the most interesting characteristics of the extended education programs is the cluster system. Groups of students (clusters) begin their programs at various times throughout the year at different locations in the greater Bay Area. These groups take all their classes together one evening a week for an 18-month period (for the undergraduate programs) or 24 months for the graduate one. Each cluster includes from six to 20 students, the average size being 14. This cluster system provides a mutually supportive learning environment that is especially suited to adult learning.

A cluster of extended education students represents a true diversity of people in terms of age, gender, ethnicity, regional origin, experience context, socioeconomic background, and religion, but the students also share some characteristics: most of them work full time in responsible management positions; they have had an interrupted college career for a variety of reasons; their main problem is "time"; and they struggle among family responsibilities, the demands of their jobs, and their studies. While the management programs are evenly balanced in terms of gender, the health administration programs are predominantly female.

THE LIBRARY INSTRUCTION PROGRAM

The extended education programs have been in existence since 1979, and from the beginning, basic library services were offered to the students. In 1986, following a Western Association of Schools and Colleges (WASC) accreditation visit and recommendations, the library was asked to develop a library instruction component for these students. Librarians collaborated with the administration and the faculty to design a program that served the needs of adult students and was well integrated into the curriculum.

Initially, a librarian would visit the classroom at its usual location for an hour at the point in their program when the students were starting to think about the long-term project they had to complete during their program. The objectives of the session were to help the students identify various types of information sources and develop a search strategy and to establish a relationship between the students and the library that would continue through phone and mail. This program worked well for a while but had its limitations: students were not in a library setting, the format was lecture only, and the students had no chance to practice with any of the sources presented to them.

In 1990 the program underwent a drastic change to become more compatible with adult learning styles and to match more closely the goals of the programs. In summary, the new program became a two-hour, on-campus library session held on Saturday mornings (outside of regular class time), and the lecture format gave way to a workshop format with hands-on experience and group discussion. The new program got immediate positive feedback from the students, even though the required Saturday session was added to their already heavy schedule. It worked because of the support of the administration but also because the session met the students' needs better: it was closely integrated into the curriculum; it was tailored to adult learning; and it reinforced transfer of learning by stressing general processes and concepts rather than specific tools, and by presenting search strategies that could be used in any library.

The new program was well accepted and the workshops were offered all year long. But soon we had to face a different challenge. The library was starting to plan for automation and was subscribing to more and more electronic resources. It became essential to incorporate the teaching of information technologies into all our instruction programs, including the extended education programs. We acquired a new instructional computer equipped with a CD-ROM drive and a projection panel, and began demonstrating Albert, our online catalog (the off-campus students can dial into Albert and request materials to be sent to them), and two CD-ROM products suitable to the extended education programs (ABI and HealthPlan). We noticed rapidly that teaching information retrieval technology to off-campus students could not be done in the same way we would teach the on-campus students. We already knew that many extended education students would be using other libraries with different CD-ROMs or online systems, so we had to teach them concepts rather than commands to ensure that they could transfer this learning to a new system. But as we became more and more involved in teaching CD-ROM technologies, we also noticed significant differences in the ways adult and younger students approach computers. We began asking ourselves, "How can we better teach technology to adult students?"

TEACHING TECHNOLOGY TO ADULT RETURNING STUDENTS

To understand how it is different to teach technology to adults, it's important to take into consideration the characteristics of adult learners. In the literature on andragogy,[1,2] it is usually recognized that:

- the adult learner is self-directed (more independent) and motivated to acquire information and skills relevant to real-life situations (or job situation);
- the adult learner is well experienced professionally and personally and expects an immediate payoff or practical application.

These characteristics seem very positive and should facilitate the learning process but, at the same time, we need to remember that:

- adult groups are never homogeneous;
- adults often lack confidence and feel isolated when they return to school;
- they are struggling with schedule and time;
- they are experience rich but theory poor; that is they need theory to make sense of their past experience.

What can we learn from this description, and how can we apply it to the teaching of technology to adults? Facing a group of adult students we need to remember, first, that the group is not homogeneous. We described earlier how the extended education clusters at Saint Mary's were very diverse. In terms of computer literacy this diversity is even more tangible: the class can include people who know more than you do about computers and others who have managed without them so far. Unlike younger students, many adults have never been exposed to technology and are often afraid of it. It is our role to quickly assess the level of computer literacy in the class and adjust our presentation and the group exercises accordingly.

When a definite lack of confidence is perceived in some of the students, one way to support them is to have them identify some of their past experiences with computers, even if it is only with word processing. It can help them make the transition to database searching. It is also helpful to use some transfer of learning techniques. For example, we usually teach the students how to use the print thesaurus (rather than the online one) when they prepare their search strategies. Using something familiar (a book) often helps students bridge the gap between the traditional tools and the technological ones.

Although adult students are usually highly motivated, they are often resistent to learning research and information retrieval skills because they don't see any value or usefulness in them. To help them recognize the value of acquiring information retrieval skills, we encourage them to make the connection with their work. We point out that these skills will enable them to keep current in their field for example, and they will also benefit from the ability to quickly retrieve information about new trends in management, industries, and companies. Another simple way to make the connection to their work is to use a real-life example to teach search strategy formulation.

Now, let's go back for a minute to the theory of adult learning. Active experimentation is considered to be a critical step in the adult learning process. Adults don't like passive situations, and they respond well to informality and collaborative approaches. They also want to know why they should learn something, and how they can apply what they learn to their job. If active experimentation is a critical step in the learning process, the ideal way of teaching technology to adults would be in a lab setting where each student has the use of a computer. If this option is not available, the demonstration should be as short as possible and followed by hands-on practice in small groups. Questions and discussion should be encouraged at all times. Peer-helping activities are particularly important and computer literate students should be paired with beginners during exercises and hands-on.

As a general rule, when teaching technology to adult students, it is useful to:

- assess their previous experience with technology;
- be sensitive to their fears, motivation levels, and abilities;
- provide hands-on experience and peer-helping activities;
- connect the experience to their life and show them how they can apply it to their work.

At Saint Mary's College, most of the students in the extended education programs work in or have backgrounds in the business and management world, an environment which definitely contributes to the way they perceive information technology. Many of them already work in a competitive environment in which computers and information play a significant role. If they possess some information technology skills, they better their chances in the job market. That fact is usually sufficient to raise their motivation in learning information retrieval skills. But we would be wrong to assume that they know all about it already. Most of them are familiar with spreadsheets, database management, and word processing programs, but they are not familiar with searching techniques on information retrieval systems. In *Teaching Technologies in Libraries* Linda Brew MacDonald describes the business people's attitude toward information technology instruction as a "just-in-time attitude" ("give me what I need now, nothing more").[3] They don't want to know everything that the software can do, they want to know what would be useful for them now. They are also results-oriented and are easily frustrated by the lack of full-text databases.

TEACHING TECHNOLOGY TO WOMEN

Another thing that has been puzzling us since we began teaching technology to adult students is the way women and men approach computers. A recent issue of *Newsweek* was dedicated to that topic. In one article, Barbara Kantrowitz claims that "in general, computer culture is created, defined, and controlled by men," that computer science is a male profession, and that there is a real gender gap in students' approach to computers. Citing Oliver Strimple, executive director of the computer museum in Boston, Kantrowitz describes the ways men and women relate to computers in the following terms:

> Men tend to be seduced by the technology itself... they tend to get into the faster-race-car syndrome, bragging about the size of their disk or the speed of their microprocessors. To the truly besotted, computers are a virtual religion, complete with icons (on-screen graphics), relics (obsolete programs and machines) and prophets (Microsoft's Bill Gates [and] outlaw hackers). This is not something to be trifled with by mere... females, who seem to think that machines were meant to be used, like the microwave oven or the dishwasher. Interesting and convenient on the job but not worthy of obsession.[4]

The articles in *Newsweek* tend to be humorous, but they certainly describe accurately the way men and women react during a CD-ROM instruction session. For example, women are not as comfortable as men with computers, they ask for help or accept it more easily than men, they prefer to work in groups, and finally they usually focus on the information found rather than the equipment. If we accept the fact that men and women relate differently to computers, we should take this into consideration when we teach information retrieval skills to women adult students. In fact, the statements in *Newsweek* are supported by the literature on female adult learning. It is not only the way men and women approach technology that is of concern, but also the different way in which adult men and women learn. Women return to school for different reasons than men. Usually they resume their education in order to prepare themselves for an anticipated change—a change in their personal life or financial situation for example. They tend to have more fears and feel less confident than men when they return to school, and they need more support to go through the experience. When we teach them technology, a traditionally male field, their need for support might be even greater. They need to feel a connection and have an interactive relationship with their teachers.[5] Studies have shown that the collaborative approach is more congenial to women and that they feel more confident in a cooperative learning environment. A cooperative learning environment can be described as "a team of students working together to accomplish learning objectives."[6] Using cooperative learning techniques, women help each other solve problems and progress together. In *Adult Learning* Terry Massin suggests the following techniques to create a supportive environment for women adult learners: "Use a lot of pair and small group work; design cooperative learning exercises to encourage full participation by everyone; call on specific women; enforce gender parity to prevent the domination of a few strong (male) voices."[7] According to our experience, these techniques work well and should be applied when teaching technology to women.

Now that we have discussed what our library instruction program for extended education students consists of and how our teaching has taken into account some of the research about adult learners, we would like to explain in a more practical way those parts of the workshop content related to teaching technology.

WORKSHOP CONTENT

We have two hours on Saturday morning plus an additional hour or so that most stay to work with us individually on their topics. Some of the students drive two hours just to get to the workshop site, so we try to provide a comfortable environment with coffee and muffins for the lecture/discussion part of the session which occurs around large tables in a fairly cozy space in the Reference Room. In fact, we have selected this time because the library is not yet open, so the normal rules about eating/drinking in the library are suspended for them. Because most of them attend with their cluster, they know each other well, as this workshop occurs about three months into their 18-month program. It is quite common for them to kid around with each other and make jokes. We try to build on this dynamic and make the session "feel" informal by fostering a relaxed environment both in the space we use and our style.

The "electronic environment" in which the learning takes place is rather modest by research library standards but typical for libraries of our size: we have an Innovative Interfaces OPAC and circulation system; public access stations to the Internet and our Web site and MELVYL, the University of California system; and eight CD-ROM databases. Our CD-ROMs are not yet networked, so the remote users have dail-in access only to our opac and the Internet/Web resources.

Given all of the above mentioned aspects of the learners and the learning environment, we aim to accomplish in the workshop session these *goals:*

1. reinforce transfer of learning by connecting information retrieval concepts to what they already know about library research and stressing general processes and concepts, rather than particular features of specific tools;
2. present search strategies that they can use effectively in most any library;
3. familiarize them with the services and resources of SMCL, especially the electronic ones and those just available to remote users;
4. support the overall program goal of enhancing students' critical thinking skills.

The workshop session objectives are detailed in Overhead Transparency 1. While this may look overly ambitious, we do have a full two hours of group time and another hour or so where we work individually with them or in pairs. However, as we have begun to introduce Internet resources, we realize that we need to redesign somewhat the workshop session, as there really is not adequate time to include this presently.

How do these objectives determine the content and teaching methods of the workshop? The "Workshop Session Outline," Overhead Transparency 2, identifies the content areas covered in the two-hour workshop, the instructional methods employed, and the learning objectives addressed. Some of these nine content areas will be elaborated on for this presentation to more clearly reveal how the workshop is conducted, how we teach these adult learners about certain information technologies, and to illustrate how we

Overhead Transparency 1. Workshop Session Objectives

1. Learners will know or know how to find out about the services and resources available to them and how to take advantage of these.
2. Learners will be exposed to two search strategies that can be used in any library.
3. Learners will identify the variety of types of information sources useful for their projects and by means of the workshop will learn the categories of information retrieval tools to access those types.
4. Learners will be exposed to a process for searching an electronic periodical index and gain experience practicing individually, and in pairs, their own search strategies.
5. Learners will be exposed to and use the OPAC.

Overhead Transparency 2. Workshop Session Outline

Content			*Teaching/Learning Method*	*Objective*
I.	Introductions, Assessing Computer Use and Explanation of Session Objectives	•	Lecture/Questioning	1
II.	Highlights of Services and Resources Available	•	Lecture/Discussion with packets	1
III.	Types of Information Sources; How Used; Access Tools	•	Questioning and Examination of Background Sources	3
IV.	Search Strategies: A. Covering Your Bases B. Following Citations	•	Questioning/Lecture	2
V.	Specific Periodical Indexes—papercopy vs. CD-ROM	•	Hands-on Lecture and Group Demo of CD-ROM	4
VI.	Translating topic/question into languge and logic for CD-ROM system	•	Lecture/Demo and Written Exercise	4
VII.	OPAC Searching	•	Group Demo, Exercise	5
VII.	Review of Key Points			—
IX.	Putting It To Practice	•	Individual and Pairs Hands-On	3-5

use active learning techniques, such as questioning, small-group, and hands-on activities.

The first part of the workshop is an introduction and quick assessment of their previous experience using computers. After introductions, three questions are asked:

1. Do they use a computer in their work or at home?
2. Do they use e-mail or other network services?
3. Have they ever done or had a librarian do for them a computer search for books/articles?

The show of hands provides a general sense of how much computer experience they've had. This also offers an opportunity to build on their previous experience by telling them that they may notice some similarities and differences in the experience they'll have today using library computers for information retrieval.

An overview of the workshop is then given, and a big point is made of acknowledging how valuable their time is, stressing that one outcome from the workshop is their knowing how to save time in doing library research.

The second content area, "Highlights of Services and Resources Available," is an opportunity to direct their attention to certain pages in a packet distributed at the workshop. What is emphasized is the dial-in instruction to our opac and the variety of ways they can communicate with us during the course of their academic program. The main idea here is to emphasize that special services are available to them, and in some cases (e.g., document delivery and electronic request of books), only to them.

Up to this point, which is about 15 minutes into the workshop, the pace and content are quite relaxed and conversational. The next part of the outline requires more active participation, still trying to build on what experience they may have had with traditional types of library resources in making connections to electronic equivalents.

This third part, "Types of Information Sources and Their Access Tools," begins by enlisting their help in filling in an empty circle on the blackboard labeled "Universe of Information Sources." Questioning them about the types of information sources they may have used in the past and what they think will be useful for their projects results in their offering many examples. Then various types of access tools (e.g., catalogs, indexes, etc.) are identified and connected with arrows outside the circle to the information sources within the circle. Usually someone in the group suggests the reference librarian or some other human "expert" as an information source or access tool.

It is interesting to find that misconceptions about computerized information retrieval will be exposed at this point, such as the idea that there is one computer which will contain everything they might need or that all computerized periodical indexes also contain the full text to the articles. It gives us an opportunity to explain that while our library does not yet have a single computer that provides access to both books and articles, some libraries they may use will, pointing out that the reality of a single computer station providing a gateway to a variety of types of electronic information sources is certainly on the increase. Since many of them work in a corporate or hospital setting, we try to solicit examples from them about the types of information retrieval sources they have available in the workplace. At least one person in the group usually volunteers a business or medical information retrieval system. This provides an entree to discuss the importance of first determining what is the database coverage for any computer they walk up to. Does it just lead them to books or just to articles or multiple types of publications? Does it cover just one discipline or many? This concept of database coverage/scope, while obvious to us, appears to be new to some of them. They begin to realize that a preliminary step in their search is to determine what is the best electronic (or print) database or catalog to use. Questioning the coverage/scope of the information retrieval systems they use is reinforced later when we walk out to the index area, and the signs on each of our electronic systems are pointed out.

In order to reinforce the concept and value of background sources as a useful type of source for their projects, a hands-on exercise is used at this point to involve them more actively. Seven or eight handbooks or one-volume encyclopedias from the bibliography in their packet are passed around. They work in pairs for only three or four minutes to look over the source to see how it might be useful for their project papers.

The "Workshop Session Outline" (Overhead Transparency 2) includes two content areas dealing with "Specific Periodical Indexes" and "Translating Topic/Question into Language and Logic for CD-ROM Systems." Periodical article access instruction occurs in three locations and at three different times. The concept of indexes in book or electronic format has already been introduced while they were seated in the Reference Room. After about 40 minutes in the Reference Room, we change location to the index/CD-ROM/opac area where a very brief tour provides the visual and spatial reinforcement to the names and titles they've heard during the lecture. Another hands-on activity occurs at this point using bound periodical indexes, followed by a short break, and then the final segment spent in the third location, a classroom setting on the second floor where a computer/CD-ROM projection station is located for group demonstration. Since we don't have a classroom with a computer station for each learner, we combine a group interactive demonstration followed by individual or pairs conducting their own searches in the reference/index area.

As a lead-in to the lecture, a question is posed asking how many have previously done searching and in what databases. The point of this questioning is to assess again how many, or few, have done any database searching and to elicit comments that can be incorporated into the explanation. Typical examples of their responses include comments that express frustration about finding too many citations or too few.

The next overhead previews the universal concepts that we deal with through our lecture, questioning, demonstration, and hands-on activities (see Overhead Transparency 3). Since we don't know which libraries and retrieval systems they may ultimately use, it's important to cover these concepts verbally and via the demonstrations and individual hands-on. Before walking them through the steps in the construction of a database search at the blackboard, their attention is focused on four major points:

1. Idea of how a complete article is represented in a database by means of a record;
2. Idea that doing an effective database search is a process that requires their best critical thinking skills and advance mental preparation before even touching the keyboard;
3. Idea that even though there are tips and strategies they can learn for doing these searches, there is no one best way—that it's normal to try one way and then another;
4. Idea that this is a skill, like driving, that they won't really get good at without practice.

Overhead Transparency 3. Universal Concepts for Teaching Electronic Information Retrieval

1. Lack of standardization among systems
    - functional similarities however
    - need to be creative and critical
2. Database scope and coverage
3. How documents are represented in database—effects on retrieval
4. Preparation and process involved in constructing a search strategy
5. Natural language vs. controlled vocabulary—effects on retrieval
6. Use of relevant record(s) retrieved to improve search strategy

To stimulate discussion, a question is asked about how the computer actually finds the CD-ROM articles about John's topic on how total quality management in long-term care facilities improves staff morale. All sorts of ideas are presented here: "Just type in the topic statement, and the computer finds all the words and makes a match," to "Type in just some of the words and then skim through all the abstracts," to someone who knows about using *or* or *and*. This kind of discussion always provides an entree to explain that the CD-ROM only contains a representation of the article, called a *record*. A record is illustrated at this point with either an overhead or an on-screen example and their attention is focused on the pieces of the record, the *fields*. We have found that it's more effective for adult learners to start off with the outcome of their search, showing them what their search will yield. We then move into a visual schematic that they have in front of them as a kind of worksheet or memory aid to illustrate the process (see Overhead Transparency 4).

This overhead illustrates how we structure the explanation of the process of doing a database search. Using one of their topics, steps 1 through 3 are modeled at the blackboard, getting them to help figure out the key concepts from the topic statement and problem/question they want to answer. We then tell them they can skip step 4 and just use their own language from step 3 as keywords to do the search. This leads to pointing out that not all

1. Topic Statement ____________________________

2. Question/Problem you want to address ____________

____

3. Concept(s) that represent the topic *

   3. A. ________________ 3. B ________________

4. Database Subject Heading/Vocabulary Terms

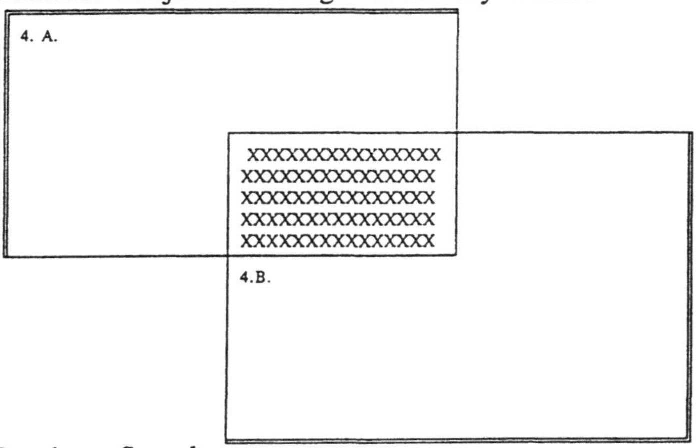

5. Database Search

6. Evaluation of Citations. Does the search need to be revised (broadened, narrowed)?

Note: * The number of concepts and/or descriptors will vary and is determined by complexity of topic/question.
Source: Model based on Michael Tilman's "Search Strategy Worksheet."

Overhead Transparency 4. Database Search Process

databases are made the same: differences between those with special vocabulary lists/subject heading/descriptors and those that have none. Again, we stress this is one of the "universal" features of databases besides coverage or scope of which they need to be aware. Since the ones at Saint Mary's in health administration and business/management do provide that added value of vocabulary control, they are encouraged to take a few more minutes and translate their own language into the language of the database.

A volunteer is recruited to look up the words from step 3 in the appropriate thesaurus. This part of the activity sometimes generates a bit of discussion, as they may argue gently about the meaning of the concept, or whether or not the suggested thesaurus term really equates with the natural language in step 3. Or, someone will usually suggest other terms as equivalents. Adult students are wonderful in this regard. Unlike most undergraduates, they have opinions and they freely offer them.

Before explaining the use of *and*, the area of overlap in the diagram is highlighted and they are asked how they think the computer can be made to find both of the keywords/phrases in the record. It is really interesting to listen to their ideas—"just type all the keywords in one after the other, or type in the most important words first." The point of the questioning is to get them to focus on the need for an overt action. We do not refer to Boolean logic; rather we usually just explain that for these databases (not all that they might use), it is necessary to type *and* to accomplish the combination of both concepts. We don't spend time at this point explaining *or* or the use of parentheses. From this point we move to the workstation and, if possible, recruit a female to do the sample/search, since our experience and readings indicate that they, as a group, may be less comfortable using computers. This part of the lesson can occupy about 15 to 20 minutes depending on how many questions are posed. We usually illustrate the use of *or* and the parentheses in these real searches, especially when too few citations are retrieved. This is where step 6 is emphasized, that is, the need to evaluate their results and make decisions about the need to broaden or narrow. The "How to Use" guide in their packet is pointed out as a resource to use when they go downstairs and actually do their own searches.

Only three or four minutes are dedicated to a quick demonstration of our OPAC. After pointing out from the main menu the several options to search by and stressing *W* (Word Search), the "Request an Item" feature is demonstrated. This allows for reinforcement of an earlier statement about document delivery of books requested electronically.

Before leaving the classroom and going downstairs to use the various tools, individually or in pairs, a few questions are asked to verify their understanding of some of the key points presented during the workshop.

EVALUATION OF THE PROGRAM: ARE WE EFFECTIVE?

We have various ways, formal and informal, of evaluating our program for extended education students. An evaluation form is distributed at the end of the workshop which gives us their immediate feedback, but we also send a library services survey to all students when they finish their program. This gives us a better idea of their overall satisfaction with the library services and of the impact of the library instruction program.

The workshops have been consistently rated high by the students, 90 percent of whom claim that it was very useful. One of the questions on the form relates to the skills which were learned or improved during the workshop. Almost 100 percent declare that the electronic sources were new to them. The survey of library services also shows a high level of satisfaction with our services, and a recent WASC team has praised the program. But it is harder to determine if the students retain and use the skills we teach them during the workshop, in particular electronic information retrieval skills. Does transfer of learning really occur? Do they use these skills in other libraries? We know that more and more students connect to our online catalog and retrieve books, and the number of students communicating with us through the Internet increases steadily every month. But at the moment, our CD-ROMs are not networked, and the students don't have dial-in access to them. They often use our computer search services, which means that we do the search for them. When they are able to dial into our CD-ROM network and perform their searches themselves, we will be in a better position to evaluate the effectiveness of our teaching.

The program developed for extended education students at Saint Mary's has had other benefits that were not expected at the beginning. We learned from a guide to planning distance education programs that:

> ...in some cases, it appears that the use of technology, coupled with a librarian designated to serve off-campus students, may create a level of service beyond what is currently being offered to campus-based students" [Then in a second phase], "benefits accrue to on-campus students as a result of the innovative uses of technology within the distance education context).[8]

This is part of what happened at our college. The special needs of these students forced us to develop new services, such as document delivery, telefacsimile communications, and online book requests that will benefit all our constituencies eventually. We also integrated the teaching of technology into the extended education workshops first, then later into all the on-campus programs.

THE FUTURE

Our goal for the next few years is to use the technology to increase the level of services for extended education students. Right now, we teach them skills that they have to transfer to another setting. With the networking of our CD-ROMs and the implementation of our Web server, students could theoretically connect to our campus network and fulfill most of their information needs while sitting at home. Our connection to the Internet has definitively opened a whole new range of possibilities for the off-campus students. They can obtain an Internet account from Academic Computing Services, communicate with the librarians through e-mail, and connect to our Web server. We first tried to include a short Internet component at the end of the Saturday workshops, but we could teach so little of it that it was a frustrating experience for the students. We finally decided to offer separate Internet workshops in a computer lab. Based on our experience of teaching technology to adult students, we have tried to adapt these Internet training sessions to adult learning styles. We soon realized, though, that teaching the Internet presents its own sets of specific problems. The quantity of information available on the Net is so overwhelming that teaching critical thinking skills to assess and evaluate all this information should be a priority. But that is another story...

REFERENCES

1. Malcolm Knowles, *The Adult Learner, a Neglected Species,* 5th edition (Houston: Gulf Publishing, 1990).

2. Stephen Brookfield, *Understanding and Facilitating Adult Learning* (San Francisco: Jossey-Bass, 1986).

3. Linda Brew MacDonald, *Teaching Technologies in Libraries* (Boston: G.K. Hall, 1991), p. 243.

4. Barbara Kantrowitz, "Men, Women and Computers," *Newsweek* (May 6, 1994): 48-55.

5. Marie Alice Wolf, 1993. "Mentoring Middle-Aged Women in the Classroom," *Adult Learning* (May-June 1993): 8-9, 22.

6. Jerry Olivas, "Using Cooperative Learning to Teach Word Processing," *Adult Learning* (November 1991): 22.

7. Terry Massin, "Unlearning to Not Speak: Adult Education and the Female Learner," *Adult Learning* (September-October 1992): 303.

8. Vicki York, *A Guide for Planning Library Integration Into Distance Education Programs* (Boulder, CO: Wiche, 1993), p. 7.

THE LITERATE LIBRARIAN AND INFORMATION TECHNOLOGY:

OVERSELLING THE INTERNET

Thomas W. Leonhardt

The Internet has become as important to conducting our business as the telephone. We use the Internet electronic mail capability on a daily basis to conduct professional business. Thanks to the Internet we can communicate and exchange articles with colleagues in Israel, Australia, and Venezuela with full confidence that the data sent or received is error free. The expense, when prorated on a per use basis, is negligible compared to long distance telephone charges and the cost of postage or overnight delivery.

But when it comes to other uses of the Internet, there is no convincing evidence that any more than 20 percent of the stuff (and I use the word advisedly) available on the Internet is worth the disk space it consumes.

I subscribe to selected LISTSERVs and use the delete key more often than not as I look at the subjects on the screen. Even PACS-L, one of the best of the lists and the one that I immediately suggest to newcomers, occasionally reaches the point of diminishing returns. In the tried and true American tradition of beating a dead horse, many lists don't know when enough of a subject is enough and to even suggest that we ought to move on brings even more flogging. Once the nuisance level exceeds the usefulness level, it is time to unsubscribe.

Over the years, as the Internet has become more and more popular, and as use has increased, so too has the hype, the hyperbole, and the hypocrisy about the Internet. The promise of the Internet, as expounded in the popular and the more serious media, far exceeds reality to date. In fact, a serious study of all that is available on the Internet may suggest that, as happened with television, the entertainment value is coopting the educational and instructional value. How many people, initially lured to the Internet by the flood of Internet articles, guides, and promises of success at parties once they learn cyberspeak, find out that the cyber-emperor is virtually naked—the emperor's virtual clothes!

In our full, uncritical embrace of the Internet and all that it stands for, librarians may have inadvertently done harm by presenting libraries in an unfavorable light. By extolling the unsubstantiated virtues of what is on the Internet and ignoring the riches found in all kinds of libraries, funding for libraries locally and at the national level has been hurt. More and more of what monies are available to libraries are for networking, as if books and buildings no longer matter.

One example that comes to mind is the Clinton administration's failure to support the HEA Title II programs while embracing anything associated with electronic networks and information technology in electronic form. This wholesale switch of allegiances is premature and short-sighted, but given the technological optimism that has prevailed in this country since its beginning, it is not surprising.

One bit of hype and hypocrisy that is particularly bothersome and that has also been harmful for libraries is the notion that access to information is just as good or better than owning the information. Electronic access to indexes and tables of contents are valuable tools, but they are often presented in misleading ways as if they provided the articles themselves. And those that do provide full text or copies of articles do so at costs that are not negligible. Access and ownership are not the same things and should not be juxtaposed as either/or propositions. We librarians may think we know what we mean, and we may distinguish in our minds between an index and what it points to, but there are many who do not and many who do not control purse strings and are reluctant to loosen them for obsolete technologies like the book.

Many of us own scores or even hundreds of books, many unread, many not meant to be read cover to cover, page by consecutive page—reference books, cook books, art books, song books, picture books, joke books. How many of us have been asked, by non-bookish friends, if we have read all of those books? No, we tell them and, to get them away from the subject, suggest that when we retire... But it doesn't matter if we get around to reading all of them, the important thing is that we intend to, we want to, and we are comforted by their presence. Unread books on my shelves are my security blanket. Often read books on my shelves provide additional security and an extended memory. I know that I am not alone.

The notion that, because the books in an academic library are not being charged out constantly, they are not necessary or useful, that they are museum pieces, should be anathema to all educated persons, not just librarians. Those books need to be there to preserve our many cultures, to provide material for teaching and learning, and to tempt faculty and students alike to go beyond the boundaries set for them and by them in required and recommended readings. Those books ought to be used, and bibliographic instruction can help foster use—reading is the old-fashioned term. Those books, too, help libraries provide a sense of place that many need in order to study or in order to survive.

Thanks to the Internet as a tool, I was able to send a note to John H. Lienhard at the University of Houston. I had heard him talk about a quiet place on his public radio show called *The Engines of Our Ingenuity*. I told him how the piece had moved me and asked if he could he send me a transcript of the program. He graciously did so, via electronic mail.

I cannot duplicate the theme music or his pleasant radio voice but I can relay his message.

Lienhard talks about the University of Houston library's workshops for inner-city honor students where they learn about library research. But first they fill out a questionnaire asking what they will study in college, what they like least about libraries, and what they like best:

> One set of answers was startling. What do you suppose these students liked best about libraries? Of course many gave the obvious answer. Libraries are places to get information. They house books, encyclopedias, and friendly information-givers.
>
> But two-thirds of the students said something else entirely. Two-thirds said they liked libraries because they're a quiet place—a peace-filled environment.
>
> Smart students from a tough school! Their lives are not filled with quiet. These students want to study science, engineering, medicine, and law. They know they'll need a mental oasis. The library is their metaphor for that need.
>
> Those students reflect a tension that stretches any creative person. Pain and trouble work like grains of sand in an oyster. Without disturbance, we don't grow. But neither do we grow, or create, without internal quiet. The trick is to come to that peace in the middle of the marketplace. A wonderful poem by Yeats catches the idea:
>
> My fiftieth year had come and gone.
> I sat, a solitary man,
> In a crowded London shop,
> An open book and empty cup
> On the marble table top.
> While on the shop and street I gazed
> My body for a moment blazed,
> And twenty minutes, more or less,
> It seemed, so great my happiness,
> That I was blessed, and could bless.
>
> Still, now and then, we have to go to a real quiet place. Endless distraction kills something inside us. On rare occasions we meet our quiet place, our deep creative content, with another person. Maybe you find your quiet place in physical exercise.
>
> But find it you must. Find it or die! You'll never know how to find it in the middle of the whirlwind, if you haven't first learned to find it in a quiet room.
>
> People who spend their entire life responding to the external world die inside. That's what these smart students sensed at some very deep level. The library was their perfect metaphor for a place apart. And they knew they'll to have find such a place—on the way to forming themselves.[1]

The University of California, Berkeley, has such a place within its main library. The Morrison Library, just inside the north entrance to the Doe Library, contains *belles lettres,* coffee table magazines, listening stations and sound recordings, and prints that one may borrow for a term. Textbooks must be checked at the doorway for studying is not allowed in the Morrison Library. It is a place for meditation, thinking, browsing the classics, looking at sophisticated but non-scholarly magazines. What better, more appropriate place for a student to hide on a rainy day or to regroup after that last final exam has been taken?

Vartan Gregorian, President of Brown University and formerly the President of the New York Public Library, speaking at a conference on technology, scholarship, and the humanities remarked that:

> While it is true that attention to detail is the hallmark of professional excellence, it is equally true that an overload of undigested facts is a sure recipe for mental gridlock. Undigested facts do not amount to knowledge. Our universities, colleges, libraries, learned societies, and contemporary scholars have a fundamental historical and social task and responsibility to ensure that we provide not training, but education. We must provide not just information, but its distillation—namely knowledge—to protect our society against counterfeit information disguised as knowledge ... In addition to an explosion of information and knowledge, we also face dangerous levels of fragmentation in knowledge. But without opportunities for creative discourse among educated persons, both within and outside the university, and without the broad understanding of the premises and assumptions of various academic disciplines, it is not easy for either students or faculty members to pursue complex problems that cut across the artificial barriers between disciplines.[2]

Academic librarians should understand his message well, and by listening to him, perhaps we can find the wisdom and the courage to listen to our collective inner voice, the voice that led many or most of us into librarianship in the first place. Notice that I did not say into the information business. Information is only part of what we do, and it is not the *sine qua non* of what we are about. We are about literacy and learning, and the tools that we use to help people find information should not overshadow our role in the educational process.

We select books, we catalog books, and we direct people to indexes of one kind or another that lead students and faculty to books. We can go beyond those roles and assume greater responsibility for directing students to books that contain the distillation of information that Gregorian is talking about.

HYPE OF THE INTERNET

When I first began using the Internet, it was not well known outside of university settings and not readily available. As it gradually became recognized in newspaper and magazine articles, I felt smug because I not only knew about it, I was using it. In 1992 I was asked to do a workshop on the Internet for beginners. I was pleased and accepted before I really knew what I had done. I used the Internet, but I really didn't know that much about it.

My next step was to begin reading about it. I bought books and borrowed books and subscribed to lists for beginners and for those teaching about the Internet. The articles I found were mainly by or for librarians. It was still a closed world, to a large degree.

Between the time I agreed to give the talk and the talk itself, more stories about the Internet began to appear with increasing frequency. Stories and cartoons about the Internet began appearing in the *Chronicle of Higher Education,* the *New York Times,* and even *The New Yorker.* We are now way past the saturation point in the grand American tradition of overkill, and I have begun to dread seeing the latest attempt to convince us that the second coming will be via the Information Superhighway.

As I began to learn more about the Internet and as I subscribed and unsubscribed to many lists, I began to see a discrepancy between the hype about the Internet and what was actually there. As I became more at ease with the mechanics of the Internet, I became ill-at-ease with what I saw—a gap, really a chasm, between what it seemed to be with what it was touted to be.

The business world has been criticized for going after the quick profit rather than investing in workers and a steady but less spectacular profitability. The same might be said of higher education in the past few years. That is, instead of careful analysis of what our problems are and what we need to do to prepare for the future, we grab onto the quick fix, the electronic panacea—electronic snake oil in some instances.

Part of the hype of the Internet and the Information Superhighway, not to mention hypertext, interactive videos, virtual reality, the virtual library, the library without walls, fiber optics, and broadband communications giving us instant access to 500 channels and hundreds of films, comes from America's long history of technological optimism that can be seen as utopianism and millennialism. The millennial drive has not been this strong for a hundred years as evidenced by the tag "2000" we find on everything from sporting events to commercial products to the information industry. Again in typical American fashion, we have overindulged ourselves with predictions of the future not even stopping as the year 2000 gets ever closer and the predictions move further away. You cannot extend the present further than tomorrow with even a modicum of certainty.

Part of the problem with the Internet/Information Superhighway hype is that the technology is being credited with powers that it does not have. Claims are made that assume or would have us assume that simply by being connected things will get better, we will learn more at a faster rate, and life will be rosy once again.

There are endless examples, but I will use only two and will suggest that the claims being made are made a priori and without evidence to back them up, mainly because there has not been time enough to gather any evidence. Looking to the past, however, as I shall do in a minute, further suggests that we may be prognosticating through a clouded crystal ball, and there may be no evidence to gather.

In a February 14, 1994 press release, Pacific Bell announced an education initiative that will allow it (Pacific Bell) to "link public schools and libraries to [the] communications superhighway." The term communications superhighway is used five times in the press release, superhighway is used twice, and information superhighway is used once. A telecommunications system, which is what is really being talked about, is mentioned just twice, once as a state of the art telecommunications system and once as a modern telecommunications system. Broadband network is used once and interactive broadband network is used once as are the terms "on ramp" and "full speed" as in "full-speed superhighway access." And by the way, "linkage for computer communications and videoconferencing" is the "first lane of the superhighway."

California governor Pete Wilson tells us that "Pacific Bell's announcement will help ... California have an affordable, state-of-the-art telecommunications system to make [Californians] competitive, to improve the quality of our lives, and to expand the opportunities for our children to learn."

Not to be outdone, Assembly Speaker Willie Brown challenged Pacific Bell to "lead businesses, regulators, and legislators in an initiative to ensure that every classroom in California is wired and equipped for full-speed superhighway access by the year 2000." Millennianism is alive and well in California.

Brown goes on to say, "I am delighted that Phil Quigley (CEO of Pacific Bell) has accepted my invitation to lead this technology initiative for our schools and libraries, and that Pacific Bell is taking a significant first step by providing an on-ramp to the communications superhighway. I firmly believe that affordable access to Information Age technology is essential to ensure that California students are prepared for the challenges of the twenty-first century."[3]

This press release is full of terms like "telecomputing and interactive telelearning." In a related press release we are told, probably because California schools are close to 50th in quality and support for school libraries and where over half of reference books are more than 15 years old, that telecomputing involves dial-up connections between schools and libraries or to remote databases "allowing students to access educational resources virtually anywhere in the world without leaving the classroom. This includes access to the Internet, the network of networks connecting millions of users around the world to education and research databases." This will in turn provide "access to continually updated information in an age when textbooks are outdated before they even go to print," and will encourage "collaborative learning and personal networking among users from diverse backgrounds, through forums such as the worldwide electronic mail system of the Internet or via online discussions groups," and will develop "computer skills to enhance students' marketability in a business environment."[5]

Vice President Al Gore, in a speech made in Royce Hall at the University of California in Los Angeles and released over the Internet on January 11, 1994, tells us that "[o]ur new ways (he really means what we have had access to for decades) will entertain as well as inform. More importantly, they will educate, promote democracy, and save lives. Virtually every business will find it possible to use these new tools (never defined) to become more competitive (more competitive than what or whom?)."[5]

Neither the press release, with limited distribution, nor the Gore speech that was sent all over the Internet really defines what is actually being proposed and how it will promote everything from business prosperity to intellectual prowess.

What is really being proposed is that broadband telecommunications be made available for everyone as cheaply as possible and the Federal Communications Commission will make sure that the power (and we are talking about incredible power) is not abused.

Gore tells us that having broadband access in all homes and schools and libraries will make us more competitive, more democratic, smarter, better looking, more sophisticated, more civil to one another, and less likely to do drugs, riot, rob, assault our fellow citizens, and so on.

In short, big government and big business together are going to provide all of this free entertainment (how much was your last cable bill?) and free information (have you done any free Dialog searches lately, ordered any free UnCover documents lately?) to free us from the shackles of our humdrum, unfulfilled lives.

By hyping the Internet with little or no critical analysis or acumen, we have created a monster. I can use Gophers and the World-Wide Web, and I can find out what the weather is like in Salem, Oregon, without leaving Norman, Oklahoma, but for speed and accuracy I can just as easily call the Salem Public Library and ask a librarian. Is that wasting a resource? Perhaps, but no more so than using the Internet. The difference is that when I call a public library or an academic library, the chances are that I will get a warm, friendly response from a human being.

We have already put too much stock in the Internet and its associated Gophers, Veronicas, Archies, and Jugheads, not to mention the software tools that let us play with the World-Wide Web. What is needed is critical analysis of what is actually available and compare it to the resources at our disposal in our own libraries. Part of library instruction can be the hard facts, the plain truth, the rest of the story about the Internet. This can be done while demonstrating the realistic value of the electronic tools that we have at our disposal.

I would like to suggest just two ways that library instruction can promote the books in libraries and impart to students that the key to becoming an educated person and lifelong learner is reading and reading books above and beyond what is required.

BROWSING

In a study of browsing as related to classification schemes, Losee writes, "A number of other conclusions are supported by the results of these experiments. One that is most important and might be missed because of its obviousness is that classification is here experimentally shown to have worth; it does cluster together documents that patrons are willing to circulate together."[6]

It is no secret that in addition to subject headings, patrons need to go to the shelves and look at what they found listed in the catalog and at what is shelved on either side and perhaps even above and below the works for which they have call numbers. So while I am not suggesting anything new, I am suggesting that browsing be emphasized more and that in discussion of online catalog enhancements, browsing capabilities should be noted as important to a patron's success in finding materials for research and perhaps for pleasure. As an additional value to browsing, I recommend that book jackets be left on books, even though it means added expense, because book jackets provide information about the contents and the author that would otherwise be lost to the reader. Public libraries have always recognized the value of the book jacket, not only for the information provided but for the appeal of the jacket to the reader. An attractive book jacket cries out for attention. In addition, book jackets protect the books from ultraviolet rays from the sun and artificial light.

NON-REQUIRED READING

A List of Unrequired Reading Selection Committee at the Undergraduate College, University at Buffalo, asked professors, librarians, advisers, and administrators from the University at Buffalo an unusual question:

> Instead of asking, "What are The Great Books that all students should read," we asked for a more personal recommendation: "What have you enjoyed reading? What books have been important to you, as a scholar and as a person?"
>
> Their answers may surprise you. Plato, Dante, and Emerson did not make the final list—but a cookbook (*The Joy of Cooking*), a science fiction novel (*Fahrenheit 451*), an account of a famous scientific expedition

> (Darwin's *Voyage of the Beagle*), and a history of Coney Island did. Some of the books on the list were published a year or two ago, while a few have been around for over a century.
>
> Out of nearly two hundred nominations, the Selection Committee chose 48 books for this list—enough to keep you reading for pleasure, at a rate of one book per month, for four years of your college career. We hope you'll enjoy reading these books as much as we enjoyed reading them and building this list.[7]

David Farmer, director of the DeGolyer Library at Southern Methodist University, teaches a course called "The Tri-ethnic Heritage of Northern New Mexico in Fiction and History." The readings and the video are selected to reflect Native American, Hispanic and Anglo points of view, along with a diversity of genres ranging from history, to fiction, and personal reflections on the life and folkways of the region.

CONCLUSION

One of my literary heroes is Christopher Morley. I like him not only for the pleasure his books bring me but also because of his indefatigable efforts to promote books, authors, reading, literacy, and literary sensibility. When being interviewed about himself, Morley would invariably turn the conversation to some author or book he had just discovered. He was instrumental in getting William McPhee's *Casual's of the Sea* published in this country, drew early attention to Joseph Conrad's novella *Below the Line*, and was one of the founders of the Book-of-the-Month Club when people in small towns and rural areas did not have the access to books and bookstores that we now take for granted.

There was a lot of librarian in Morley, and I hope there is a lot of Morley in librarians. Certainly public librarians are proud of the heritage that he so strongly promoted and so lovingly depicted in *Parnassus on Wheels*. Our libraries are full of books, the original information technology and the ultimate virtual reality—losing oneself in a book of vicarious experiences. Go forth and multiply, literate librarians of the world.

NOTES AND REFERENCES

1. John H. Lienhard, "A Quiet Place," in *The Engines of Our Ingenuity* (Houston: The University of Houston), Program no. 671.

2. Vartan Gregorian, "Keynote Address," in *Technology, Scholarship, and the Humanities: The Implications of Electronic Information* (Irvine, CA: American Council of Learned Societies and the J. Paul Getty Trust, 1993), p. 9.

3. Pacific Bell, press release (February 14, 1994).

4. Ibid.

5. Albert Gore, "Address on the National Information Infrastructure," Royce Hall, The University of California, Los Angeles CA, transcript on PACS-L (January 11, 1994).

6. Robert M. Losee, "The Relative Shelf Location of Circulated Books: A Study of Classification, Users, and Browsing," *Library Resources and Technical Services* 37(April 1993): 207.

7. *The Undergraduate College List of Unrequired Reading: One Good Book a Month for Four Years* (Buffalo, NY: Undergraduate College, University at Buffalo, 1993).

INTERNET RESOURCE DISCOVERY:

THE ROLE OF CRITICAL THINKING

Craig Gibson and John Meade

The enormous growth and increased use of the Internet in recent years have many unexplored implications for librarians, libraries, computing professionals, and campus computing centers. Most campuses are well on their way to solving technical and networking problems related to providing Internet access; many are addressing administrative and training issues as well, including, in some cases, providing merged service points between libraries and computing centers, or perhaps more frequently, joint Internet training and education programs. The Internet is such an unwieldy, rapidly changing, and ambiguous environment, that it takes a wide range of expertise to understand it and to provide some structured approach to it—the expertise of the technical computing expert, that of the scholar, and that of the information professional or librarian.

What is less frequently addressed in our approach to the Internet, both for ourselves as computing professionals, as librarians, and as disciplinary experts and for our students and other clienteles, is our ability to think in a fundamentally new way when we deal with the Internet. One of the commonplaces in learning theory is that we learn new concepts and ideas only in terms of what we already know, hence the numerous analogies and metaphors describing the Internet in more familiar terms—the Information Highway, the Information Autobahn, the Virtual Community, the Matrix, and most recently, the Web. All of these metaphors fall short of describing the true nature of the Internet, as do such similes comparing the Internet to an unorganized warehouse, a universal switchboard, or a virtual library. All of these comparisons suggest some elements of the true nature of the Internet, but all of them also limit our ability to understand it. We need to learn to think critically about the Internet in order to make sense of it; we will then be better able to help our clientele think critically about the Internet and use it more appropriately.

We hear it said often that the most difficult aspect of using the Internet is knowing where a needed resource is located. After all, the Internet is only beginning to be indexed and categorized in a truly useful fashion. Computing professionals have invented a term for tools and skills needed to identify useful information on the Internet: the process of *resource discovery*, or *resource discovery tools*. A more elaborate definition of "resource discovery" includes the following:

- A process of locating, assessing, and acquiring information resources,
- An approach which enables the seeker to navigate an electronic world cluttered with confusing, redundant, and often less-than-useful information,
- An accompanying process of identifying the most useful information repositories and forums.

Librarians will find this definition of resource discovery for the Internet similar in some ways to their more traditional notions of search strategy and information evaluation in a mixed print, CD-ROM, and online service environment. The concepts of search strategy and information evaluation are the two primary vehicles through which librarians have sought to teach critical thinking; librarians will certainly find common ground with computing professionals in the allied concept of resource discovery. Both librarians and computing professionals should have a common interest in helping Internet users develop organized, useful search methodologies as well as useful criteria for evaluating information resources.

If resource discovery is related in some way to search strategy, and if information evaluation is a common concern of both librarians and computing experts, what should be the common intellectual bond uniting both groups, in designing systems and in developing training for their users? That common bond should be critical thinking—a sometimes overused term and not-well-understood educational concept, currently of enormous concern in schools, colleges, and universities; in the business world; and in such professions as medicine and nursing. Critical thinking is a complicated concept for many reasons, but one has only to understand the essential elements of it to realize its indispensability as an educational tool for computing and library professionals in coping with, and training users in, effective Internet use.

This definition of the term conveys some of its essential elements. Critical thinking is a disciplined process of:

- Asking informed questions,
- Posing problems in various ways before attempting to solve them,
- Examining assumptions,
- Solving ill-structured, messy, "real world" problems,
- Evaluating sources of information,
- Assessing the quality of one's own thinking and problem-solving.

This definition of critical thinking is obviously wide-ranging. It incorporates a related concept, problem solving, but is broader than that rather technical term (as cognitive psychologists use it). For librarians, the one very familiar component of this definition, when they think of critical thinking, may well be evaluating sources of information. However, critical thinking is more expansive in its usefulness and its implications. The ability to frame a good research question (to ask an informed question) is a prime critical thinking skill, as are bringing multiple perspectives to bear on the research question; examining one's own assumptions to eliminate biases about possible search paths and sources; accepting the ambiguity of the research question and how well it may or may not be mapped into the information tools and resources; and evaluating and modifying one's own search strategies. Critical thinking should permeate the research process because that process, whether using the Internet or more traditional resources, is fundamentally a thinking process.

What, then, is an appropriate way of thinking critically about the Internet? We must first of all understand it as a *global data network integrated by common standards of addressing, navigation, and user interaction*. The Internet is often described as a chaotic, rapidly changing environment, and it is obvious that the constant change characterizing the Internet makes previous information environments seem utterly glacial in their pace of change and extremely well-organized in comparison. But the common standards developed early in the history of the Internet provide some degree of predictability about using the Internet, even when using the Internet is fraught with frustration and difficulties. Servers go down, bottlenecks develop at crucial routers on the Net, and information repositories are assigned new addresses overnight as they are moved from one host computer or server to another. The informed Internet user is aware of these contingencies and works around them or lives with them. It is because of the addressing, navigation, and interaction standards that we have some degree of confidence about using what otherwise seems like a totally unpredictable maze of confusing, conflicting, redundant, self-referential sites, repositories, with a cacophony of voices on the Internet itself giving us advice and helping us troubleshoot and otherwise navigate through the maze. Internet standards provide a foundation for beginning to think critically about this environment. Before thinking about any environment, issue, or problem, some foundation of knowledge is required. Thinking does not exist in a vacuum.

However, the Internet possesses some special characteristics that challenge our ability to think critically and also *require*s us to think critically. The Internet is fundamentally a new communication medium. We can have the foundation of knowledge about the standard Internet protocols, conventions, and addressing schemes, and still not know how to navigate successfully in this environment. This is because the Internet is marked by tremendous ambiguity and uncertainty; because its resources resist easy classification, though some very fine efforts have already been made to classify and organize those resources; and because it is, most of all, an organic, open-ended, evolving system, or collection of systems, that defeats final, definitive explanations but is always offering new trends, tentative explanations, temporary and quickly outdated solutions for resource discovery, and limited, although sometimes extremely useful, information about itself in the form of LISTSERV and Usenet archives, a collective memory of the virtual community about itself. All of these features of the Internet make for a very uncertain, messy environment fraught with much ambiguity.

The ability to think critically is essential in dealing with uncertain, ambiguous situations and problems. Cognitive psychologists like to make a distinction between well-structured and ill-structured problems. In their view, well-structured problems are those that have a clearly defined set of constraints, a clear solution path, and a clear goal or set of goals. Working a mathematical equation is an example of a well-structured problem. There are definite rules, principles, and procedures that allow the equation to be solved. Ill-structured problems, in contrast, have no such certainties. Often it is not even clear what the problem to be solved really is. There may be multiple solution paths, and there may not be any real certainty if the problem has actually been solved once a solution path is followed. Most of the problems we face in our daily lives have that messy, ill-structured quality. Many of the problems our leaders face (consider the national health care problem, for example) also are ill-structured. Formulas and rigid thinking simply will not work in solving problems of this nature. The appropriate kind of thinking in dealing with ill-structured problems is critical thinking.

We often hear it said that the Internet, in addition to being ambiguous, is also complicated. We know this is true even if we have begun to use intuitive point-and-click interfaces like Mosaic and Netscape. Even if we are shielded from the complexity of seven layers of network protocols, we can readily understand that a highly distributed, global network of networks and data resources depends on a highly complicated set of understandings, physical infrastructures, and interactions. We do not have to be network experts to fathom something of that complexity, and if we are able to grasp some important characteristics of the Internet that further augment that complexity, we will be better able to use the Internet as critical thinkers, which in turn will allow us to teach others to use the Internet in a critical thinking mode.

These dimensions of complexity and uncertainty characterize the Internet:

Dynamic resource pool—The growth of the Internet is well-documented on the Internet itself through such organizations as InterNic. Web sites, FTP archives, full-text databases, MOOs, and virtual reality environments, as well as more traditional resources such as library catalogs, are added to the Internet at a dizzying pace, at a rate that makes much of the information unusable by most of us. Dealing with this dynamism can be a full-time job. The critical thinker learns to manage the dynamism and the information overload and stops worrying about missing the latest hot new site because it is rapidly replaced by another hot new site.

Many interconnections—The Internet is a great self-referential engine, especially through the use of browsing tools such as Gopher, Mosaic, and Netscape. One hypertext link leads to another. It is very much like getting lost in a virtual fun house. The interconnectivity allows for a serendipitous browsing gone mad, if one allows total serendipity to take control. The critical thinking response to this problem is to control one's individual Internet use through informed search strategies, which include using search tools like Veronica and Hytelnet and Web search engines such as Webcrawler, Lycos, and Opentext.

Radical software—The browsing and searching tools currently in use on the Internet are radical in the sense that they depart fundamentally from the primitive Internet protocols of Telnet, file transfer protocol, and simple mail transfer protocol. Gopher and Veronica software, now considered passé in many quarters compared to the newer World-Wide Web search tools, were truly innovative only three or four years ago because they sought to incorporate the "virtual system" concept into the Internet, whereby the complexity of the network is concealed from the user, and the need to know sometimes arcane commands and the Internet addressing schemes was obviated. The World-Wide Web, based on the hypertext model and using markup language to construct home pages, has expanded Internet use at a phenomenal rate. These new software tools are not a problem in the sense that they challenge the user to solve a difficult situation. Rather, they shield the user from complexity and don't allow a view of what is occurring behind the scenes to make information from thousands of remote sites available so seamlessly. When the user does not understand *why* a Veronica search has returned nothing useful on a particular subject or *why* he cannot find a World-Wide Web site dealing with Finnish linguistics (after all, is not all information available on the Internet?), then the need for knowledge about the network and a critical thinking response arises. The critical thinker will not allow new, attractive search software to fool him into thinking that the Internet works better than it does or that it is a universal repository of all knowledge and information.

Context mysteries—Lack of context for understanding Internet resources and sites is not a new problem. Of course, when only research scientists, university professors, and military experts were using the predecessors of the Internet in the 1970s and early 1980s, context for understanding usually was not a problem because of the tightness of that particularly community, because of its shared knowledge base, vocabulary, and its secretiveness. With millions of non-specialists and "newbies" using the Internet now, alongside veteran Internet users and hackers, with almost everyone able (theoretically) to become Internet publishers through creation of Web pages, a great electronic Tower of Babel is being erected. Fundamental to making sense of an environment and the information in it is understanding of context, of clues about the cultural or political background of an information resource, of indications of its provenance and its intentionality. Librarians are very familiar with the problem of decontextualized information and data, having seen the migration of finding tools such as catalogs and indexes from print to electronic formats over the past 15 years and the accompanying elation of users about those tools and their frequent uninformed use of them. It is partly the loss of physical, tangible form of information tools that has been one of the major problems for library users (though certainly not the only one) as they struggle to make sense of electronic information resources such as CD-ROMs and online catalogs. The Internet poses the same challenge manifold—a distributed, global network of electronic resources. Here is loss of physical contact and context with a vengeance. However, context mysteries have even more to do with the ways in which information on the Internet is presented to the user or retrieved by him. Most users do not understand the workings of highly structured databases with controlled vocabularies and fairly predictable retrieval strategies. How well can users deal with finding information in an environment that lacks control and relative predictability? Veronica searching is another good example of loss of context. Retrievals from these searches are of cryptic (Gopher menu items themselves are given strange and whimsical names) and mysterious. The creation of World-Wide Web pages has restored much of the context to Internet sites and searching because full-text descriptions obviously provide much greater context for understanding, even with Web pages, although the user is at the mercy of the page designer for understanding.

Context mysteries for Internet information and searching will continue to be a problem. The critical thinker will have to develop a site orientation to Internet resources in order to invest them with meaning. Retrievals in cyberspace have to be placed in some kind of mental framework created by the searcher. Various kinds of mental frameworks can be created, including classifying Internet resources by origin or provenance, type of data, need for special manipulation or file management, or even an intellectual seriousness scale that would presumably locate certain Usenet groups at the low end of the scale while placing the Oxford Text Archives or the Coombspapers archive at the high end of that same scale. Critical thinkers will invent frameworks that help create context in what often seems like a context-free environment.

Uncertain quality—Lack of context is related to this dimension of the Internet's complexity as well. In the less frenetic and more predictable world of only five years ago, information resources, whether on the Internet or not, could be more readily evaluated and assessed. The advent of publishing on the Internet, the tremendous growth of networked resources, some residing on campus mainframes, others on mini-computers and small servers, even desktop computers, have all created an uncontrolled situation where the traditional channels of publishing and information dissemination can be circumvented. The gatekeeping function of traditional editorial boards will undoubtedly remain to ensure that quality research and writing get published. But increasingly, information resources developed by almost anyone can be made available on the Internet, assuming connections to the Internet are in place, adequate computing power is available, and an Internet address is assigned. Evaluating Internet resources will become a major challenge for librarians and computing professionals in the near future. This problem is already very much with us and will only increase because of the uncontrolled nature of the Internet. Evaluating Internet resources will not be extraordinarily different from evaluating more traditional information resources. Criteria will include date, currency, frequency of updates, internal organization and logical consistency, balance and objectivity (with a special eye to political and cultural agendas), authoritativeness (deciding what is truly authoritative on the Internet may be problematic indeed in newer areas of research), and originality. To these criteria might be added standards such as credentials or reliability of the individual or organization maintaining the information resource and presentation of the information, an increasingly important factor, especially in designing Web pages. Internet resources should also be evaluated for their ease of use, the extent to which they duplicate more traditional information resources, and whether they are truly unique and provide data and other information not available elsewhere. Anyone using critical thinking skills in using the Internet will necessarily conduct a cost-benefit analysis to decide whether time and effort are necessary to use the Internet and deal with its often redundant, confusing complexity.

These, then, are the major dimensions of complexity that challenge our critical thinking skills and also require us to use those skills. Librarians and computing professionals will need to cultivate those skills in dealing with the constant change coming upon them. Remaining technologically up-to-date may well be the easiest part of our professions in the future, although that is be no means an easy task. Developing the critical thinking skills to manage complexity, to understand how our users are at once fascinated and baffled by the Internet, to help them find logic, structure, and meaning in messy, ill-structured situations that the Internet constantly presents—these are our true challenges. Information professionals have always had the need to use critical judgment and discernment and to deal with ambiguity. The information environment traditionally has been somewhat ill-structured and messy. The problem of the Internet, however, is that it is a new communication and publishing medium requiring extraordinary ability to ask informed questions, question assumptions, use flexible reasoning when solving problems, and evaluate the information found. Using the Internet effectively, instead of casual browsing and surfing, both requires these skills and refines them.

Internet training and education in the future will necessarily involve a critical thinking emphasis. Technical training will always be needed. Teaching for critical thinking, however, will extend the competence of Internet searchers beyond the technical skills into an arena of genuine usefulness where the quality of their searching and the information they find will have a greater effect on the curriculum, in the professions, and in everyday life.

INTERNET: THE GOOD, THE BAD, AND THE UGLY

Billie Joy Reinhart and Gary B. Thompson

BACKGROUND

Gareth Branwyn, author of *Mosaic Quick Tour*, estimates that there are more than two million Internet sites and 20 million Internet users worldwide.[1] The potential information value of the Internet is astronomical. The Internet has several obvious advantages as a communications medium. It provides instantaneous transmission to a wide audience, eliminates temporal or geographic restrictions, increases interpersonal exchanges of information, and creates new forums for the dissemination of ideas. However, the ease of use results in an unfiltered transmission of much information which is unverified and unedited. For example, a study of a discussion group of cold fusion scientists suggests that the Internet may be a double-edged sword with positive and negative sides:

> On the positive side.—Though the information on which they act may be unstable and changing, they are nonetheless making progress while other researchers, still awaiting information through more traditional slower channels, have not yet begun to work.[2]

> On the negative side.—Because so many active users of the newsgroup are not themselves experts in the field under discussion, misinformation is common. Many of the messages ... consist of corrections to previous messages.[3]

In the July 12, 1993, issue of *Nation*, Kevin Cooke and Dan Lehrer discuss the feeling of being lost in the "irrelevant chatter" of cyberspace. To them the challenge of "getting information off the Internet is like taking a drink from a fire hydrant."[4]

The Internet has it all, from esoterica to news to erotica. If the Internet is to become a reliable and valuable resource for current information and academic pursuits, then users must develop coping mechanisms to sort through the good, the bad, and the ugly to locate the real gems of knowledge.

TEACHING CRITICAL THINKING AND EVALUATION OF INFORMATION

Like other programs of library instruction, the objective of the Cleveland State University program is to teach students to think critically and to evaluate print and electronic sources of information. We concur with Emily C. Kisane and Daniel J. Mollner about the importance of teaching critical thinking:

> Without the ability to discern between good and bad research the undergraduate is currently faced with hundreds, perhaps thousands, of search matches and lacks the most important instrument for weeding through those matches: informed judgment.[5]

Cerise Oberman notes the particular importance of these skills in this age of expanded access to information from CD-ROMs, electronic full-text sources, and the Internet when she states:

> The information world, particularly the electronic world, is like a supermarket stocked with limitless varieties of resources. In this environment it is imperative that students face the choice on the "shelves" with the ability to discern which of the available products are appropriate. The alternative is that students, much like my friend facing the endless shelves of cereal, will turn and walk away.[6]

Martin Kesselman and Mary Page, likewise, note the imperative to teach patrons to be critical in assessing Internet resources:

> The tricky part about teaching patrons about the network is that it lacks the stability of a physical text ... The network is truly a shared resource: on the positive side it is constantly expanding and evolving; on the negative side it can be unreliable.[7]

THE EVOLUTION OF TEACHING EVALUATION FROM PRINT TO ELECTRONIC

In 1989 Hannelore Rader, Billie Reinhart, and Gary B. Thompson put together a brochure for evaluating information for use by students at Cleveland State University. In 1990 The American Library Association accepted this brochure for publication with the title *Evaluating Information: A Basic Checklist.* Recently revised, it is still available from the American Library Association. The checklist was intended to be applicable to all print and electronic formats. It puts forth a series of questions about the source of the information. For example:

> Is it scholarly, popular, government, or private?
> When was the information published?
> What is the reputation of the publisher, producer, or distributor?

It also lists the key questions to assess the information content:

> What facts and opinions are presented?
> What are the major findings?
> Are the conclusions justified?

In teaching the evaluation of information, we have developed exercises so that students can learn to evaluate information. For example, we have used a simulated research project on national health care to show students how to assess popular and scholarly journal articles. We have given other students reports of the results of public opinion polls and asked them to evaluate the source of the data and the biases of the survey. When there was an important current event like the Rodney King trial, we have asked students the following questions:

1. What are your main sources of information on this topic: TV? radio? newspapers? magazines? friends?

2. How would you rate the information from these sources in terms of accuracy, reliability, clarity, and depth of coverage?
3. Can you identify the main facts and differing viewpoints on this topic?
4. Do the news sources change your opinion or add to your knowledge of the subject?

There is so much out in cyberspace, so many resources on Gophers, and so much of it is ephemeral notes and comments and items only of local interest. Standards of editing and verification are sorely lacking. The Internet started as an informal network to allow individuals at different universities around the world to talk to each other. Then it developed discussion groups so that specialists in technical fields or aficionados could share ideas or information. Then local universities realized that they could put course syllabi and other general campus information on this network. Researchers then started putting some of their research databases on the Internet. Only recently did librarians and others realize that the Internet could be used as a general information network and that the important information could be organized into Gophers and Webs for quick access to the important files.

The University of Michigan's Clearinghouse for Subject-Oriented Internet Resources Guides has greatly assisted Internet users with finding materials of special subject interest. As the guides are produced by members of the Internet community, they vary in scope and format. Some guides are evaluative annotated lists of resources and some are non-evaluative lists of listservs on specific subjects. The University of Michigan issues the disclaimer that the clearinghouse guides undergo no review process and ask that any errors be reported.

Internet provides special challenges for student evaluation of sources. This is due to the following:

1. Origins of the material often are not cited.
2. Editions and dates are not cited for each resource.
3. Many sources are not edited for publication.
4. The many types of resources for one subject are not arranged in an organized manner.
5. Bibliographies or references to electronic resources are seldom included.

6. Few sources are refereed.
7. The difference in format is not clear—newsletters, discussion groups, journals.
8. The qualifications of the authors are seldom available.
9. The perception, "If it is on the Internet, it must be right," must be questioned.
10. The vast array of data is difficult to sift through for the needed information.

There is very little written detailing how to evaluate electronic sources as differentiated from print sources. The 1986 New Jersey Governor's Teacher Grant Program produced a very interesting manual titled *Critical TV Watching*, which contains exercises for students to use to assess the objectivity, credibility, and quality of all kinds of television shows.[8] In 1990 Gail Dickinson provided a checklist for evaluating a CD-ROM encyclopedia.[9] In recent years a number of library, education, and popular journals started publishing critical reviews of CD-ROM products. Then Internet resources started to mushroom. They began to be noticed by the educational community. *The Chronicle of Higher Education* introduced a column "On the Internet," with general news about the Internet and the sources out there in cyberspace. In 1993 *C&RL News* started publishing a series of critical reviews of the literature on Internet resources for different disciplines (psychology, women's studies, etc.) and in 1994 *C&RL News* started doing actual reviews of Internet sources. These reviews are quite long and set a new standard for reviews of Internet files and Gophers. Also in 1994 the Library and Information Technology Association (LITA) started an electronic journal titled *Telecommunications Electronic Reviews* which provided reviews of Internet sources.

Now that there are resources on the Internet that can be used readily by students and faculty to answer research questions and general information inquiries, we must teach students how to evaluate Internet sources critically. When they call up an Internet source, they must answer these questions:

1. Is there a text file to explain the source. If not, is the purpose of the file clearly stated?
2. Do you understand the material? Is it applicable to your research?

3. Do you know who the author is? Is the author an authority on the subject? Is the materials refereed? Is it possible for anyone to contribute to the database?
4. Is there a subject or keyword access to the material? Is the information arranged logically—chronologically or by subject division? Are you able to move easily between screens?
5. Is the material dated? How often is it updated? Are the files complete?
6. How does it compare with other electronic databases or printed resources?
7. Is the resource available on a Gopher or a Web? It is possible to FTP it?

In conclusion, librarians must build upon their past experiences teaching students to evaluate printed sources to develop appropriate criteria and exercises for students to use in evaluating the growing Internet resources.

REFERENCES AND NOTES

1. Gareth Branwyn, *Mosaic Quick Tour* (Chapel Hill, NC: Ventana Press, 1994).
2. Bruce C. Lewenstein, "The Changing Culture of Research: Processes of Knowledge Transfer," (unpublished report to the U.S. Congress Office of Technology Assessment, September 21, 1992), p. 47.
3. Ibid., p. 40.
4. Kevin Cooke and Dan Lehrer, "Whole World is Talking," *Nation* 257(July 12, 1993): 61.
5. Emily C. Kissane and Daniel J. Mollner, "Critical Thinking at the Reference Desk: Teaching Students to Manage Technology," *RQ* 32(Summer 1993): 487.
6. Cerise Oberman, "Avoiding the Cereal Syndrome; or Critical Thinking in the Electronic Environment," *Library Trends* 39(Winter 1991): 200.
7. Martin Kesselman and Mary Page, "Instruction for Networked Resources: U.S. Experiences," (a preprint of a paper for IFLA 1993, Barcelona, Spain, August 22-28, 1993), p. 4.
8. Ed Stanley, *Critical TV Watching* (Red Bank, NJ: Red Bank Borough Board of Education, 1987).
9. Gail Dickinson, "Choosing a CD-ROM Encyclopedia: How to Critically Evaluate the Product," *Library Software Review* 9(September-October 1990): 277-282.

REMOTE ACCESS AND ACTIVE LEARNING IN CONTEXT: TEACHING AT TIME AND PLACE OF NEED

Lori Arp, John Culshaw, and Keith Gresham

While teaching poses many challenges, perhaps the most intriguing is how to effectively teach at the time of need and in the place of need while living in an environment undergoing radical pedagogical and technological transformation. From a practical point of view, many questions occur on a daily basis. For example, how do you use a lab of computers effectively? What happens when you only have space for one workstation and LCD equipment? How do you prepare when the library's instruction laboratory is booked, but the student's homeroom electronic classroom is available? How much log-in information is enough? How much is too much? What do you do when the students all need to use different files simultaneously, and you want to teach concepts? How do you teach concepts rather than skills when the F1 key doesn't work? These practical yet important questions have been raised repeatedly in the last decade. In many ways, these daily concerns have resulted in a willingness to re-examine and question commonly held theoretical views and look to new and innovative solutions. The similarity in the concerns is that they can be characterized as issues that revolve around providing instruction in context, whether the context revolves around timing or location.

This paper will review both practical and theoretical issues about providing instruction "in context" by looking at the questions of time of need and place of need for instruction. Active learning will be shown to be a practical result of time of need and remote access a question of place of need. Arp will review the literature to date on these questions; Culshaw and Gresham will then provide case study examples from the University of Colorado of applications of this research.

The question of when to provide instruction most effectively was one which was examined from a number of perspectives in the last decade. In particular, research focused on two areas:

1. "In context" learning of the individual from social and cognitive perspectives, and
2. "In context" teaching through curriculum transformation, course integration, and active learning techniques in the classroom.

IN CONTEXT: TIME OF NEED AND THE INDIVIDUAL LEARNER

Placing learning "in context" at time of need could certainly be considered the pressing issue of the 1980s in educational theory. During this period, pedagogical and theoretical precepts of the last fifty years were questioned and often rejected. In learning theory, the movement from behavioralist paradigms to new cognitive approaches was introduced to the library community with immediate and significant effect.[1] Older paradigms of learning in vogue until the 1980s were based on certain suppositions:

1. The student was an empty vessel or blank slate.
2. Knowledge and learning were additive processes.
3. Learning could be measured by behavior.
4. The teacher was the absolute authority.[2]

The new cognitive and social paradigms proposed in the 1980s placed learning "in context." The previous experiences, present attitudes, abilities, and intellectual views held by the individual learner were seen as essential components to understanding the learning process. Analyzing and synthesizing these components on a case by case basis were considered paramount to creating a successful learning environment. In other words, the teacher could no longer assume "one size fits all." Rather, each individual's place in the learning process and in society needed to be put in context and carefully considered. In the new traditions, the theoretical precepts which emerged included:

1. The student brings preconceived views based on previous experience to the learning environment. These views are often called schemata or mental models.
2. The student actively participates in the learning process and transforms schemata. Learners can and do construct and transform knowledge. In fact, new knowledge may be created which goes beyond the material taught and instructor's knowledge.
3. Learning is not an additive process in which each piece of knowledge is incrementally added to create a whole. In the new view, learning is seen as holistic. Students go back and forth between parts and the whole to understand a topic.
4. There is no absolute authority. The teacher is a coach, moderator, or facilitator who encourages and guides the learning process.[3]

Some research even went beyond generalizing about the student or the learning process. Some researchers experimentally studied individuals directly at the time when they were engaging in the learning process. One important study by Glaser[4] experimentally examined the difference between the way experts in a field (or domain) and novices reason through to a solution of a problem. Glaser found that experts displayed:

1. a coherence of what is known (relatedness);
2. knowledge of domain-specific patterns or principles;
3. use of patterns and principles in problem-solving;
4. recognition of situations and conditions for using knowledge;

5. highly efficient performance; and
6. use of self-regulating skills (meta-cognitive strategies).

Novices did not display these traits.

Transformation of learning theory by cognitive theorists in the 1980s, then, focused on the importance of the time in a learner's life experiences when instruction is occurring and how to successfully translate this knowledge into the educational arena. No less important in understanding learning at time of need, however, was the work being done by psychologists examining the social element of providing education "in context." This focused on the importance of an individual's socialization and the impact on learning.

Richard Tiberius called "social context" the entire spectrum of roles, responsibilities, expectations, and interaction between students and teachers and among students."[5] He advocated that only by developing alliances between teachers and students could successful learning occur. These alliances were characterized by "mutual respect and commitment to goals, shared responsibility for learning, effective communication, willingness to negotiate and to understand one another, and a sense of security with the process."[6] Interestingly enough, he also stated that technological change was the most critical factor redefining the social context of learning.

Learning theory from the cognitive and social traditions examined the question of what is "in context" from the view of the individual. The 1980s transformed our view of the importance of understanding the individual's role in society and ability to relate to one's peers and coaches, and relegated theories of learning in isolation, both cognitively and socially, to the Dark Ages. The importance of understanding the time frame in which information is taught and the context from which the learner derives perspective were brought to the forefront of the discussion.

Time of need and the context in which information is provided were also the critical concerns of teaching theory of the 1980s. Transformations occurred in the classroom through the introduction of collaborative and cooperative (active) learning techniques. In course structure, the impact of research on time of need was seen in the library community through the widespread adoption of course integration and team teaching as teaching methods. In overall management of curricular development, the emerging notion of curricular integration was also a precursor of the importance of time of need from an overall higher education perspective.

IN CONTEXT: TIME OF NEED AND TEACHING

The question of how to teach and when to do so in context had three components in the 1980s. Questions and research focused on classroom activity, course structure, and overall curricular design.

The importance of engaging students in active discussion and learning has its roots in the educational literature where it has appeared for well over a decade. But its strong emergence in the library community appeared in the late 1980s through the introduction of collaborative and cooperative learning techniques and their practical application to daily activity. There are numerous examples of excellent articles in the literature on this topic[7], including works by Ridgeway, Oberman, Wilson, and Petrowski. One of the overall messages within these articles is that, in order to engage students effectively, the conditions or context in which teaching occurs are of paramount importance.

In the design of course structure, the 1980s saw the strong emergence of course integration and team teaching as preferred and often the most practical approaches. The first *Bibliographic Instruction Handbook,* published in 1979 and now out of print, defined course integrated instruction as "any instruction which is part of a course's objectives. [The] instruction is viewed as essential to knowledge of the subject and therefore to successful completion of the course. The integration is usually achieved by discussion between faculty and librarians at the time the course is designed."[8] John Lubans, in his column titled "Library Literacy" in *RQ*, often discussed course integration as a practical approach to instruction. Arp and Wilson also anticipated five possible structures of instruction and the political conditions necessary for each to succeed.[9] Jacobson strongly advocated this approach for science students because of its success from the cognitive perspective.[10] Perhaps course integration has proven to be a successful mode of instruction precisely because its very existence is dependent on timing—it is tied very closely to the course's objectives and occurs precisely when information is needed. Obviously course integration is "in context"; it is tied to the assignments and success students achieve in a course.

The emergence of the question of curricular integration, or timing library instruction precisely to when it is needed within a student's educational career, was also an important issue of the 1980s. The recent publication by the ACRL Bibliographic Instruction Section titled *The Evolving Educational Mission of the Library*[11] reflects this trend.

Yet, in many ways, the trend could actually be considered a re-emergence of the question of time of need as it relates to the overall curriculum. As early as the 1960s, the Monteith experiment was lauded as an excellent example of innovative approaches to integrating library education into the curriculum. Perhaps the most impressive work in this area, however, was by Evan Farber and Tom Kirk at Earlham College.[12] In their remarkable program, course integration was the structure used throughout all of the curriculum. In this case, all instruction was delivered in context and at time of need throughout a student's career. The longevity of this program speaks strongly to the success of this approach.

At Colorado we have recently begun to examine time of need and providing information in context throughout all of our service offerings in the Central Reference Department through an approach called diversity in services. Over seven different services provided at time of need, ranging from extensive one-on-one help to large-scale group instruction, have been developed. An important component to the success of these services is determining the appropriate context and level of instructor. Three of the services are peer-based (taught by students) and directed at undergraduates. Others focus on different user populations.

Time of need and providing information in context, then, were important in research and practice in the 1980s. But if providing learning experiences "in context" at time of need was the issue of the 1980s, perhaps providing information "in context" at place of need will be the question of the 1990s. This issue is generated by technological change and the reason why instruction librarians are now members of CD-ROM selection committees, deciding what is appropriate for tape-loading or a gateway, negotiating with vendors, or looking at the Internet with a somewhat jaundiced eye.

It also leads, finally, to the other part of this paper, remote access "in context," or the place of need.

IN CONTEXT: IDENTIFYING PLACE OF NEED

What is place of need? In one view it is active learning "in context," that is, identifying where best to simulate the real research experience of the user. If it is a remote user, it should probably be a remote site. This sounds obvious, but the issue is not as simplistic as it sounds.

Prior to the recent development of networks, the variety of options for teaching at place of need was not extensive. There was the library's classroom or the student's regular classroom in which one provided materials that simulated or prepared the student for the "real" research experience in the library—usually in the reference area. Some classrooms contained materials—such as indexes—that emulated the reference room. And, of course, there was the no longer standard example of bringing the library to the classroom on a booktruck—much in the same way that CD-ROM disks are brought to the LCD setup of today. Some instructors brought the students to the collection in "hands-on" or follow-up sessions conducted in the reference room. But opportunities for changing place of need were limited due to technological constraints. You could demonstrate how to use technology, but students couldn't work simultaneously and in groups on the technology. Networks and licensing has changed this.

What is revolutionary "in context" for "place of need" in the 1990s is that the real research experience can be simulated outside of the library. This option truly creates the classroom without walls and leads to enormous opportunity. In recent literature, classroom design and the placement of technology has been extensively reviewed, and much has been adapted from active learning research. Student-centered clusters have proven to be more effective organizations for physical space than linear organization of terminals and isolated locations. To date, most work has focused on the layout of the classroom itself—valuable and important information, but only the first step.

What is missing in the literature about place of need is data about the actual site selection. At Colorado, five possible locations in which a "real research" experience can be emulated have been identified. These locations were chosen on the assumptions that group instruction was occurring and that it was desirable for the instructor to be physically present. While diversity in services in creating the electronic educational group experience is possible through e-mail and computer conferencing, it is presently not an option in our environment to engage groups in this activity simultaneously. This is, in all likelihood, the next question for review. When is electronic instruction enough, and when will the physical presence of the group or instructor be critical to educational success?

Possible group sites now include:

1. A reference room with clusters of public catalog terminals and CD-ROM index terminals;
2. An electronic classroom in library (networked PCs with access to library catalog, electronic periodical indexes, the Internet, and other electronic resources);
3. An on-campus computing lab used primarily by campus users for word processing but which also provides access to the library catalog, electronic periodical indexes, and Internet resources through a campus network;
4. A computer lab in a campus dormitory, linked to the library's electronic resources through a campus network; and
5. A remote-site computing lab, located off-campus but connected to the Internet.

These environments can each simulate the library experience or provide direct hands-on experience. But what are the characteristics that determine the best site selection, and what is best taught once there? To date, experiments have occurred at more than 10 sites at the University of Colorado. Within these locations, the most successful teaching and learning experiences have resulted when the following characteristics were present:

1. Small groups were used rather than one student per terminal.
2. Instruction was guided but not structured. There was no expectation of numerous students engaging in the same steps simultaneously.

3. The psychomotor or skill aspects were acknowledged, but instruction focused on cognitive issues.
4. The context of "why" was introduced prior to the hands-on experience on the terminal.
5. The instruction simulated the experience of the location in which research would continue at a later time. For example, students were given the log-on instruction that they would be using throughout a project's duration, rather than specialized instructions created for the day of class.
6. Follow-up options were offered through other services.

CASE STUDIES

University Learning Center Writing Program (Keith Gresham)

The University Learning Center Writing Program of the University of Colorado at Boulder is an introductory expository writing workshop designed to prepare provisionally admitted students for college-level coursework. The program consists of two sequenced four-credit writing courses that use collaborative learning approaches to teach students how to create, analyze, revise, and refine college-level papers.

Approximately 225 students participate in the program each year. The students are ethnically and culturally diverse, and for many English is a second language. Most of the program participants tend to be first-generation college students whose prior educational experiences have been less than successful. Also, most have had limited exposure, if any, to libraries and library research.

After spending the first half of the semester discovering their own voice in a series of writing assignments, students are introduced to the basic concepts of academic discourse and library research. For their final paper, students are required to locate, evaluate, and incorporate two to three scholarly articles into their own papers.

Instructional Sessions

Working with the program coordinator and course instructors, librarians from the Central Reference Department have integrated a library research component into the writing program. Through a series of small-group activities and hands-on work with CD-ROM periodical indexes, students explore the process of library research and learn about academic disciplines, search strategies, electronic database searching, and evaluation of information sources.

During the 1993 fall semester, the library research component consisted of two separate sessions. During the first session, students were introduced to the characteristics of information and were guided through the steps of the research process using their actual paper topics for context. This first session also included a brief demonstration of a CD-ROM index and the library catalog. The second session consisted of hands-on practice using CD-ROM indexes appropriate for individual topics. This second session allowed students to put the conceptual processes of library research into practice by physically locating citations and periodical articles relevant to their paper topics.

Time of Need

The library research components took place only after course instructors worked extensively with students on the basics of expository writing. The instructional sessions were given once students had selected final paper topics and were ready to incorporate the ideas of others into their writings by locating research articles in the library.

Place of Need

The first session, which focused on providing a conceptual understanding of the research process, was held in the library's instruction room. The room is arranged with several collaborative group tables and contains a computer, CD-ROM drive, and LCD panel used for demonstrating CD-ROM databases and the library catalog. The room is also two floors above and on the other side of the building from the central reference room where most of the library's public CD-ROM terminals are located. The second session, the hands-on component with CD-ROM indexes, was held in the reference room.

The instruction room, it turns out, was not the ideal place for teaching the basic concepts of library research to this particular group. The students had difficulty conceptualizing the research process because of the instruction room's physical distance from the reference room, the part of the building that students identified as "the library." In addition, the students had difficulty focusing on the small-group activities in the instruction room because the room was not designed like the student's regular classroom. In the future, this first session will be offered in the writing program classrooms.

However, the public CD-ROM terminals in the reference room were the appropriate place of need for the hands-on component. Other possible locations for the hands-on work—including a computer lab in the library building and a computer lab in the writing program classrooms—had been tried unsuccessfully. The reference room is the actual physical location where students would engage in future research.

Boulder Valley School District Internet In-service (John Culshaw)

The Boulder Valley School District Internet Project is a joint project of the school district, the University of Colorado at Boulder, Colorado Supernet (the state Internet provider), and Westnet (the regional Internet provider). Computing and Network Services, the School of Education, members of the university administration, and the University Libraries' Central Reference Department all represented the university in this collaborative venture. The goals of the project were to provide connectivity in every classroom and library and to integrate the Internet into the K-12 curriculum.

A coordinator was hired to oversee the project. The coordinator works as a liaison between the school district and collaborators in addition to assisting teachers and students in the schools.

The Central Reference Department became involved in the project in its early stages. Initial discussions with project planners focused on access issues such as who would be allowed to access the network and for what purposes or location-specific issues such as equipment concerns. Planners were also concerned with security of the administrative network. By the time of the in-service training (three months later), however, concerns shifted to Internet resources and how to locate and use this information.

Instructional Sessions

The in-service sessions were planned primarily for librarians and media specialists from elementary, middle, and high schools. Each person would be using the network from his or her own location—some with Macintosh computers and others with IBMs or clones. The sessions were held in February and March of 1993.

The in-service was planned as an all-day workshop. In the morning session, the project coordinator covered basic Internet skills including electronic mail (including Netnews), remote log in (Telnet), and file transfer (FTP). This session was designed to provide all the skills required to navigate the network via the district's Unix mainframe. The afternoon session concentrated on cognitive issues such as resource discovery and critical analysis of sources and search engines.

The afternoon began with a review of the basic skills and an introduction to the print and electronic tools that could help to locate networked sources. Discussion centered primarily on the availability of free resources, including library catalogs (such as the CARL system) and other services (such as the Weather Underground) but also included fee-based tools such as OCLC's FirstSearch. Each participant was given a handout describing a variety of free network resources for individual exploration.

Time of Need

Timing of the in-service was perfect. Each of the participants had just received computers and network connections and were very anxious to begin traveling the network.

Place of Need

The in-service was held in a typical computing lab on campus. Each of the workstations had word processing and other productivity software in addition to ethernet connections to the Internet. In this situation, the ideal teaching situation would have been the home environment. But with more than seventy people from all over Boulder County, the ideal was not possible. It was understood, however, that each person had a different setup and would be working with different remote resources.

The lab worked because everyone got into the same remote mode. The morning session taught skills for logging in to their system. Once they had connected to the BVSD mainframe, it was no different that working from home. The lab, then, emulated the home situation.

The afternoon session was not very structured. We were available to answer questions and guide through problems. This type of experience encouraged people to learn in different manners; some worked independently, some worked in small groups, and some relied on printed documentation. No matter how a person or group choose to investigate the Internet, all experimented with several different resources.

Follow-Up

No formal follow-up activities were planned for the workshop attendees. The participants were encouraged to take advantage of the Central Reference Department's Expanded Reference Service (an appointment-based service for detailed or lengthy reference questions) or to make appointments for individual consultation with the workshop presenters either in person, via e-mail, or phone.

It should be noted that the Boulder Valley Internet Project was an incredible success. The project has been used as a model for networking school districts and schools nationwide.

APPENDIX

The following active learning scenarios are presented for discussion.

Exercise: Teaching at Time and Place of Need

Given each of the following user profiles and possible instructional sites, determine:

- Which instructional site(s) would you choose for the library session?

- Which three concepts would you want the users to learn from the session?
- Provide a preliminary outline of how you would structure the educational experience within either a single two-hour session or two one-hour sessions.

User Profile #1:

Group:	Graduate students in history
Academic Setting:	Large state-supported university
User Need:	Learn about discipline-specific electronic reference resources as part of a Research Methods in History course

Possible Instructional Sites:

1. *Reference room* with clusters of public catalog terminals and CD-ROM index terminals.
2. *Electronic classroom in library* (networked PCs with access to the library catalog, electronic periodical indexes, the Internet, and other electronic resources).
3. *On-campus computing lab* used primarily by campus users for word processing, but also provides access to the library catalog, electronic periodical indexes, and Internet resources through a campus network.
4. *Computer lab in campus dormitory* linked to the library's electronic resources through a campus network.
5. *Remote-site computing lab* located off-campus but connected to the Internet.

User Profile #2:

Group:	Local high school students
Academic Setting:	Regional state-supported liberal arts college
User Need:	Introduction to academic library research for senior honors

Possible Instructional Sites:

1. *Reference room* with clusters of public catalog terminals and CD-ROM index terminals.
2. *Electronic classroom in library* (networked PCs with access to the library catalog, electronic periodical indexes, the Internet, and other electronic resources).
3. *On-campus computing lab* used primarily by campus users for word processing, but also provides access to the library catalog, electronic periodical indexes, and the Internet resources through a campus network.
4. *Computer lab in campus dormitory* linked to the library's electronic resources through a campus network.
5. *Remote-site computing lab* located off-campus but connected to the Internet.

User Profile #3:

Group:	First-semester freshmen in writing composition course
Academic Setting:	Large state-supported university
User Need:	Locate two scholarly articles for use in a six-page argumentative paper

Possible Instructional Sites:

1. *Reference room* with clusters of public catalog terminals and CD-ROM index terminals.
2. *Electronic classroom in library* (networked PCs with access to the library catalog, electronic periodical indexes, the Internet, and other electronic resources).
3. *On-campus computing lab* used primarily by campus users for word processing, but also provides access to the library catalog, electronic periodical indexes, and Internet resources through a campus network.
4. *Computer lab in campus dormitory* linked to the library's electronic resources through a campus network.
5. *Remote-site computing lab* located off-campus but connected to the Internet.

User Profile #4:

Group:	Education Department faculty
Academic Setting:	Private liberal arts college
User Need:	Education Department is getting Internet connections in offices, and faculty wish to learn about Internet resources that they can incorporate into education curricula

Possible Instructional Sites:

1. *Reference room* with clusters of public catalog terminals and CD-ROM index terminals.
2. *Electronic classroom in library* (networked PCs with access to the library catalog, electronic periodical indexes, the Internet, and other electronic resources).
3. *On-campus computing lab* used primarily by campus users for word processing, but also provides access to the library catalog, electronic periodical indexes, and Internet resources through a campus network.
4. *Computer lab in campus dormitory* linked to the library's electronic resources through a campus network.
5. *Remote-site computing lab* located off-campus but connected to the Internet.

NOTES AND REFERENCES

1. Raul Aluri and Mary Reichel, "Learning Theories and Bibliographic Instruction," in *Bibliographic Instruction and the Learning Process: Theory, Style, and Motivation,* edited by C.A. Kirkendall (Ann Arbor, MI: Pierian Press, 1984).

2. Glenda B. Thurman, "The Evolution of Behavioral Objectives" (Ph.D. dissertation, University of Colorado at Boulder, 1982).

3. An excellent review of these issues is in Raymond S. Nickerson, "On Improving Thinking Through Instruction," *Review of Research in Education* 15 (1989): 1-57.

4. Nancy S. Cole, "Conceptions of Educational Achievement," *Educational Researcher* 19(1990): 2-7.

5. Richard G. Tiberius and Janet Mancini Billson, "The Social Context of Teaching and Learning," *New Directions in Teaching and Learning* 45(1991): 67-86.

6. Ibid.

7. See, for example: Trish Ridgeway, "Active Learning Methods in the One-Hour Bibliographic Instruction Lecture," in *Defining and Applying Effective Teaching Strategies for Library Instruction* (Ann Arbor, MI: Pierian Press, 1989); Mary Jane Petrowski and Lizabeth Wilson, *Cooperative Learning and Bibliographic Instruction: A Workshop for Librarians* (Baltimore: Johns Hopkins University, Center for Social Organization of Schools, 1991), ERIC Document Reproduction Service No. ED 338 268; Cerise Oberman, "Avoiding the Cereal Syndrome, or Critical Thinking in the Electronic Environment," *Library Trends* 39(1991): 189-202.

8. Association of College and Research Libraries, Bibliographic Instruction Section, *Bibliographic Instruction Handbook* (Chicago: American Library Association, 1979).

9. Lori Arp and Lizabeth A. Wilson, "Structures of Bibliographic Instruction Programs: A Continuum for Planning," in *Integrating Library Use Skills Into the General Education Curriculum,* edited by Maureen Pastine and Bill Katz (New York: Haworth Press, 1989), pp. 25-34.

10. Frances F. Jacobson, "Library Instruction and the Science Classroom: The Ideal Laboratory," *Journal of Youth Services in Libraries* 2(1989): 235-240.

11. *The Evolving Educational Mission of the Library,* edited by Betsy Baker and Mary Ellen Litzinger, (Chicago: American Library Association, 1992).

12. Evan Farber, "Library Instruction Through the Curriculum," in *Educating the Library User,* edited by John Lubans, (New York: Bowker, 1974), pp. 145-162.

TEACHING THE LIBRARY AND ELECTRONIC RESOURCES ON TELEVISION

Naomi Lederer

COURSE CONTENT AND OBJECTIVES

The Use of Research Libraries course teaches research skills and a knowledge of information access tools. Furthermore, students learn how to analyze, interpret, and use the information they find. Through the homework assignments, students gain hands-on experience with a variety of library resources that go well beyond those used in first-year composition courses. Through these experiences, students gain information literacy skills that enhance lifelong learning as well as academic success. The research project, an annotated bibliography, requires students to demonstrate the library research skills learned in class.

The course moves from introductory topics through a recommended research strategy with homework that applies directly to each student's annotated bibliography. Paper, electronic, CD-ROM, Internet, and other formats are presented, as relevant, throughout the semester. Special topics such as company research and science resources for the lay researcher make up the latter part of the course. The included syllabus provides the details (see Appendix).

STUDENTS

LIA 390 is offered through the College of Liberal Arts and Sciences; cable access is provided through the College of Extended Education. The class, by its number and content, fulfills upper division requirements for graduation. Additionally, it now fulfills the General Studies requirement for Literacy and Critical Inquiry (L1). Many students admit that they are taking the course to fulfil graduation requirements. On the other hand, they will acknowledge a need to learn library skills.

Seniors with graduate school plans also take the course; over the years, a number of them have begun their thesis or dissertation research, giving themselves a great head start for graduate school. Honors students with research projects ahead of them sign up for the course. Students who want to learn how to use the library because of previous intimidating experiences make up another part. Older students who are returning to school after years (sometimes decades) want to learn how the current library (without a familiar card catalog!) works. Finally, the occasional freshman student who is often also taking a composition course will sign up so that he or she can do well on the research paper. All of them get what they want and then some.

STUDENT RESPONSE TO COURSE

Course evaluations and comments from students have indicated that generally the students think that the course is a lot of work. (These comments have lessened considerably now that the course is three credits). The hands-on homework in the library is time consuming. On the other hand, students say it is worth it—they now can do better research in a fast, efficient, and thorough manner. The time saved in later semesters and for other courses makes up for the demands of one semester. Cable students have written in response to evaluations that they feel that they are participating in the course (although not as much as the students in the classroom) and do as well academically as those in the classroom.

CLASSROOM SET-UP

The classroom used to teach the course is outside the library. Fixed long tables face the front of the room with microphones placed so as to be used by two students. This means furniture

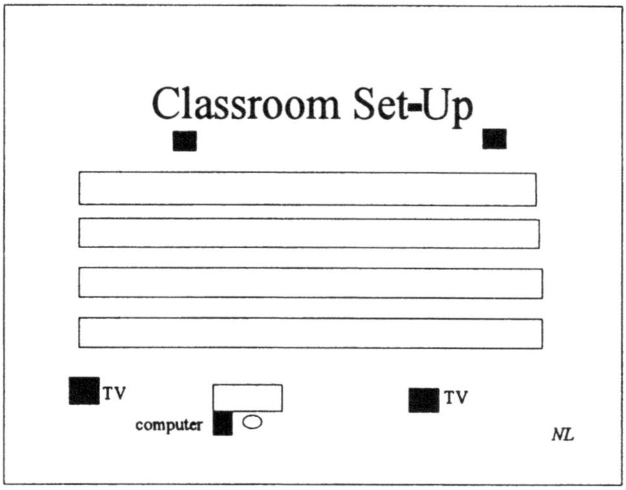

Figure 1. Classroom Set-Up

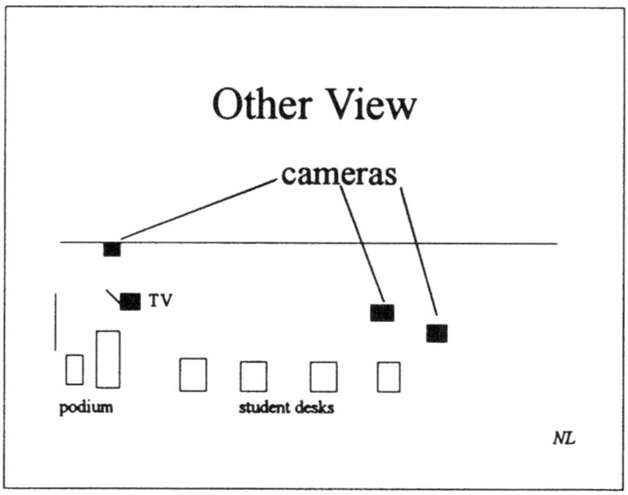

Figure 2. Other View

rearrangement for cooperative or other learning exercises is impossible. At the front of the room is a fixed podium for the instructor (see Figures 1-2). There is a studio from where the cameras are operated by extended education staff. Students are in the classroom and also watch via cable at home, at a remote classroom, or watch the class later on videotape.

CLASSROOM EQUIPMENT AT ASU

The cable classrooms at Arizona State University are equipped with chalkboards, an 11" X 8.5" writing pad, a computer with its screen hardwired so that it can appear directly on monitors or televisions, three cameras, two or three television monitors (depending on the size of the classroom), and a telephone.

The chalkboard is supplied with fat chalk that forces the instructor to write in large letters that can be seen on TV. Additionally, instructors are asked to write within specific camera lens spaces so that everything fits on the television screen.

The writing pad is on the podium, and there is a camera directly above it, so everything that is on the pad can be transmitted over the air—this can be writing, photographs, books, or other objects.

The three cameras provide classroom shots, close-ups of the instructor, and show the pad or chalkboard. Sometimes when the pad or computer is used, the instructor's head is "boxed" and put in a part of the screen. Occasionally, the camera in the ceiling (over the pad) is tilted so that the faces of the students can be seen.

The student microphones transmit over the air so that students watching offsite can hear their classmates. The instructor's microphone hangs around his or her neck, and the long cord allows moving about the front part of the classroom. The telephone enables remote students to call in during class. Their calls are routed through the studio to prevent the general public from calling in and using up class time. What they say can be heard both in the classroom and on the air.

The camera operator generally chooses the shots, but the instructor can direct this, up to a point, by saying, "Show the pad," or "Now, we will go to the computer," to cue him or her. Options generally are: the pad, the computer, the chalkboard, visuals, or "me." Being on television is not for the faint of heart—occasional camera operators have shown *very* close-up shots!

PROBLEMS AND SOLUTIONS

There are most definitely difficulties with this kind of teaching arrangement. Materials can't be handed out to all students as part of the class. Certainly the students in the classroom can get them, but remote and cable students need to have items sent or mailed to them, and there are additional delays when sending things through campus mail to go "outside."

Another major concern is copyright issues in a new medium. Can the instructor show copyrighted books over the air? Special permission must be granted (or paid for) to show movies or CD-ROM products. Some of these issues are still up in the air (educational fair use), so sometimes there is a tendency to err on the side of *not* showing things, just in case. On the other hand, I consider that showing a reference book is free advertising or promotion, but then again, the publishers might not think so.

Another difficulty is that students cannot just walk out into the library and see where things are. Educational television has certain video quality standards, so ordinary videotape cannot be used to show the library on the air. To combat this, I found it useful to require students to take an audio library orientation tour. The audio tour includes a hands-on online catalog search so that students have an opportunity to see the catalog before it is introduced in the classroom. Photographs of the library or sections thereof are also useful. I can show what the biography indexes, book review indexes, or other reference sources look like on the shelves in the library, even if the students can't see them live in class. This is helpful because students don't always do homework when there is someone around to give directions.

As for classroom discussion, this can get dicey. As we move towards a cooperative learning environment, we want all students to participate. Bolted down tables hamper group work. Student microphones that don't work keep cable viewers from hearing what is going on. Involving cable viewers is another problem because many of them tape the course and watch it later, while others watch it later in the Video Resources Library on campus. One cannot get immediate feedback or questions from students who aren't watching when you teach.

I have seen one example (at the University of Utah's Utah Education Network "Reaching and Teaching Through Television" day-long workshop on teaching on television, April 24, 1992) of a teacher who pulls names out of a bowl, and students are required to call in at that moment. However, this may defeat one of the objectives of distance learning—providing instruction when and where it is convenient for the learner. The bowl idea could work with the contingency that if the student isn't watching live that he or she calls, writes, e-mails, or faxes with the answer by next class time. Unfortunately, this isn't going to keep a discussion moving along, and short answers to questions will need to be available right away or render that portion of the class meaningless. There are many ways to get an entire classroom of students actively engaged, but the distant learner is not necessarily going to be engaged at the same moment.

Use of electronic discussion mechanisms may partially solve the problem of classroom discussions. Operating like ongoing electronic mail, student comments are available for all to see. The instructor monitors this, asking questions designed to promote feedback, thus the location and time the student watches become irrelevant. Also, this is an excellent mechanism for students to have practice writing for an audience, and they will want to look good in front of their peers.

Another way I have started to get remote students at least somewhat involved is to require them to supply answers (on debatable topics) to two or three of the homework questions a few hours before classtime (via e-mail, fax, or drop off); then their answers can be contributed by the instructor in class. This works well. If they are watching live they can call in their participation—the remote fixed-site students are required to do so. However, there is another difficulty—if there is a lively discussion, we still have to finish on time because of the cable schedule. So teaching the class does involve some clock watching. Afterthoughts mentioned in the classroom after the broadcast are missed by those at remote sites or watching on cable.

ELECTRONIC RESOURCES

A major problem with teaching the course on cable is that the computer screen is too small to see the online catalog, Internet, or CD-ROM screens clearly (see Figures 3-8). A large screen projection system is not an option when teaching on television. At the same time, interactive live demonstrations are valuable because they show students how things work (or do not work).

SMALL SCREEN PROBLEM SOLVING

One way to enhance the online catalog demonstration is to prepare certain screens in advance to show the class on the 11" X 8.5" pad. After dumping screens to the hard drive, I open the file in WordPerfect ® and, after changing the page layout to landscape, enlarge the font (to *Large* or *Very Large* or 16-20 points, depending on how much is on the screen), tidy it up (things have a way of shifting), and print it out on my laser printer. Then, as I am doing

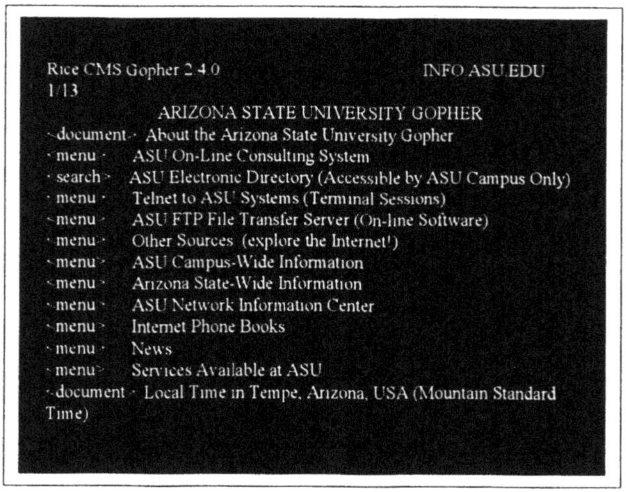

Figure 3.

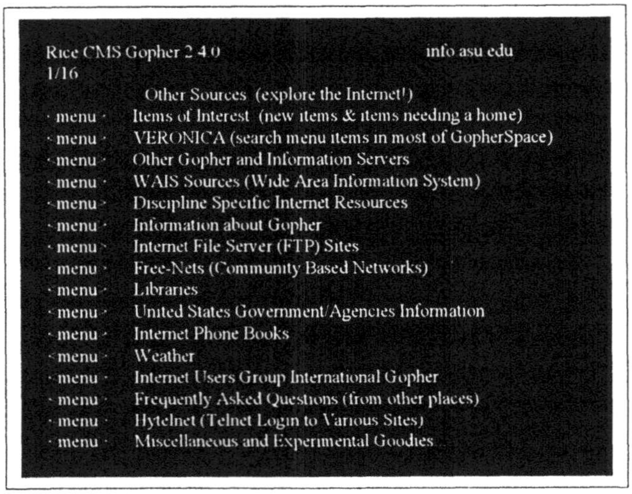

Figure 4.

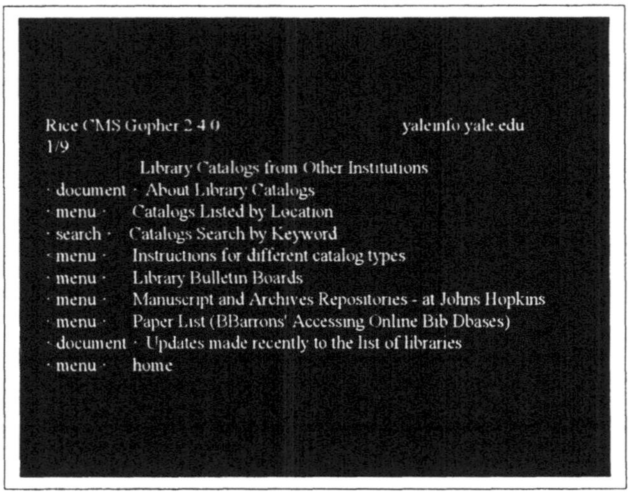

Figure 5.

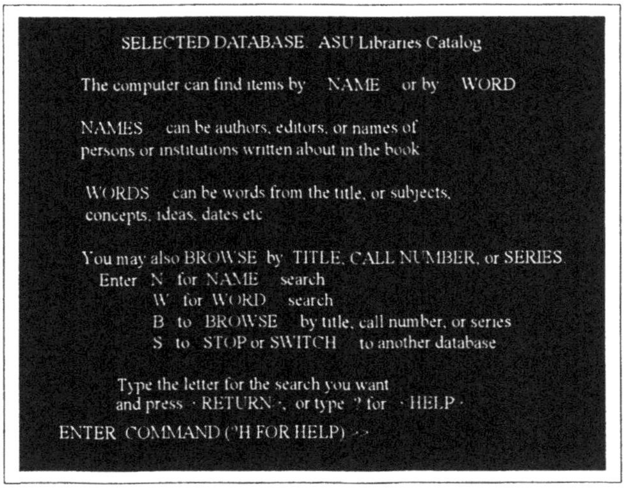

Figure 6.

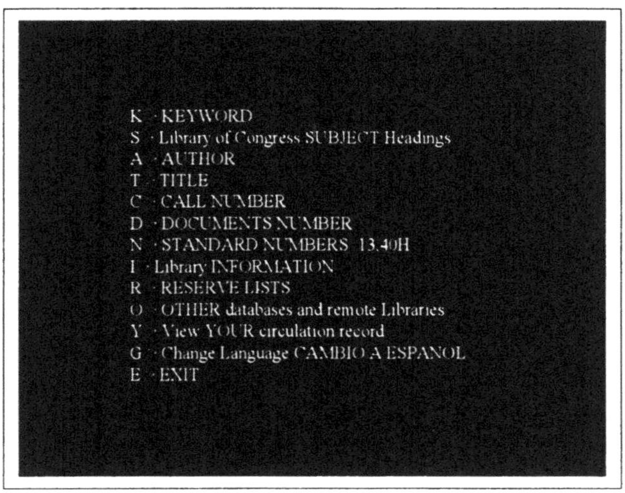

Figure 7.

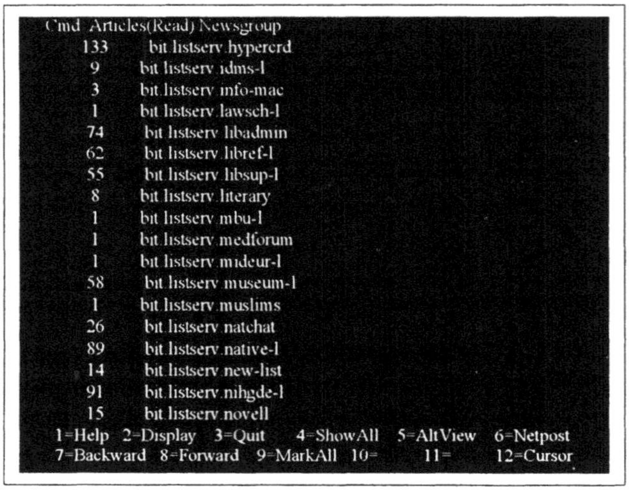

Figure 8.

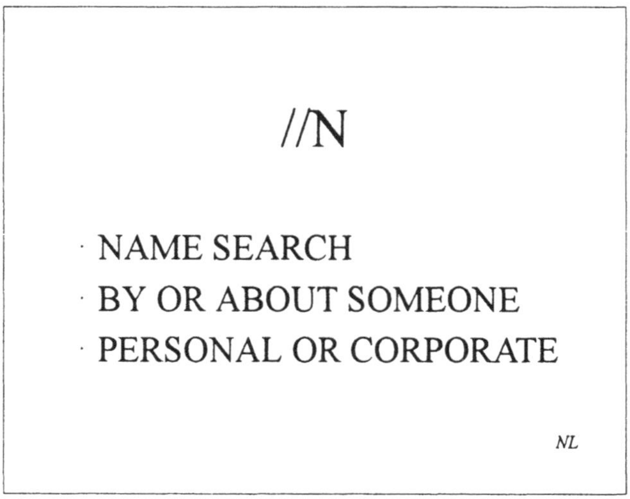

Figure 9. //N

1. ASU LIBRARIES CATALOG (books, journal titles, other cataloged materials)
2. OTHER ASU LIBRARIES SPECIALIZED COLLECTIONS AND DATABASES (AZ & SW, Maps, Solar Energy, Song Index...)
3. JOURNAL INDEXES, ERIC, & UNCOVER (Article Access) NOTE: SEE LIBRARY NEWS (#8) FOR JOURNAL CANCELLATIONS
4. ENCYCLOPEDIA (Grolier's Academic American, c. 1992)
5. INFORMATION DATABASES (AZ Statistics, Child Car...)
6. ARIZONA LIBRARIES
7. OTHER LIBRARY CATALOGS (including Gov. Publications, 1976-)
8. LIBRARY NEWS, HOURS, AND INFORMATION (Including Journal Cancellations)
9. NEW BOOKS

Enter the NUMBER of your choice, and press the
< RETURN > key > >

Screen 1. Online Catalog

the interactive demonstration, I can ask the camera operator to switch to the pad and show the dumped screens—these show up rather well—and give students another view of the screens (see Screens 1-4).

Not only do I show the screens, I say what I am doing and describe the screens. Certain aspects are not intuitive ("Now, I am pressing return"), so details are important. In addition, I have found that talking my way through the screens slows me down so the students have a greater chance of seeing them.

Another way to help students learn how to use online catalogs and other electronic resources is to create slide shows in large fonts (48-72 points) that demonstrate the electronic resources. The enlarged size ensures that everyone is able to see the words. These slides are reproduced in the course textbook so that students do not need to rush and copy down the screens but can add their own comments or those extras I supply (see Figure 9). Aldus Persuasion ® software has been marvelous for this. I have used it

SELECTED DATABASE: ASU LIBRARIES CATALOG

The computer can find items by NAME OR WORD

NAMES can be authors, editors, or names of persons or institutions written about in the book

WORDS can be words from the title, or subjects, concepts, ideas, dates, etc.

You may also BROWSE by TITLE, CALL NUMBER, or SERIES

Enter	N	for	NAME search
	W	for	WORD search
	B	to	BROWSE by title, call number, or series
	S	to	STOP OR SWITCH to another database

Type the letter for the search you want.
and press < RETURN >, or type ? for < HELP >

SELECTED DATABASE: ASU Libraries Catalog

ENTER COMMAND (?H FOR HELP) >> //w internet resources

Screen 2. Online Catalog

since I began teaching on television. The handouts (see Identifying Key Journals in a Professional Field on pages 185-186) have four screens per page with room for notes and are automatically generated by the software, so all I have to press is "print." (Note: Aldus Persuasion ® is a Windows ® program; there is a Macintosh ® version as well.) The outline format is automatically generated and can be used as instructor's notes. Persuasion ® also has "Notes" that show one small slide per page, and then speaker's notes can be typed in and printed out. The full "Slide" screens can be printed out as well. In fact, I try to print out the full slide screens in case the computer breaks down or cannot transmit for some reason. I can use the print out on the 11" X 8.5" pad. Sometimes I create slides specifically for the pad.

Showing the slide shows works very well. You can go backwards and have fun with them. Much to my great disappointment, however, I cannot be as creative with the backgrounds as I would

INTERNET 50 ITEMS   ASU Libraries Catalog
patience—RESOURCES is a long one....
INTERNET + RESOURCES   3 ITEMS

Set of 3 will display on one page—proceeding with display....

1 Braun Eric Eric Eu   ASU SCI REF   1994
The Internet directory   TK51056.875.I57   B72 × 199

2 Krol Ed   ASU LAW LPROF   1993
The whole Internet user's guide & catalo TK5105.875.I57 K76 1993

3   ASU see record   1992
Library resources on the Internet: strategies   Z687 .L53×   1992

ALL ITEMS HAVE BEEN DISPLAYED.
Enter < Line number(s) > To Display Full Records (Number + B for Brief)
< P > revious For Previous Page OR < Q > uit For New Search

Screen 3. Online Catalog

like. Persuasion ® allows this—and I have created some real beauties—but transmission over the air distorts colors; therefore, I must stick to single color backgrounds. Bright yellow, blue, and green work well. White works, too, but it's a bit bland—I do want to dress it up for people with color televisions! Nonetheless, I think the Persuasion ® software is fabulous (although the manual leaves much to be desired). Rather than having only a dull talking head, the slide show adds variety to the class and appeals to different learning styles. The slides also save the students from reading my bumpy handwriting on the pad. I still write on the pad a lot because one cannot anticipate all questions. The large font printouts help.

Another way the students see the screens is when they do their homework. The online catalog is going to be large enough to see while they are completing their assignments. As the small screens are shown repeatedly in class they become more familiar to the students. The online catalog and the Internet are taught more than once, so students have ample opportunities to become comfortable using them.

__________ASULibraries Catalog __________
AUTHOR(s): Krol, Ed.
TITLE(s): The whole Internet user's guide & catalog / Ed Krol
Minor corrections.

Sebastopol, CA : O'Reilly & Associates, c1993,1992.
xxiv, 376 p. : ill. ; 24 cm.
Includes index.
Contents: What is this book about—What is the Internet—How the Internet works—What's allowed on the Internet—Remote login—Moving files: FTP—Electronic mail—Network news—Finding software—Finding someone—Tunneling through the Internet: Gopher—Searching indexed databases: WAIS—Hypertext spanning the internet: WWW—Other applications—Dealing with problems—Resources on the Internet.

OTHER ENTRIES: Internet (Computer network)
Whole Internet user's guide and catalog

LOCN: LAW LPROF STATUS: Checked out—
CALL #: TK5105.875.I57 K76 1993
____ 2 of 3 __________ ASU Libraries Catalog ______
< R > epeat this display, < Q > uit,
< X > for Express, < H > for Search History, <O > for Owners
? for HELP>

Screen 4. Online Catalog

TEXTBOOK

The textbook plays an important role in keeping students aware of what is going on. The textbook is written by the course instructors and revised every semester to ensure up-to-date information. Homework assignments are included in the book so that they do not need to be mailed (cable students have a postmark due date to turn in assignments). As mentioned above, the Persuasion ® slides are included so even if the slide show goes by too fast due to time constraints, students don't need to worry about

Identifying Key Journals in a Professional Field

1. Magazines for Libraries • over 6,000 titles • by subject area • identifies audience	**1. Magazines for Libraries** ________________ ________________ ________________ ________________ ________________ ________________ ________________ ________________
Magazines for Libraries (cont.) • tells where indexed • however, verify if journal still publishing	**Magazines for Libraries (cont.)** ________________ ________________ ________________ ________________ ________________ ________________ ________________ ________________
2. *Encyclopedia of Associations* • gives associations' publications, if any	**2. Encyclopedia of Associations** ________________ ________________ ________________ ________________ ________________ ________________ ________________ ________________
3. Current Contents • weekly • has most frequently cited journals in the field	**3. Current Contents** ________________ ________________ ________________ ________________ ________________ ________________ ________________ ________________

5. Guides to the Literature

- some disciplines have a handbook that identifies sources in that subject area

5. Guides to the Literature

6. Ulrich's International Periodicals Directory
- guide to journals arranged by broad subject areas
- publication information

6. Ulrich's International Periodicals Directory

Ulrich's (cont.)

- indicates where indexed
- keeps up to date as an annual with 3 updates

Ulrich's (cont.)

Finally, use your own expert judgment

Finally, use your own expert judgment

Outline (Persuasion ®)

- Online Catalog Searches
- //W
  - WORD SEARCH
  - KEYWORDS
- WORD SEARCH
  - if there are 300 or fewer items
    - items are displayed in reverse chronological order
    - (newest items at the top)
  - if there are more than 300 items
    - they are not sorted
- //N
  - NAME SEARCH
  - BY OR ABOUT SOMEONE
  - PERSONAL OR CORPORATE
- NAME SEARCH
  - if there are 300 or fewer items
    - sources are displayed:
      - books by the author
      - books where the author is the second author
      - books about the author
- NOTE
  - if doing research ABOUT someone, it is a very good idea to do a WORD (subject) search on him or her, too.
- //J { } AND { }
  - JOINT AUTHOR SEARCH
- //T
  - TITLE SEARCH
  - alphabetical listing
  - used first to identify journal titles
  - finds books and other materials' titles, too
- //N /
  - NAME/WORD SEARCH
  - author/word(s) from title
- //C
  - CALL NUMBER BROWSE
  - (shelf browse online)
- //S
  - SERIES BROWSE
- FULL RECORD
  - AUTHOR
  - TITLE
  - OTHER ENTRIES
    - (LCSH terms)

(continued)

Outline (Persuasion ®) (continued)

- CALL NUMBER
- LOCATION (LOCN)
- STATUS
    - checked out or not checked out

- ASU LIBRARIES CATALOG
    - database on the Online Catalog
        - books
        - journal holdings
        - other cataloged materials
- JOURNAL INDEXES
    - identify journal articles
- You must check the *ASU Libraries Catalog* database for journal holdings (except Government serials)
- //H
    - SEARCH HISTORY
    - shows last 10 searches

missing them. The textbook has a table of contents and an index, so students can find what they need when doing homework or later on when doing research for another course.

THE FUTURE

The future has some exciting possibilities. Many students have told me that they think the Use of Research Libraries course should be required of all students. The hopeful goal is for this to happen some day, but given budget cuts and other unknowns, this might not happen. The workload for the instructor(s) is heavy; one of the reasons the course is so effective is that students research topics of interest to *them*—bubble answer sheets could never replace the personal touch.

In a more electronically advanced (or to be more accurate—better funded) future, students in the classroom or watching from home will have their own computers so that they can type in what the instructor does, and the size of the screen or the type size on the monitor will not matter. Technology wherein students' screens match the teacher's exists, so students can have right in front of them exactly what the teacher is typing or showing (although I imagine it will not work for remote sites). Again, the problems are funding, not technological.

CONCLUSION

It is possible to teach library and electronic resources on television effectively. A little imagination, some flexibility, and a huge sense of humor helps. Sometimes (as in any classroom) the equipment lets you down and you are back to the chalkboard; nonetheless, by planning ahead, problems can be anticipated. By providing elegantly prepared screens in the textbook, one can use them as teaching tools, even if you cannot show the fancy slide show with neat slide changes in class. And, I believe the most important tool in the classroom is still the instructor. Textbook, technology, and teacher can work together in a cable—or any other—course.

APPENDIX

NEED TO DO LIBRARY RESEARCH?

Sign up for ASU's LIA 390,
Use of Research Libraries course
Spring 1995
Three credit hours; fulfills General Studies L1 requirement

Via cable television!

— Learn

Skills for effective library research

*research methods
*critical thinking
*research methods

How to use library tools

*Online Catalog databases
*reference tools
*indexes
*CD-ROMs

Acquire information age skills now!
Register for LIA 390, line #07044

Tues. & Thurs. 12:15-1:30pm

Course available on Dimension Cable in Phoenix, Tempe, Fountain Hills, and Litchfield Park; Insight Cable in Phoenix. For additional information, please call ASU's College of Extended Education, 965-6738.

Taught interactively from ASU's Main campus; to attend on campus register for line number #42193.

LIA 390 Use of Research Libraries
Course Content

The Use of Research Libraries course teaches research skills and a knowledge of information access tools. Furthermore, students learn how to analyze, interpret, and use the information they find. Through the homework assignments, students gain hands-on experience with a variety of library resources that go well beyond those used in first-year composition courses. Through these experiences, students gain information literacy skills that enhance lifelong learning as well as academic success. The research project, an annotated bibliography, requires students to demonstrate the library research skills learned in class. In addition to regular homework, there is a midterm and a final exam.

Literacy and Critical Inquiry Components

The Use of Research Libraries is basically a course in critical inquiry. The core of the course is learning how to access, evaluate, and synthesize information. The course requires students to construct effective search strategies and demonstrate efficient retrieval techniques as they identify and examine a variety of print and non-print sources. Of critical importance is discovering what to do with information once it has been found. Therefore, students analyze books, articles, and other sources evaluating them for veracity, authority, bias, value, and relevance.

With few exceptions there are no "right" answers for the writing assignments—all that matters is a well-written argument backed by solid evidence.

Information Literacy Competencies for Students

Information Literacy competencies can be addressed within the following major ability categories:

The ability to ACCESS information:
articulate information needs;
construct effective search strategies;
select appropriate resources;
use efficient retrieval techniques; and

consider issues relating to access to information—privacy, copyright, preservation, censorship, electronic access, exponential growth, and issues yet to come.

The ability to EVALUATE information:
critically examine for veracity, authority, and bias;
and judge the value and relevance of information.

The ability to SYNTHESIZE information:
comprehend meaning and interpret material;
integrate and organize effectively;
apply to problem solving and decision making; and
communicate information successfully.

Required Texts

Library Research Skills

Gibaldi, Joseph, and Walter S. Achtert. *MLA Handbook for Writers of Research Papers.* 3rd ed. New York: MLA, 1988.

Syllabus

1

Topics: Introduction, course policies, student introductions, overview of syllabus, and course goals. Explanation of Encyclopedia/Dictionary Assignment.

2

Topics: Library Resources overview. Information Superhighway. Libraries in the 1990s.

Do: Information Superhighway and Encyclopedia/Dictionary Assignments

3

Topics: Discussion of Information Superhighway and libraries in the 1990s.

4

Topics: Types of libraries, jargon, terms, research project described, LC classification.

Do: Visit Libraries, Contemporary Library Issues, and LC Classification Assignments

5

Topics: LCSH, thesauri, controlled vocabulary, research topic selection, and search strategy.

6

Topics: How to find books on the online catalog, CARL and generic: author/subject/keyword/title/call #; Access points

Complete: LCSH, Online Catalog Assignments,
Read: Bok article
Write: Summary and abstract of Bok article
Acquire: E-mail account and do E-mail Assignment

7

Topics: Journal Indexes: paper, Online Catalog, CD-ROM; Scholarly vs. Popular journals; Interlibrary Loan; narrowing topics; identifying key journals.

8

Topics: Research guides; Primary and secondary sources; Basic reference sources—encyclopedias and dictionaries; bibliographies; evaluation and synthesis.
Choose: Research project topic
Meet: With instructor regarding topic. Do this in person or over telephone; then complete Topic Selection Assignment;
Do: Paper Index and Abstracts, Journal article, Identifying Key Journals, book evaluation, bibliography, encyclopedia Assignments
Read and write abstract of article in textbook

9

Topics: Research on current issues; Table of Contents; Newspapers and news media; Media Resources.
Do: Current Issues Research Assignment and Media Assignment

10

Topics: Book reviews; Archives and manuscripts.
Complete: Book review Assignment
Find and read: Articles on assigned topics (given in class) from Contemporary Library Issues topics
Write: An abstract and annotation for articles

11

Topics: Hands-on library research at Hayden and Fletcher Libraries

12

Topics: Government documents; documents on Internet; Maps.
Complete: Government documents and Map assignments

13

Topics: Discuss government documents; Privitization of government documents; documents on Internet; Maps; Freedom of Information; Statistics.

14

Topics: Advanced Online Catalog Searching, Contemporary Library Issues Discussion, Almanacs.

Study: For Midterm exam

Complete: Advanced Searching, Almanac, and Persuasive Letter Assignments.

15

Midterm exam

16

Topics: Research strategies; pulling things together; style manuals; biographical sources; midterm overview.

Read and write summary and annotation of Contemporary Library Issue (assigned in class).

Complete: Biography assignment

17

Topics: CD-ROM, LAN

18

Topics: Internet and Gopher

Complete: CD-ROM search method and CD-ROM hands-on Assignments

Start and try to finish when possible: Internet Assignment

19

Topics: Discuss CD-ROM, Internet, and Gopher; Libraries without walls, "virtual" library.

20

Topics: Science and Technology, non-major.

Complete: Science and Technology Assignment

21

Topics: Discuss Science and Technology.

22

Topics: Humanities for the non-major.

Complete: Humanities Assignment

Read and write annotation of article on Contemporary Library Issue

23

Topics: Discuss Humanities; Reading; Support of Public Libraries.

24

Topics: Business and Industry Research.

Complete: Business reference sources Assignment

25
Topics: Discuss Business and Industry.
26
Topics: Real life research—college and graduate schools, grants, careers, cities, cars, children's. **RESEARCH PROJECT DUE**.
27
Topics: Other online catalog systems.
Do: Other systems on the online catalog Assignment
28
Topics: Internet, Gopher, ongoing technology, updates.
29
Topics: Class overview, overview of final exam.
30
Final Exam due 2 p.m.

THE GATEWAY TO INFORMATION:

MEETING THE BI NEEDS OF 54,000 STUDENTS (NOT TO MENTION FACULTY, STAFF, AND COMMUNITY USERS) WITHOUT WORKSHOPS, FLYERS, OR STAFF ASSISTANCE

Fred Roecker

INTRODUCTION

While driving to this conference I heard a radio interview with Stewart Brand, founder of *The Well*. In this interview, he said he considered the Internet not a superhighway but an epidemic that everyone is catching. Huge amounts of time, money, and personnel have been utilized to help understand this epidemic, control it, and manage its growth. He felt that, while this epidemic was currently out of control and difficult to fully grasp, it will become manageable in the future. Once the initial excitement and panic fades, he said, the Internet will become an integral part of everyone's lives.

If the Internet is likened to a fast-spreading epidemic, then basic library research skills can best be described as the common cold that still requires day-to-day attention from librarians. At The Ohio State University, staff face the real world of library users who do not know the basics of library research, much less how to use the Internet. Many users struggle with such library skills as choosing between a periodical index and the online catalog to identify relevant resources, identifying whether a citation refers to a book or a journal, and locating a book buried in our huge collection. With downsized budgets, staff reductions, and reduced library hours, attacking this basic illness is more difficult than ever before. Yet without attacking this basic illness, the complexities of the Internet epidemic cannot be addressed.

BI NEEDS IN THE UNIVERSITY LIBRARIES

In 1985 Virginia Tiefel, Head of the Office of Library User Education at The Ohio State University, recognized this urgent need of our library users to acquire effective information-seeking skills. She examined the current state of bibliographic instruction in the University Libraries and found several problems:

- Although about 35,000 students per year were receiving some form of bibliographic instruction, half the student population as well as the staff received none.
- Students taking a one-hour workshop could not be considered "information literate," ready to confidently undertake research in the University Libraries or search the new computer databases.
- Workshop attendance was steadily dropping.
- There was a growth in continuing education students and other remote users who could not attend workshops and had no access to our User Education instructional materials.
- Electronic resources were on the increase.
- Budget cuts in all areas, including personnel, made it impossible to offer more workshops, print more brochures, or staff the reference desk with more people for longer hours.

Tiefel reasoned that computers might provide the answer. A computer information system could provide huge numbers of students with consistent, on-demand assistance to organize a search strategy, identify relevant materials regardless of format, search available CD-ROMs and the online catalog, and then locate the materials by examining library floorplans and campus maps. A critical thinking component could help users evaluate these materials for relevance. Tiefel felt the ideal computer system would:

- Display a search strategy for guiding novices through their first steps in organizing research.
- Direct users to relevant materials regardless of format and assist them in evaluating those items.
- Provide easy access and front end to all OSU Libraries catalogs and databases.
- Show other library information such as hours, addresses, floorplans, etc.
- Provide access in every university library and remote sites
- Require no further assistance in the form of manuals, staff, or workshops.
- Allow easy modification of screens and content

FUNDING AND TECHNOLOGY

The University Libraries had no money available for creating such a revolutionary system. Tiefel and other library personnel therefore submitted (and won) a formal grant proposal to the Fund for the Improvement for Post-Secondary Education (FIPSE), a U.S. Department of Education agency. FIPSE bought into an idea which had no programmers, no computers, no idea of what type of system would be used...just a great idea. FIPSE supported this concept of creating a "one-stop shopping" computer for research needs. Three other grants were also received. Two grants were from Title IID (U.S. Department of Education) and one from the William Randolph Hearst Foundation for a total of about $500,000. The project was named "The Gateway to Information."

Susan Logan, Coordinator of Automated Library Systems, directed the technology aspects and William Studer, Director of the University Libraries, contributed tremendous encouragement and staff time for the project. Grant funds paid for equipment, CD-ROMs, and a programmer. John Salter, Senior Programmer/ Analyst, was hired to oversee the programming. Eight Macintosh

IIcx computers and ImageWriter printers were also purchased. Apple Computers, Inc. was also very supportive and donated two additional Macintosh computers for programming.

Four consultants from outside Ohio State worked for four years on the project. Evan Farber, Earlham College; Karen Drabenstott, University of Michigan; Judith Sandler, University of Delaware; and Brian Nielsen, Northwestern University visited OSU yearly (thanks to grant funding) to monitor progress and offer suggestions. On-campus volunteer consultants included Marjorie Cambre, College of Education; Philip Smith, College of Engineering; Wayne Talarzyk, College of Business; and Joseph Foley, Department of Communication. Each consultant was committed to the idea of assisting users and creating a unique, quality computer program.

Other Gateway committees composed of library personnel were formed to develop the content, the evaluations, and the technology. With Virginia Tiefel keeping the project focused on the needs of the users, John Salter directing the programming, and Nancy O'Hanlon, head of Reference in the Undergraduate Library, editing the pathways and screen displays, The Gateway slowly took shape.

CREATING THE NARRATIVE

Reference librarians in the Undergraduate and Main Libraries provided information on topics most often researched by The Gateway's target audience of undergraduates and library research novices. Ninety subject areas ranging from advertising to zoology were selected as the subjects most often explored by the targeted users. The librarians also suggested core reference materials, regardless of format, that would provide relevant information for these subject areas. The Gateway narrative was constructed to guide users from these subject areas to 90 relevant encyclopedias and 70 periodical indexes. Users could also follow pathways to 90 other titles covering biographical, statistical, or review materials. Each resource had a source card with call number, abstract, and location including access to the holding library's address, hours, floorplan, and campus map.

Additional sections were created for users not sure of what type of information tools were needed. In "Time Saving Research

Strategies," users could follow pathways to relevant materials based on their need in a fashion similar to a reference interview. Users without topics were guided to materials listing ideas for research papers. Those users with topics that were too broad were lead to encyclopedias and dictionaries to focus their search. Other screens helped users define their needs through questions about the currency of information needed, whether users wanted background or specific information, and whether they needed in-depth materials or quick facts. A critical thinking component also was accessible from every source card to help users evaluate the items found.

USER-FRIENDLY ELECTRONIC ACCESS

The Gateway provided direct links to OSU's online catalog, LCS (Library Control System), and 18 locally networked CD-ROMs. Electronic resources could be searched from the source cards by clicking on a special button marked "Search This Index." Programming invisible to the user then sends the request from the library computer over the local area network (LAN) to the servers and CD-ROM towers housing the information disks or to the university's main frame computer to the online catalog. The Gateway used MacTCP software to allow the Macintosh computers to send and read information from DOS databases over the LAN.

Front-ending these electronic resources was critical to the success of The Gateway. Users were faced with the variety of database search engines and screen displays from Wilson, SilverPlatter, UMI, and Grolier, as well as the difficult interface of LCS. For novice researchers to succeed, they needed to be able to search a variety of databases and the online catalog.

Fortuitously, MitemView software became available in 1989 allowing customization of DOS information onto one template. The Gateway student programmers "grabbed" a field such as the search line from a DOS CD-ROM and wrote a script to place it in a certain area on a HyperCard template screen. Buttons were added to replace commands such as "Search," "Print," and "Go to Next Record." Each database was customized to be similar in appearance, searchable with common commands, and identical in displaying records. Using The Gateway, users could be guided to *Applied Science and Technology Index,* (a database they might previously not have known existed), look at library floorplans and the campus map for libraries holding the print version, evaluate its relevance to their needs, then successfully search it using keywords. Even the cryptic LCS commands were simple to use. Instead of users having to remember to type "TLS/" to search the catalog by title and then "DSL/" to display holdings, they now merely click on a button marked "Title," enter the title wanted, and click on the "Search" button. With The Gateway, novice users could confidently locate and search an electronic database with no more skill than clicking on a button or typing in a few words.

TESTING AND EVALUATION

In January 1990 two prototype Macintosh IIcx computers were placed in Ohio State's Main Library for public testing a few hours a day. Gateway developers asked passersby to test the system, search LCS, and explore floorplans and then observed the users' reactions. Two additional computers were installed in June that year and left unattended to test the system's stability. In January 1991 the five remaining grant-purchased computers were installed in the Undergraduate Library.

Evaluation forms were placed by each computer to gather comments, problems, and suggestions. Evaluations showed that users rated their searches as "completely" or "mostly successful" 79 percent of the time, while 82 percent rated The Gateway "very" or "mostly" easy to use. Over 89 percent felt the screens were "very" or "mostly" clear, and 86 percent said they would use The Gateway again. Later evaluations were gathered electronically with users filling out questionnaires and comments on the Gateway screen itself. Over 8,000 evaluations were recorded in four years. These evaluation results have had a major impact on the project's revisions and further development. Noting the success of The Gateway with library users, the University Libraries purchased 50 additional Macintosh computers to replace all Telex terminals (which had been dedicated to LCS only). The libraries now had one-stop shopping computers.

IMPACT OF THE GATEWAY ON USERS AND STAFF

Some librarians in the University Libraries felt The Gateway might eventually replace them. Their fears were lessened through a series of open meetings where they were reassured that The Gateway was designed to free librarians from repetitive, basic questions about directions, core materials, the catalog, and University Libraries' procedures. Reference librarians could now be used as research experts to assist users with more challenging questions rather than repeatedly show them how to perform a title search on LCS or enter a subject search in *Readers' Guide Abstracts*.

University librarians soon began to create special sections to highlight their own collections beyond the core materials available in The Gateway. Expanded sections for "Business," "Communication," "Latin American Studies," and "Women's Studies" added hundreds of research titles, descriptions and locations for users desiring more specific information materials. The business librarian constructed the expanded business section to answer questions for users on weekends and evening hours when the business reference desk is not staffed. The Latin American studies section details encyclopedias, periodical indexes, and other resources found in a collection not widely recognized by novice users. Each of these expanded sections is updated by the subject librarian as new resources are made available.

Users have been very pleased with The Gateway over the last five years. Comments taken from student evaluation forms show their enthusiasm:

- This system is phenomenal! I wish I'd had it when doing my dissertation here a few years ago.
- Excellent! Best system I have used.
- A great source of information. Excellent for weeding through OSU library maze.
- Everything you need is at your fingertip.
- I'm in information heaven.

Faculty comments have been equally praiseworthy:

- What a wonderful resource for our students. Bodes well of OSU students who will be light years ahead with this.

- This will be very useful for my doctoral students who are learning to review the literature. Excellent possibilities.
- The Gateway to Information promises to be the great equalizer in terms of providing effective access to information for the many.
- I have seen the future...and it works!

In addition to meeting the needs of traditional library users, The Gateway has been successfully incorporated into two existing programs. The Freshman Library Instruction Program requires that all new students complete two hands-on library assignments during their required one-quarter orientation course. Each year over 10,000 new freshmen and transfer sophomores take this course designed to introduce them to all aspects of the university. In September 1993, The Gateway became the primary research tool used to complete these assignments. The change in the Undergraduate Library after using The Gateway for these assignments was remarkable. The Undergraduate Library staff recorded a 47 percent drop in questions asked by students doing the assignment. This drop included a 30 percent drop in instructional questions, a 62 percent drop in questions regarding the online catalog, and a 45 percent drop in directional questions.

The Young Scholars Program, OSU's summer college preparation program for minority 6th-12th grade Ohio students, also uses The Gateway for an introduction to the University Libraries. The Gateway successfully addresses the research skill level of each age for the 2,400 Young Scholars during the six summers when they study at OSU. The Gateway provides the younger students with an introductory library experience and helps the older students search the online catalog and databases to find basic resources on a designated topic. Evaluations of their experiences closely match those of the university students, with 80 percent finding it easy to use and 87 percent feeling their searches were successful.

FUTURE DEVELOPMENTS

The Gateway has been termed by Virginia Tiefel as a "Forever Project," one that will continue to expand and develop in response to users' needs and the growth of technology. Currently, a World-Wide Web version of The Gateway is under development. This version will be available on any DOS or Macintosh computer connected to the Internet running any of the new Lynx, Mosaic or Netscape software. The first prototype of this version will be tested on selected OSU audiences and library personnel during spring 1995. Full implementation is scheduled for fall 1995.

Using the Web, remote access to The Gateway pathways, maps and floorplans, library information, and access to electronic information databases will be possible from any Internet computer. The University Libraries can assist continuing education students who need access (and assistance) to research information when the reference desks are not staffed or the libraries are closed. The 7,500 fall quarter freshmen can choose to complete their two library assignments in campus computer labs or dorms to avoid the crowds in the Undergraduate Library. As with the Macintosh version, brochures, workshops, and staff intervention will not be required. Web software also expands The Gateway's capabilities by offering color display, sound, graphics, multimedia, and other exciting features.

Much of the current software on the Macintosh version is costly to purchase and install and requires ongoing maintenance. The Web version will eliminate MacTCP, MitemView, and HyperCard. Web version itself is a free software, further reducing the costs of the new version. Most of the new programming is done by the Office of User Education and its undergraduate students, all of whom previously had no computer programming experience. The Office of Library Automation will create the final programming scripts for the difficult connections.

The Internet resources can also be made available without complex programming. The Web Gateway will display pathways and direct access to items beyond the University Libraries' collection for the first time. The Web platform will lend itself to easy expansion to highlight new Internet resources suggested by users, especially faculty researchers. The Gateway will still provide assistance in creating a search strategy for research novices, but will soon simplify access to the Internet resources for more experienced graduate students and faculty users.

CONCLUSION

The Gateway to Information has successfully addressed the needs of novice and experienced users for five years in the Ohio State University Libraries. The project has remained true to the initial goals to assist users focus their research topic, then help them identify, locate, and evaluate relevant materials regardless of format. Most importantly, The Gateway has never required training outside of the program itself, such as workshops, manuals, or staff intervention, for users to achieve success with even their first-time searches. During the ongoing cutbacks in budget and reassignment of personnel experienced in the University Libraries, The Gateway continues to offer quality research assistance and electronic access throughout the University Libraries.

Providing instruction to core research skills is vital to making library patrons independent information users. Once the concepts of a search strategy are understood and the information-seeking skills mastered, the "common cold" of novice library researcher will be controlled and addressing the "epidemic" of the Internet can be possible.

USE OF MACROMEDIA DIRECTOR™ AND QUICKTIME™ FOR MULTIMEDIA CLASSROOM PRESENTATIONS

Paul T. Adalian, Jr.

INTRODUCTION

I began my work in multimedia development using simple Hypercard stacks for classroom presentations in a biological literature class. I used a liquid crystal display (LCD), overhead projector, and a Macintosh SE running Hypercard™ as a black board. Since I am a visual learner, it was easy for me to plan and organize the stacks that would provide graphic presentations for the students. I designed stacks to demonstrate the proper way to cite using the Council of Biological Editors style manual and how it can retrieve articles by highlighting indexed keywords in the title and subject fields of a typical bibliographic citation. I even created a jeopardy game to review the previous week's works and to reinforce student learning and understanding.

As the technology progressed, I moved from using Hypercard™ to using Macromedia Director,™ a true multimedia program.

Macromedia Director™ provided color, enhanced motion and movement, animation, scanned images, and integration of QuickTime™ movies. Using Macromedia Director™ has proven to be more than a presentation "slide" software program. With the assistance of a library colleague, I developed three multimedia classroom projects that are equal to any commercially available multimedia programs.

These programs provide a general overview to Lexis-Nexis, MEDLINE information through the Lexis-Nexis search engine, and BIOSIS through DIALOG.

THE TYPICAL CLASSROOM PRESENTATION

Classroom multimedia presentations do not simply stand by themselves. For effective learning to occur, it is necessary to provide sound handouts that parallel the presentation, follow-up online exercises that reinforce key concepts, and worksheets that can be used to assist students when using the online databases during or after the class presentation. Bibliographic Instruction (BI) librarians have been involved in developing these aids for years.

The typical classroom presentation starts with students receiving various handouts prior to being given a brief overview of the session. After this introduction, the students know what to anticipate and are prepared for the following:

a. Receiving the various handouts in the order in which they will be used.
b. Viewing a multimedia program projected on the screen in front of the class.
c. Asking questions at any time throughout the program.
d. Having an opportunity for hands-on experiences within the class period.
e. Completing an assignment due at next week's class (only if this is for a credit-bearing class).
f. Describing how they can access the database after the class session has concluded.

The handouts usually include the following:

Command Sheet	A list of commands for the system. The presentation is arranged in the same order as the commands are displayed on the handout.
Log on/Log off Handout	Procedures for getting on the system through our library Gopher. These are simple and easy to follow screen-by-screen displays. The presentation also includes the same screens which demonstrate log on and log off techniques. Students log on in the classroom the same way they will log on remotely or from within the library.
In-Class Assignment	The assignment is keyed to the same search strategy as displayed in class. The students are asked to find a number of elements within the citations and to limit the search by various methods. This way they will experience how to navigate through the system and use advanced features. If an individual or group of students completes the in-class assignment, they are then free to conduct their own searches. I have found that students conducting their own searches do not use many of the advanced features of the system. For this reason a specific in-class assignment is given.
Worksheet	The worksheet is a helpful guide to searching once class is over, and students are required to use the system on their own.
Homework	Students have an opportunity to conduct their own searches in conjunction with a thesaurus, such as MESH or the *Biological Research Guide of BIOSIS.* Students can use these systems remotely. They use the log on and log off handouts, plus they have the experience of logging on in class.

The handouts are significant. If the handouts can parallel the presentation and the in-class experiences, they will act to not only serve as a guide to proper search and protocols, but they will reinforce the presentations every time a student uses them to search.

The large screen presentation is viewed by all of the students. As I click through the multimedia screens, the program is so visual that I say much less than if I were giving a lecture utilizing a black board along with handouts (or even if I were online, displaying searches in front of the class).

After the large screen presentation and during the next class session, students are asked about their searches and if they have any questions. Students turn in the actual printouts of relevant full records and circle words and codes on the full records that match the search statement. This is an excellent way for students to reinforce their knowledge of fields and how words and codes can retrieve specific records.

LEXIS-NEXIS (GENERAL PRESENTATION)

The basic introductory section to Lexis-Nexis describes the content of the database. The program is divided into the Nexis (news, etc.), Lexis (legal sources), and Medis (medical) component. Within each of these three sections, specific source categories are listed. These include such categories as magazines, newspapers, and annual reports and are displayed along with scanned images of the sources. Thus, students see the word Magazines along with a cover of a magazine. This pattern is used to describe numerous categories of information within each of the three components.

An outline of the structure of the database is displayed by using "Libraries," "Group Files," "Files," and "Documents." Examples of each are presented. Students can clearly see, for example, the relationship between the newspaper group file and individual newspaper files.

Traditional Searching vs. Full-Text Searching is described next. Book, article, and newspaper citations are displayed, and students easily see how traditional searches require that the citations be searched on our OPAC to determine if California Polytechnic State University holds the source before finding it. A description of a full-text database is given along with a list of many of the full-text documents available on Lexis-Nexis, such as articles, annual reports, court cases, laws, etc.

Next, students see the library menu. Each group of libraries can be highlighted yellow with a simple click. Students can get a good feel for the libraries on the library menu. I go over each set of libraries and describe them. The yellow highlight catches a student's eye.

Then we simulate selecting the "NEWS" library and go to the "NEWS" group file menu. Each group file is highlighted yellow so students can gain a good understanding of the relationships between "CURNWS" and "MAJPAP", and how to enter an individual file.

Print documentation is also presented. Both the Library Alphabetical and Contents directory and the Product Guide are displayed. Covers have been scanned along with sample pages using yellow highlights to focus on relevant sections.

Free-text searching is described next. A short newspaper article is displayed with several words highlighted yellow within the text. The program explains that a search statement using the words highlighted will retrieve this article along with any other articles using the same words.

The visual aspect of the program really hits home, and the students see the power and danger of free-text searching in the data base. The dangers are displayed as too many hits (the Lexis-Nexis phrase, "your search has been interrupted because it will probably retrieve over 1,000 records,") and false drops.

To demonstrate a false drop, a search statement is displayed (Chrysler and Third Quarter) along with a corresponding article. The appropriate words are highlighted in the article to demonstrate the false drop (Ford's third quarter earnings rather than Chrysler's).

From this point on, the search commands are presented to avoid false drops and seeing the phrase, "Your search will probably retrieve over 1,000 hits."

To assist in the process, I created an original command sheet. It is a one-sheet, two-sided handout with searching commands on the front of the page and online commands for browsing, changing files and libraries, and modifying on the back. The program progresses in the same order as the command sheet. The command sheet has sufficient room for the student to take notes, if needed.

Lexis-Nexis connectors are displayed first in the multimedia program. A single column article from a newspaper is displayed on the right side of the screen. The left side of the screen displays the various connectors, one at a time, used in a brief search statement. The connectors (and, or, and not, w/n, w/s, w/p, etc.) are a different color from the words in the search statements. The specific words used in the search statement are highlighted on the article. Highlighting terms is an excellent way to teach the concepts of Boolean logic and proximity operators used by Lexis-Nexis, such as the w/n (term used within so many words of another term), w/s (words used within the same sentence), and w/p (words used within the same paragraph). When w/s is demonstrated, the sentence in the article is highlighted yellow with the words in the search statement a different color from the rest of the text. The w/p command is demonstrated the same way. Students quickly learn the significance of proximity operators.

Truncation shows words using the "!" and the words that be will retrieved (for example, "bank!" will retrieve banks, banking, bankers, bankruptcy, etc.). Different color letters used after the stem bank help students understand the truncation process.

Date limiters are displayed and explained on the screen as well.

Segments are taught next using the same article. Hlead, person, and company segment examples are displayed. After highlighting hlead segments and comparing them with search statements, students quickly learn the power of segment searching to narrow the focus of the article.

After segments, the first side of the command sheet has been completely reviewed. We now work on a typical search statement. A question for the search is displayed, and then a search statement is created using all aspects of the commands (connectors, truncation, date limiter, and segments). The search statement is constructed, section by section or word by word, so that the students can see it being developed. Once completed, the search statement is then compared to an actual article retrieved. Each part of the search statement is highlighted in the article. This provides students with a visual representation of how truncation, proximity operators, and segments work together in a single search statement. This reinforces these searching commands displayed earlier.

The next part of the program is a simulated search in which screen dumps are placed in the program. Log on procedures are displayed, and several searches are prepared to use all the command features located on the back of the command sheet. These include displays, browsing through displays, changing (new search, changing files or libraries), and modifying a search. Since the screen dumps do not take up the entire screen, the commands can be displayed clearly . Thus, students can see the command codes and the screen displays at the same time. Yellow highlighting is used in screen displays throughout the simulated search to point out a number of variables.

The multimedia program usually takes about twenty minutes. Once completed, I actually get online, so that the students see an actual log on process and a real search.

After the short online demonstration, students get online to practice their skills. They go through the same log on process as demonstrated in front of the class through our Gopher. The Lexis-Nexis temporary classroom account is used within the classroom so all students have an opportunity to use the system.

Students have access to Lexis-Nexis through two workstations in the Reference Department, and two passwords available remotely through the library's Gopher. Students using the remote password are verified as bona fide students with a current student identification card. Passwords are changed periodically.

MEDLINE (LEXIS-NEXIS SEARCH ENGINE)

The MEDLINE program is similar to the general Lexis-Nexis presentation. Description and contents of the database are displayed. In addition, a scanned-in photograph of the National Library of Medicine and scanned covers of major medical journals provide a colorful introduction to MEDLINE.

Covers of *Index Medicus* are displayed alongside a computer to show the print and online version of the same source.

Commands, logging onto the system, simulated searches, and yellow highlighting are all included in this instructional module.

The major emphasis of the MEDLINE program focuses on the significance and use of Medical Subject Headings (MESH).

A medical research topic is placed in the form of a question and is displayed near the top of the screen. The cover of MESH is displayed on the far right. The significant words within the question to be searched are circled in red. MESH pages are displayed to find corresponding or similar words to construct an effective search statement. When a relevant heading is found, it is highlighted, and the word or phrase is literally pulled off the page and placed on another part of the screen forming a list of appropriate search terms.

When all the headings have been identified and are displayed, they are moved from the list to create a search statement. The visuals of this process have been very successful. Students learn how to focus in on the major concepts and words in a search question. They next learn how to use MESH to find the proper headings. And finally, they learn how to construct the words and phrases found in MESH into a search statement.

A simulated search follows this process. The same search is used and students see the results of the search. At this point they are shown the various commands for displaying, browsing through displays and modifying a search. Yellow highlighting is used extensively. Several free-text searches are also demonstrated.

When the program is completed, students get hands-on experience conducting the same search. This exercise provides a number of opportunities to experience commands, displays, and to navigate and to start a new search.

BIOSIS

The BIOSIS on DIALOG program is similar to the MEDLINE program. There is a basic introductory section on the contents of the database, and the program displays the size and comprehensiveness of the database. There is also a simulated search through the use of screen dumps and relevant sections which are highlighted yellow.

The focus of the BIOSIS program is on using the *BIOSIS Research Guide*. Similar to the MEDLINE program, a research topic is placed in the form of a question at the top of the screen. The significant words are circled in red.

By using the Master Index in the *BIOSIS Research Guide*, students are led through finding the proper terms, concept codes, biosystematic codes, and super taxonomic groups.

Throughout this process, students see the search question, the cover of BIOSIS search guide, pages of the search guide that correspond to the keywords circled in the question, and the creation of a list of words and codes that will be used to construct a search statement. Finally, students see how to take the list of words and codes and place them into a search statement.

The same search is used for the lab exercise. Students are asked to perform various functions and commands so that they may gain broad experiences in using BIOSIS through DIALOG. Students using this program have been successful in creating search statements, conducting searches, and retrieving a reasonable number of hits without using date or language limiters in a massive database.

Software and Hardware

Software used to develop these projects includes Macromedia Director,™ Adobe Photoshop,™ Adobe Illustrator,™ Adobe Premier,™ and Infini-d.™ A Macintosh Centris 650 with an EndView large screen projector is used within the classroom.

The Classroom

The classroom is a long narrow room. It contains desks in the front part of the room and 16 dumb vt100 Wyse 60 terminals connected to our library Gopher in the back of the room. Four terminals are clustered on each of four tables. This arrangement has worked well for collaborative learning assignments and projects. It also provides the students with some change. Once a presentation is over, they leave their desk and head back to the terminals. This arrangement also prevents students from using the keyboards during a presentation and forces them to pay attention during the program before beginning their actual hands-on experiences.

GRACE UNDER PRESSURE:
COPING WITH MULTIPLE DATABASE PERSONALITIES

Linda Friend and Bonnie Osif

The information world in which we all work has increased in complexity. There are more resources available in multiple interfaces and languages. Librarians and staff voice concerns about the vast number of databases to learn and the rapidity of additions available locally, as well as the changes that occur to existing resources. If this proliferation of resources and constant enhancement is a challenge to the library staff, it is even more intimidating for the library user. This presents a second challenge to librarians in the new information environment: how do we not only learn systems ourselves but teach them to staff and students so they can utilize the new resources to the fullest? The University Libraries at The Pennsylvania State University have been facing these challenges for years. However, the rate of growth in the 1990s is necessitating innovative action to assist staff in coping with the rapid changes. For this paper, the resources discussed will be limited to those accessible through the online catalog.

THE PENNSYLVANIA STATE UNIVERSITY LIBRARIES

Penn State is an institution of approximately 70,000 students and 5,000 faculty. About 39,000 of the students attend the main campus at University Park. Some freshman and sophomores are at University Park, as well as most upper class students and graduate students. The remaining 31,000 students attend one of the additional 21 campuses distributed throughout Pennsylvania. Size of the campuses varies, and most have one or two librarians. Many are a substantial distance from University Park, which presents travel difficulties and the resultant training difficulties.

The University Libraries at University Park have a main library which houses the general collection, life sciences, business, humanities, social sciences, arts, and documents. Education, physical sciences, mathematics, architecture, engineering, and earth and mineral sciences are located in the buildings housing the appropriate discipline. Each branch library provides the same services as the main library, and the separation and staffing levels need to be considered in the training picture.

DATABASE/SYSTEM FEATURES AND QUIRKS

Motivated users will tolerate a certain level of frustration in order to identify the resources or information they want, but multiple systems and unfriendly-appearing system messages make the instructional job an even bigger challenge. Some examples from Penn State:

- The LIAS system has a generic banner screen when a user logs in. Unless someone was introduced to the concept or browsed online help, until very recently, there was no transparent way for a user to know that "select" is the command that brings up the full menu of choices and routes a user to databases, Gopher and World Wide Web connections, or electronic journals.
- Users sometimes have access to more than one version of a database. At Penn State, they have a choice of two means of reaching ERIC or COMPENDEX. Both are available in

the library as CD-ROMs (using SilverPlatter or DIALOG software). It is also possible to reach the same databases via any LIAS terminal in the library or through a remote connection. An additional potential confusion for consumers of engineering information is that while EI Page 1 (EIP)is a version of COMPENDEX available through the online catalog, it is actually a Z39.50 connection to the Research Libraries Group, (RLG) so *most* but not *all* of the familiar LIAS commands are functional.

THE CATALOG INTERFACES

Major changes have occurred to the online catalog in the last several years that need to be considered in educational efforts. Penn State's online catalog is LIAS (Library Information Access System), a system developed at Penn State. Relatively recent enhancements have included both keyword and Boolean searching. In addition to the search enhancements, access to databases has been provided, creating a true information access system for its users.

The databases use a variety of interface types, although the goal is to keep interfaces to a minimum. Decisions on the best platform for each database necessitated the number of interfaces. For example, ERIC and Table of Contents (TOC) both use the same interface as the online catalog. Both are tape loaded on the mainframe and have most, but not all, of the same search capabilities as the catalog. This difference also presents an educational challenge since students often believe that a system that looks like the catalog must behave exactly like the catalog, and they can be confused when it does not.

A second interface that is very heavily used is the UnCover connection. Before TOC was made available in 1994, UnCover was the only free table of contents service available online and widely used. Many still use it because of familiarity or the greater number of titles indexed. The third major database interface is that of CD-Plus, used for MEDLINE and PsycLIT. Both novice and expert modes are available, adding to the challenge for users.

A major interface initiative has been with the Z39.50 protocol. In cooperation with RLG, Penn State has been at the forefront of work with this protocol in libraries. The available

Z39.50 databases include Anthropological Abstracts, Avery, EIP, ABI/Inform, Newspaper Abstracts, Periodical Abstracts, PAIS, and RLIN.

The basis of Z39.50 is to allow two different computer search engines to communicate with each other so that a user of one system does not need to know the search commands of another computer system to search and retrieve results (see Figure 1). The commands at one computer location are translated to a common language, transmitted via the Internet to the remote computer, retranslated and the database is searched. Results are than sent back to the user. In many ways the search is completely transparent; the patron does not realize translations are occurring, and the results are arriving from a remote computer that "speaks another language." The exceptions concern those commands available on the user's system that are not translatable. For example, LIAS searches the author's last name, then first name. Z39.50 databases available via the RLG platform search first initial, then last name. This is reduced to a minor problem once this is known but can be confusing to patrons at first. To further complicate the issue, Z39.50 is an evolving standard. Improvements are made with the resulting need to update the user. For example, when EIP (the first Z39.50 database) was brought up, there was no functional limit command. Shortly thereafter, limit by date and language became available and information needed to be conveyed to staff and the public.

Penn State has added a significant number of enhancements and databases to the catalog within recent years. While these have provided the library staff and patron with a number of valuable resources, it has also required the user to become "multi-lingual," learning at least one or two search languages beyond the standard LIAS that they had used for years.

DATABASE IMPLEMENTATION PROCESS

The educational and training process for new databases begins as soon as a database is chosen for investigation. An outline of our planning effort may assist others who are challenged by the multiple interface environment. Decision points include selection of a database, selection of the database interface, and the implementation process.

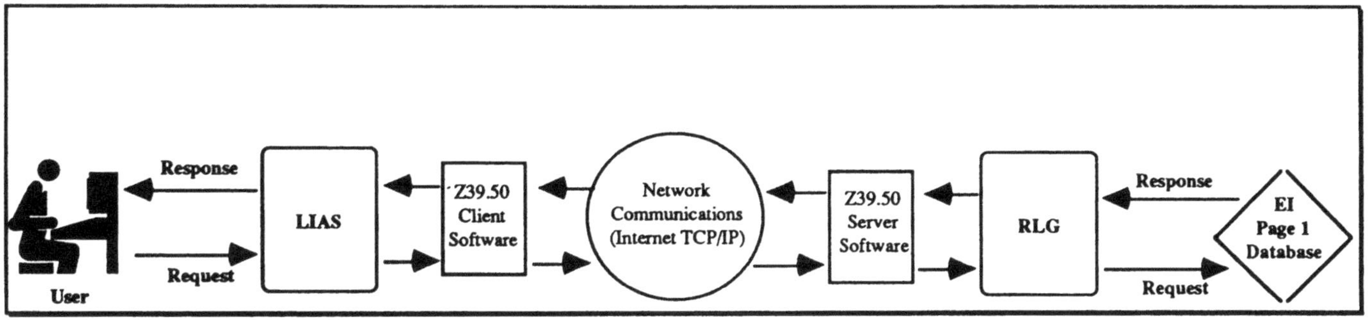

Figure 1. Penn State Access to EI Page 1 Via Z39.50

Choice of database is often the first decision that must be made. A library beginning to consider local mounting will most likely take its cues from the most popular indexes in print or CD-ROM. Typically these "heavy-use" files are the ones that will be used most effectively in a networked environment as well. With the size of our institution and the diversity of the student population and faculty needs, the initial choices of databases have been designed to link users with some of the larger, most popular files (Periodical Abstracts, Newspaper Abstracts, MEDLINE, ERIC, AGRICOLA, etc.). More specialized needs will gradually be met as financial and staff resources permit.

Once the product is chosen, an interface must be determined. Electronic products are increasingly available from producers in more than one form, including local mounting, CD-ROM, and via modem or Internet TCP/IP connections. The variety of potential access methods needs to be investigated to provide the best match for the institution. As already mentioned, at Penn State we have been fortunate to be in the vanguard of using the Z39.50 common user interface protocol to connect to other systems. We were also the recipient of a grant which allowed the purchase of a Unix mainframe to run CD Plus software for MEDLINE and other related products needing a higher level of searching sophistication. Our local programming staff has developed proficiency in taking database tapes, mapping them to MARC format, and making them available using local search commands. In addition, there is a developing local area network that is providing multi-workstation access to more than a dozen CD-ROM titles. Other factors such as cost come into play at this interface decision point, including contract negotiation for subscription costs and often the permitted number of simultaneous users, hardware concerns, and networking capabilities.

We have found that the most efficient way to provide databases via the LIAS system is to appoint a team of three to four individuals with subject expertise to see the process through from the beginning to the public release and beyond. Each team is responsible for:

- Partnering with Library Computing Services to design a workable timetable.

- Taking an active role in testing and debugging.
- Being responsible for staff training in the new database, which may include "train the trainer," cascade training, simple orientations, detailed hands-on seminars, etc.
- Providing text for all appropriate documentation for both staff and users. This has been simplified by adopting a template approach, where each handout is arranged similarly and includes critical information about the database, searching techniques, and what to do to find desired items once they are located in the database.
- Continuing "ownership" and responsibility for the database, including documenting changes and training new staff.

Unlike some library committees, people are enthusiastic about being appointed to these teams since a genuine product is the result achieved over a reasonably brief (but usually intense) time period. We have also realized our goal to have as many people as possible develop a respect for the complexity of the process and achieve a greater understanding in general about database structure and design.

STAFF TRAINING AT PENN STATE

In order to combat burnout and frustration, the Penn State Libraries have recognized system-wide, continuing staff training to be an important aspect of its strategic plan. Some of the specific programs already in place are outlined below.

Automation Skills Training

A 10-hour course for all new employees, this program is designed to provide all staff and faculty with a common grounding in automation and to insure that they are prepared with the necessary building blocks to make practical use of information technology. Each person completes a self-assessment since initial skills vary; a modular design allows staff to attend only those sessions that they need. Topics include:

- introduction to the PC, including the internal anatomy of a computer;
- basic DOS;
- introduction to PC applications (spreadsheet, word processing, data management, Windows);
- using the libraries and Penn State networks;
- overview of Internet resources;
- basics of the LIAS system for cataloging, collection development, reference uses; and
- accessing remote services (RLIN, DIALOG, Gopher, World-Wide Web, other online catalogs).

Database Training

Each new database has its own training program, as mentioned earlier. Updates are offered at regular intervals.

Open Labs

At least once a week, experts are available in a library lab on a drop-in basis to answer all kinds of specific questions about word processing, constructing a homepage, and setting up a spreadsheet.

Road Shows

Visits by staff trainers are made on a regular basis to all the Penn State locations to train staff at these outlying campuses, to foster communication, and to lessen the physical distance. Campus teaching faculty and computing support people also attend these sessions on occasion. Library staff from the main campus who assist in this training return with a better idea of the challenges of the campus situations, where hardware and staff are usually at a premium.

TRAINING PUBLIC USERS

Our support for the public user of LIAS follows a similar pattern of varied instructional methods. The University Libraries continue to provide traditional bibliographic instruction. This will vary somewhat by the unit and the librarian, since there is a great deal of autonomy in the different subject units. Some subject specialists advertise the service widely, while others depend more on teaching faculty initiative. In many cases course related bibliographic instruction will be done in properly equipped classrooms in the main library. When correct wiring and equipment is available, the sessions will be done in a university instructional classroom. A second type of successful instruction has a somewhat different target group. Several years ago several librarians, particularly in the sciences, began to notice students coming to the libraries with similar questions. These questions followed a pattern of mentioning specific books or databases with a factual error of use or purpose. A little investigating revealed partially correct information being presented by teaching assistants in a particular program.

To try to solve this problem and to better acquaint the teaching assistants with the library, librarians campaigned to meet with the teaching assistants during their pre-semester group meetings or during their credit teaching assistant seminar. The first groups targeted were the English and engineering teaching assistants. Presentations tend to be a survey of the catalog and the databases that would be most useful to the particular group. Help sheets are available, and the sessions encourage questions. In general, this has been very successful. Misconceptions have been corrected, new features introduced, and the sessions have provided excellent feedback. Requests for bibliographic instruction in classes taught by these teaching assistants have increased. An additional benefit has been the increased visibility of the librarians to the teaching assistants and continued contact if problems or confusion arise.

In addition to the traditional classroom instruction, the libraries have developed a series of topical workshops. These are coordinated through public services but rely on the expertise of subject specialists, the Computer-Based Resources and Services Team (CBRST) and the Public Information and Relations department. These workshops are publicized in a variety of ways, including newspapers, flyers, direct mailings, and electronic announcements. Open to faculty, staff, students, and the community, these workshops are held in the libraries' instructional computer lab. Hands-on experience can be provided to a dozen participants. LIAS and its search language is the foundation workshop and recommended for most users. Covered are basic search strategy, keyword, Boolean, limiting, and some of the lesser known but useful commands.

Following the LIAS workshop, or if the individual is an experienced LIAS searcher, interested participants can choose from a variety of subject workshops ranging from astronomy to women's studies. Some subjects are obvious workshops since they cover LIAS databases, others less so. For example, astronomy has no specific database, but participants can consult UnCover, TOC, fee-based resources, and Internet sources. An example of a LIAS subject database is EIP. Released to the public in February 1993, there has been enough interest to offer several workshops each semester. While the seminar focuses on EIP, it also provides an opportunity to demonstrate COMPENDEX on CD-ROM using DIALOG search language and introduce participants to some Internet resources in engineering.

The Internet is not relegated to a footnote in the subject workshops. The University Libraries, with the Center for Academic Computing (CAC), has developed a popular workshop, InterNexus, which is devoted to the structure, resources, and navigation of the Internet. This is offered in the demonstration-lecture format due to class size. It is team taught by librarians and members of CAC.

Library staff also provide "one-on-one" support and information, but this is an area of largely untapped potential at this point because to do it well requires more staff than we currently have to spare. Individual users, especially remote users of systems, need specific answers, and they do not want to wait to have their questions answered. This is one area where additional personnel are needed, as well as involvement by more public services staff in providing prompt responses to phone and e-mail questions. Current methods of assisting remote users include:

- An online mailbox where users of the LIAS catalog and databases can ask specific questions.
- A telephone help line to connect a user with someone in the Computer-Based Resources and Services Team or Library Computing Services who can help or refer,
- Written guides designed to assist remote users, and
- Office visits—we make "house calls" to faculty offices, for example, if a problem can't be handled from a distance.

SUGGESTIONS FOR SUCCESSFUL TRAINING PROGRAMS IN AUTOMATED SYSTEMS

These are mostly common sense, tried, and true principles and tips.

People

- Get administrative support for the project. It is crucial to have the library's administration see training as a positive and critical activity for the success of the organization. For example, we chose managers as the test group for Automation Skills Training since they were able to experience the benefits firsthand and see the value of the entire program.
- Show that common elements exist among databases/ systems. Attempt to relate the current subject to something users may already be familiar with (e.g., compare World-Wide Web access to Gopher).
- Recognize potential stress factors for users. Every active learning experience has some level of stress associated with it, and automation topics are among the most highly charged.
- Don't assume that you already know what people need—ask them. Your training program will benefit by asking people for advice in the planning stages and then continuing to have participants evaluate the program.
- Involve as many people as possible. Being responsible for training others is the strongest incentive to learning a system, database, software package, or technique yourself.

Process

- Have an overall plan in place. The program will be much more efficient if there is some thoughtful advance planning.
- Assign priorities when you can't do everything. Try not to be too ambitious when beginning a new program but, instead, build on successes.
- Decide on the types of sessions that are needed and provide lesson plans in order to maximize the time available.
- Decide on training method(s). Will a particular concept be best presented in a lecture, hands-on lab, online tutorial, small groups, some combination?

- Provide printed or online tutorial information for use after the session. Having something concrete to refer to is important; for example, sometimes it is false economy not to buy sufficient software manuals for users.
- Expect to be in constant-revision mode, since the environment changes rapidly and trainers will also be learning from attendees about key areas to cover.
- Plan follow-up methods. Make sure session attendees know they have a contact person for later, since no one will remember everything presented, especially if the new skills aren't used immediately. Post-session exercises are highly desirable since they require people to test their recently acquired knowledge and give trainers a way to evaluate how well the training is meeting its objectives.
- Identify post-session contact people who can answer the day-to-day questions about software, hardware, and systems.

Practicality

- Provide the optimum training environment. Schedule for attendee convenience, choose an appropriate location, and attempt to have more than one trainer available if group sessions are hands-on (every attendee will find a different way to get lost in the Internet).
- Customize sessions whenever possible for maximum relevance. Try to use subject examples that students can relate to actively; don't use engineering topics with rare books staff or vice versa, or people are more likely to tune out and learn less. On a related note, be sensitive to diversity in the audience and recognize that people have different ways of processing and retaining information.

ACCOMMODATE DIVERSE STYLES

It is a given that there are different learning styles. What works well for one person or group may not work at all for another. Therefore, the libraries have made a concerted effort to address these differences. One interesting method to describe learning styles is in the research of David Kolb.[1] He views learning as an activity that is influenced by perception and process and represents these as a continuum. This continuum is determined by perceptual gradations of concrete or abstract and experimental or reflective preferences. The four different quadrants on the circle tend to prefer different learning experiences. These include individualized experimentation, guided experimentation, lecture and demonstration, and exercises.

From the brief description above it is evident that one instructional method does not fit all users. For this reason a combination of workshops, classroom instruction, online help, help sheets, suggested exercises, and individualized help at the terminals is needed to meet the needs of users with different learning styles and the different specific situations that can arise.

Some useful generalities were found that help make most of these sessions more beneficial. First, the instructor should promote a positive atmosphere. Instructors should be enthusiastic so the message conveyed during the session is positive. When EIP was a new system with very limited capabilities, it could have been presented as a crippled system. Instead, it was honestly presented for the strengths it had. The limitations were explained with some information on the changes that were to come, and the benefits were emphasized.

Second, it is important to provide information in writing so it can provide reinforcement after the session is over. Notetaking is kept to a minimum since all of the essentials are already on paper, allowing more time for listening, hands-on activities, and questions.

The delivery of material will also affect the success of the presentation. It is desirable to change pace regularly, rather than to give one example after another. Break up the presentation with a pertinent anecdote, ask for questions, use humor or cartoons, and take relevant tangents. For example, during the EIP workshops, since so many engineering faculty or students know about *Star Trek,* a comparison between Z39.50 and *Trek's* universal translator, which allows different races to communicate effortlessly, is usually successful.

All of the above are constrained, at least to some extent, by the location, environment, system problems, and the individuals involved. However, planning can circumvent some of these problems. Back-up transparencies can allow a session to continue even if the system goes down or there is an equipment failure. Exercise sheets can partially substitute for hands-on time if a lab is not available. The same planning and flexibility used in bibliographic instruction still apply in the increasingly electronic environment.

CONCLUSION

By providing timely, up-to-date instructional materials, staff and user training and support, and an atmosphere where staff automation expertise is highly regarded and rewarded, it is possible to minimize frustration and meet the challenges of multiple interfaces successfully.

NOTE

1. David Kolb, *Learning Style Inventory* (Boston: McBer and Company, 1976).

ABOUT THE AUTHORS

Paul T. Adalian Jr. is Head of the Reference Department at California Polytechnic State University Kennedy Library, San Luis Obispo, California.

Lori Arp is Head of Central Reference and Media Libraries at the University of Colorado—Boulder Libraries and is a past chair of the ACRL Bibliographic Instruction Section. She is author of several articles on learning theory, critical thinking, management of instruction programs, and information literacy.

Barry Brown is the Science Librarian and Access Services Coordinator at the University of Montana Mansfield Library, Missoula, Montana. He is an Associate Professor and has been at the Mansfield Library since 1990. In addition to Internet classes, he also team teaches a biological literature credit course with a biology department faculty member.

Gale Burrow is Coordinator of Library Instruction for the Libraries of The Claremont Colleges, Claremont, California.

Jeris Cassel is Electronic Services Coordinator and Reference Librarian at Kilmer Area Library, Rutgers University, New Brunswick, New Jersey. She is co-author of *Critical Thinking: An Annotated Bibliography* (Metuchen, NJ: Scarecrow Press, 1992).

John Culshaw is Electronic Reference Specialist in the Central Reference Department of the University of Colorado—Boulder Libraries.

Linda Friend is the Electronic Resources Specialist for The Pennsylvania State University Libraries, University Park, Pennsylvania. Her research interests include the Z39.50 protocol, client-server technology, and user instruction. Currently, she and a colleague are developing a database of the literature of eating disorders.

Craig Gibson is Associate Director for Information Services at George Mason University Libraries, Fairfax, Virginia. He was formerly head of library user education at Washington State University Libraries, where he managed the library instruction programs, coordinated the libraries' Internet classes, and developed a credit course in research skills for Washington State's distance education program. He has written articles on critical thinking and given numerous presentations on critical thinking and the Internet.

Bonnie Gratch, Head of Information Services at St. Mary's College, Moraga, California, has been active in bibliographic instruction and reference services as a librarian and manager for 17 years in academic libraries in New York, Ohio, and now California. Active in ACRL's IS and EBSS sections, she has also written articles and co-edited an ACRL-EBSS committee publication, *Teaching Information Retrieval and Evaluation Skills to Education Students and Practitioners: A Casebook of Applications* (American Library Association, 1995).

Keith Gresham is Reference Librarian and Undergraduate Collection Bibliographer at the University of Colorado—Boulder Libraries.

Randall Hensley is the Head of the Reference Center at the University of Hawaii at Manoa. He received his M.L.S. from the University of California—Berkeley, a M.A. in sociology from California State University—Chico, and a training management certificate from the University of Washington. He is past secretary of the ACRL Instruction Section, past president of the Washington Library Association, has taught user education courses for the University of Washington School of Library and Information Science, and frequently does continuing education workshops on learning styles and communication in the workplace.

Todd S. Hutton is Vice President for Academic Administration at Willamette University, Salem, Oregon.

Hélène Lafrance has been working with adult students for 10 years—first as a French instructor, then as the off-campus librarian at Saint Mary's College. Currently in charge of the library instruction programs, she has developed Internet workshops for students and faculty and is also teaching an introductory course on the Internet at Diablo Valley College. She is a member of the Modern Language Department at Saint Mary's and has recently designed an advanced conversation class using French resources on the Internet.

Naomi Lederer is an Associate Instruction Librarian at Arizona State University, Tempe, Arizona. She has taught numerous instructional sessions at three university libraries, 11 semesters of ASU's "Use of Research Libraries" course including the televised version, is liaison to the First- Year Composition Program, and is coordinator and editor of library publications.

Thomas W. Leonhardt is Director of Library Technical Services and Head of the Collection Department at Bizzell Memorial Library, University of Oklahoma, Norman, Oklahoma.

Mary Ellen Litzinger is an Associate Librarian at the Pennsylvania State University Libraries. She received a M.S.L.S. from the University of North Carolina, a Ph.D. in instructional systems and a certificate in workplace learning, both from Pennsylvania State University. She is a past chair of the ACRL Instruction Section and frequently lectures and writes on user education topics.

John Meade is Consultant in the Information Technology Division at Washington State University. He was the developer of WSU's campus-wide information system (WSUInfo), has been working in Internet training, and currently works with faculty as part of the Learning Systems Group in Information Technology.

Bonnie Osif is the Assistant Engineering/Transportation Librarian for The Pennsylvania State University Libraries. Her research interests include science/technology literacy and instruction in the electronic environment.

Vicky Pengelly has worked in Computing and Information Services at the University of Montana for 11 years. She has a B.A. in anthropology and sociology from Carleton College, Northfield, Minnesota. Besides training, some of her other duties in CIS include writing documentation, editing the newsletter, consulting, and overseeing the Help Desk.

Loretta Rielly is Sponsor of the Information Services Instruction and Training and Reference and Research Consulting Teams at Oregon State University, Corvallis, Oregon.

Billie Joy Reinhart is Coordinator for Information Literacy and Science/Engineering Librarian at Cleveland State University, Cleveland, Ohio. She has given presentations on information literacy, evaluation of information, use of electronic resources, and the Internet at local, regional, and national conferences.

Fred Roecker is the User Education Librarian at Ohio State University, Columbus, Ohio. He directs the evaluation and screen designs of The Gateway to Information.

Cynthia Snyder is Coordinator of References Services for the Libraries of The Claremont Colleges.

Gary B. Thompson is Head of Information Services at Cleveland State University. He has over 20 years of experience providing library instruction and reference assistance to students enrolled in universities and colleges in New York and Ohio.

Lizabeth A. Wilson is the Associate Director of Libraries for Public Services at the University of Washington, Seattle, Washington.

BethAnn Zambella is the Reference Librarian at Lamont Library, Harvard University, Cambridge, Massachusetts. Previously, she was bibliographic instruction coordinator and reference librarian at Kilmer Area Library, Rutgers University.

INDEX

academic libraries,
and alliances, 12, 39, 137, 198, 222, 225
changing users, 3, 15, 19, 29, 77, 106, 109, 158, 161, 172, 196
as a collaboratory, 13
and competition, 11
as gathering place, 4, 13, 129
invisible users, 3
as a mental oasis, 127, 128
and social frameworks, 5
and user-centeredness, 9, 10, 14
accreditation, 7, 107
Adobe software products, 215
affective behavior patterns, 21-22
affective learning styles, 22
Aldus Persuasion, 180-181
American Library Association,
and electronic information policy, xx
Evaluating Information: A Basic Checklist, 149
Hot Topics Discussion 1993, 77
Archie, 4, 133
Arizona State University, 172, 174
Arp, Lorie, 7
Atkinson, Hugh, 15

Baskett, H.K., 89
Bechtel, Joan, 13
Beyerman, K., 88
Bibliographic Instruction Handbook, 157
BITNET, 39
Boolean searching, 30, 120, 219
Brand, Stewart, 195
Branwyn, Gareth, 147
Broidy, Ellen, 15
Brown University, 129
Brown, Willie, 131

California Polytechnic State University, 210
CARL, xxi, 164
cataloging,
automated, 37, 45, 56, 64, 108, 116, 142, 175, 183, 217
national shared, 8
Chronicle of Higher Education, 5, 130, 151
Claremont Colleges, 93
Cleveland State University, 148
cognition, 21
and electronic literature searching, 29
cognitive apprenticeship, 89
cognitive learning styles, 22, 154
collaborative learning, 14, 80, 161
COMPENDEX, 218
conceptualization, 21
Cooke, Kevin, 148

Coombspapers, 144
critical thinking skills, 13, 107, 113, 117, 123, 138-139, 141, 145, 148
Critical TV Watching, 151
curricular design and integration, 157, 158
curriculum changes, resource-based teaching, 7

DeGolyer Library, 135
Dickinson, Gail, 151
Drabenstott, Karen, 198
Drucker, Peter, 9

e-mail, resource for collaboration, 39, 122, 125, 160, 164, 176, 226
Earlham College, 158, 198
electronic information,
  eliminates geographic restrictions, 147, 159, 176
  equal and affordable access, xx, 132
  equalizing power of, 4
  and funding for libraries, 126, 188, 196
  uncertain quality of, 144, 150
electronic village, 6
ERIC, 218, 219, 222
Estes, Clarissa Pinkola, 90
Ethnic NewsWatch, 99
Eureka, 84

Farber, Evan, 158, 198
Farmer, David, 135
Federal Communications Commission, 133
field dependence/independence (*see* field sensitivity)
field sensitivity/independence, 22
FirstSearch, 93

"Gateway to Information" project, 197
gender gap, students and computers, 28, 111
Gopher, 4, 36, 60, 83, 95, 113, 122, 133, 142, 144, 150, 151, 209, 213, 215, 218, 224
Gore, Albert, 132-133
Gorman, Michael, 14
Gregorian, Vartan, 129

HEA Title II programs, 126

Illustrator, 215
"in context" instruction, 154, 156
incidental learning, 88
Infini-d, 215
information overload, 4, 125, 138, 211
  irrelevant chatter, 148
  (*see also* critical thinking skills)
information surfers, 5
information technology,
  access vs. ownership of information, 126
  books and files, 5, 45-46, 56, 57, 132
  as a transforming opportunity, 11
information-economic underclass, xx
Innopac, 84, 85
Internet, 36, 61, 90, 125, 140, 226
  as entertainment, 126
  as epidemic, 195
  hype, 130
  and source evaluation, 139, 147
  as a teaching tool, 43, 63
  (*see also* electronic information)
Iris, 84, 85

Jughead, 4, 133

kanbrain systems, 8
Kantrowitz, Barbara, 111
Kesselman, Martin, 148
kinetic learning styles, 22
Kirk, Tom, 88, 158
Kisane, Emily C., 148
knowledge vs. knowing, 89
Kolb, David, 26, 228

learning environment,
  cluster system, 106, 159
  cooperative, 108, 156, 175
  social context, 156
learning process, 155
learning style preference, 20-22, 183, 228, 229
  and adult learners, 108, 122, 172
    active experimentation, 109
    connections to work, 109
    transfer learning techniques, 109
  experiential learners,
    accommodators, 28
    assimilators, 26
    convergers, 27
    divergers, 26
  experiential learning style preference, 26
  sensory preference, 22
    auditory learners, 23
    and instructional design strategies, 25
    kinesthetic learners, 25
    visual learners, 24, 207
  and societal groups, 28, 29
Lederberg, Joshua, 13
Lehrer, Dan, 148
librarian role, 11, 129, 201
  evaluating Internet resources, 145
  information expert and rookie, 4, 76, 138, 217
  policy maker, xxii, 16
  systems designer/purchaser, 90, 158, 220
  teaching information access, xx, xxii, 16, 60
  teaching information evaluation, 149, 151
  value-added, 15-16
  working with decontextualized information, 143
Library of Congress, 30
library funding, 126
Library and Information Technology Association, 151
Lienhard, John L., 127
Lipow, Anne, 15
LISTSERV, 39, 40, 42, 43, 125
Logan, Susan, 197
Losee, Robert M., 134
Lubans, John, 157
Lynx, 203

McLuhan, Marshall, 76
Macromedia Director, 208, 215
Marsick, Victoria J., 89
MELVYL, 93, 113
mental models, 155
meta-cognitive strategies, 156
MitemView, 199-200, 203
Mollner, Daniel J., 148
Morley, Christopher, 135
Morrison Library, 128
Mosaic, 4, 142, 147, 203

national information infrastructure, 75
Netscape, 141, 142, 203
Nielson, Brian, 198
North West Net, 36, 64

Oberman, Cerise, 148, 157
Ohio State University, 195
Oxford Text Archives, 144

Pacific Bell, 131-132
PACS-L, 125
Page, Mary, 148
Pamona College (*see* Claremont Colleges)
Pathworks, 38
Pennsylvania State University, 218
Petrowski, Mary Jane, 157
Photoshop, 215
place of need, 159
Premier, 215

Rader, Hannelore, 149
Reinhart, Billie, 149
resource discovery, 138
Ridgeway, Trish, 157
Rutgers University Libraries, 76

Saffo, Paul, 5
Saint Mary's College, 105
Salter, John, 197
Sandler, Judith, 198
schemata, 155
Schlesinger, Arthur, 6
Secor, John, 6
Sheil, B.A., 89
Southern Methodist University, 135
Stenhouse, Lawrence, xxi
Strimple, Oliver, 111
Studer, William, 197

teaching electronic information, 7
  concepts vs. commands, 108, 113
  and continuity of instruction, xxii, 107, 163
  learner centered, xvii, 20, 106, 227
    (*see also* learning style preference)
  pro-active, xxi, 82
  and self-teaching, 39
  strategies, 23, 107
  to academic departments, 39
  using research models, 94
teaching on television, 174, 190
  concerns and issues, 175
teaching vs. learning, 20
Telecommunications Electronic Reviews, 151
Telnet, 39
Thompson, Gary B., 149
Tiberius, Richard, 156
Tiefel, Virginia, 196
Toffler's electronic cottage, 4

UnCover, 84, 85, 133, 219, 226
University at Buffalo, 134
University of California, Berkeley, 128
University of California, Los Angeles, 132
University of Colorado, 154, 158, 159
University of Delaware, 198
University of Houston, 127
University of Michigan, 198
University of Montana, 35, 39
University of Utah, 176
University of Washington, 14
UWire, 14

Veronica, 4, 133, 142, 144
virtual library, xx, xxi, 11, 130, 138

WAIS, 4, 36
Western Association of Schools and Colleges, 107, 121
Wilson, Larry, 13
Wilson, Lizabeth, 157
Wilson, Pete, 131
Wired, 5
Witkin, Herman, 23

World-Wide Web, 4, 36, 60, 95, 133, 138, 142, 144, 218, 224, 227

Z39.50, 11, 219, 220, 222, 229